The Particularistic President
Executive Branch Politics and Political Inequality

As the holders of the only office elected by the entire nation, presidents have long claimed to be sole stewards of the interests of all Americans. Scholars have largely agreed, positing the president as an important counterbalance to the parochial impulses of members of Congress. This supposed fact is often invoked in arguments for concentrating greater power in the executive branch. Douglas L. Kriner and Andrew Reeves challenge this notion and, through an examination of a diverse range of policies from disaster declarations, to base closings, to the allocation of federal spending, show that presidents, like members of Congress, are particularistic. Presidents routinely pursue policies that allocate federal resources in a way that disproportionately benefits their more narrow partisan and electoral constituencies. Though presidents publicly don the mantle of a national representative, in reality they are particularistic politicians who prioritize the needs of certain constituents over others.

Douglas L. Kriner is an associate professor of political science at Boston University. He is the author of *After the Rubicon: Congress, Presidents, and the Politics of Waging War*, which received the 2013 D.B. Hardeman Prize from the LBJ Foundation for the best book that focuses on the U.S. Congress from the fields of biography, history, journalism, and political science. He is coauthor (with Francis Shen) of *The Casualty Gap: The Causes and Consequences of American Wartime Inequalities*. His work has also appeared in the *American Political Science Review*, the *American Journal of Political Science*, and the *Journal of Politics*, among other outlets.

Andrew Reeves is an assistant professor of political science at Washington University in St. Louis and a research Fellow at the Weidenbaum Center on the Economy, Government, and Public Policy. He previously held a faculty position at Boston University and has held research fellowships at the Hoover Institution at Stanford University and at the Center for the Study of American Politics within the Institution for Social and Policy Studies at Yale University. His work has appeared in the *American Political Science Review*, the *American Journal of Political Science*, and the *Journal of Politics*, among other outlets.

The Particularistic President

Executive Branch Politics and Political Inequality

DOUGLAS L. KRINER
Boston University

ANDREW REEVES
Washington University in St. Louis

CAMBRIDGE
UNIVERSITY PRESS

CAMBRIDGE
UNIVERSITY PRESS

32 Avenue of the Americas, New York, NY 10013-2473, USA

Cambridge University Press is part of the University of Cambridge.

It furthers the University's mission by disseminating knowledge in the pursuit of education, learning, and research at the highest international levels of excellence.

www.cambridge.org
Information on this title: www.cambridge.org/9781107616813

© Douglas L. Kriner and Andrew Reeves 2015

First published 2015

Printed in the United States of America

A catalog record for this publication is available from the British Library.

ISBN 978-1-107-03871-4 Hardback
ISBN 978-1-107-61681-3 Paperback

Contents

List of Tables

List of Illustrations

Acknowledgments

In writing this book, we have benefited from the thoughtful insights of many individuals who have read drafts or listened to our questions and shared their thoughts. These individuals include: Barry Burden, Ian Clark, Adam Dynes, Katherine Levine Einstein, Justin Fox, Jim Gimpel, David Glick, Daniel Hopkins, William Howell, Jeff Jenkins, Gary King, Toby Merrill, Gary Miller, Terry Moe, Ryan Moore, Max Palmer, Eleanor Powell, Jon Rogowski, and Christine Rossell.

The book was also improved by the comments and criticisms that we received at various workshops and conferences where participants and discussants challenged us to think harder about our research questions. These venues include: the University of Illinois at Urbana-Champaign, Georgetown University, Stanford University, the Harris School at the University of Chicago, the University of Virginia, and Yale University.

In particular, we wish to single out individuals who attended a book conference at Boston University, which was generously funded by Graham Wilson and the College of Arts and Sciences. Here, we had the great benefit of receiving advice from Dino Christenson, Jeff Cohen, Dean Lacy, and Frances Lee, each of whom who read the entire manuscript, offered valuable suggestions and insight, and sacrificed a Saturday to share their thoughts. We also thank chairs, discussants, and participants at meetings of the Midwest Political Science Association and American Political Science Association where elements of this project were presented and improved.

At Cambridge University Press, we thank our outstanding editor Robert Dreesen, who encouraged us and guided us throughout the project, and Elizabeth Janetschek and Brianda Reyes, who deftly steered us through the sometimes daunting publication process. We also wish to thank Paula Dohnal for editorial assistance, as well as Amron Gravett for indexing assistance.

For financial support, we wish to thank Boston University, the Center for the Study of American Politics at Yale University, the Hoover Institution, Washington University in St. Louis, and the Weidenbaum Center on the Economy, Government, and Public Policy.

Finally, for their love and support, we wish to thank our families, particularly Jillian Goldfarb, Deborah Kriner, Gary Kriner, Ann Reeves, Christopher Reeves, Harry Reeves, Michael Reeves, and Patrick Reeves.

I

Introduction

More than a century ago, Woodrow Wilson, the only president of the American Political Science Association to become president of the United States, articulated a vision of the chief executive as the only actor in our system capable of representing and serving the interests of the nation as a whole. Contrasting members of Congress who are "representatives of localities" and "voted for only by sections of voters" with presidents who are elected by the nation, Wilson concluded that the presidency "is the representative of no constituency, but of the whole people." As a result, Wilson argued, when the president "speaks in his true character, he speaks for no special interest. If he rightly interprets the national thought and boldly insists upon it, he is irresistible."[1]

Wilson's view continues to hold great currency today as scholars, pundits, and presidents themselves tout the office of the presidency as a universalistic counterbalance to Congress, whose members all too often put the interests of their constituents above those of the nation as a whole. While members of Congress are driven to pursue policies that benefit their narrow geographic constituencies, presidents alone take a broader view and pursue policies that maximize the general welfare. The contrasts are often held to be particularly acute in the realm of divide-the-dollar politics. As law professor and Federalist Society cofounder Steven Calabresi describes, the president is "our only constitutional backstop against the redistributive collective action problem."[2] Members of Congress seek to "bring home the bacon" to their own constituencies. Presidents take a

---

[1] Wilson (1908, 67–68).
[2] Calabresi (1995, 35).

holistic view and instead seek policies that maximize outcomes for the country at large.

Undoubtedly, presidents do approach policy from a different perspective than do members of Congress, and they are often uniquely positioned to view political challenges through a national lens. But is the presidency really a "constitutional backstop" defending us from parochial policies rife with inefficiencies? We argue no, and throughout the book we show that electoral and partisan incentives combine to encourage presidents to pursue policies across a range of issues that systematically target benefits to politically valuable constituencies.

Presidents do have a national constituency, and voters hold them accountable for national outcomes. But we argue that this logic underlying the universalistic framework is fundamentally flawed. Voters hold presidents accountable for the state of the nation, but as we show in this book, voters also hold presidents responsible for how their local communities fare under presidential policies. Moreover, in an ironic twist reminiscent of Orwell's *Animal Farm*, the Electoral College ensures that some voters are more equal than others.[3] This combination of forces encourages presidents to prioritize the needs of some voters over others. Every four years, presidential candidates devote seemingly endless time, energy, and resources to courting voters, but not all voters. Rather, campaigns focus their efforts like a laser beam on a handful of swing states that will ultimately decide who will be the next president of the United States. The vast majority of the electorate is all but ignored.

But what happens after the last piece of confetti from the inaugural parade has fallen and the job of governing begins? Does the single-minded pursuit of swing state voters affect how presidents behave when they turn to govern the whole nation? Most existing scholarship argues no. We disagree: the compulsion for presidents to court swing state voters does not end when the election is over. Rather, we argue that presidents have a primal desire to secure reelection or to assure their party's continued hold on the presidency to both defend and reinforce their legacy. This political impulse is so strong that it systematically causes the president to engage in particularistic behavior very much like the reelection-seeking parochialism of which members of Congress are accused.

---

[3] After overthrowing Mr. Jones, the animals issued seven commandments, the last of which read: "All animals are equal." By book's end, the seven commandments had been replaced by a single commandment: "All animals are equal, but some animals are more equal than others."

Equally important for presidential behavior is the drive to please the partisan base. Reelection is not the only force that causes presidents to deviate from defending the interests of the whole nation. Modern presidents do not stand above the party. Rather, increasingly they are leaders of their political parties with strong ties to core partisan constituencies. Presidents frequently trumpet the need for bipartisanship in Washington and hold themselves up as national figures who can transcend partisan divisions. Barack Obama was not the first, nor will he be the last president to promise that he, or someday she, will bridge the partisan political divides in American politics. Yet despite the rhetoric, in practice presidents are partisan leaders motivated to seek what is best for their partisan base and for their partisan allies across the country. This, in turn, compels presidents to pursue policies that are more responsive to the base of their party than to the needs of the nation as a whole.

As a result, we offer a different conception of the presidency – one that is particularistic. When we say that presidents engage in particularism, we mean that they pursue policies that target public benefits disproportionately toward some political constituencies at the expense of others. As we shall see, presidential particularism can take many forms and serve a variety of objectives related to both electoral and partisan goals. The particularistic president routinely pursues policies that disproportionately benefit a small fraction of his tens of millions of constituents.

What concern is it if presidents favor some constituents over others? We argue that the scope of presidential particularism is vast; consequently, it produces skewed outcomes across a gamut of policy venues. It also has stark implications for the American constitutional framework. The contemporary American political system is more polarized than it has been in more than a century. Budgetary brinkmanship, government shutdowns, debt ceiling defaults, and the repeated failures of political leaders to grapple with the pressing issues of the day have given rise to a widespread belief that the federal government is broken. Trust in government has fallen to new lows, and public confidence in the country's direction has eroded significantly.[4] To confront this institutional malaise, a growing chorus calls for the delegation of more power to the president as a means of breaking through the dysfunction that has rendered Congress all but incapable of enacting policies that serve the national

---

[4] Justin Sink, "Poll: Government trust nears record low," *The Hill*, October 19, 2013. http://thehill.com/blogs/blog-briefing-room/news/329423-poll-trust-in-government-nears-record-low.

interest.[5] To these critics we urge caution. While the presidency may have institutional advantages over Congress in taking swift action in times of crisis – as Alexander Hamilton argued in *Federalist 70* – there is no guarantee that presidents will use more power to pursue outcomes that will make the nation as a whole better off. Rather, our analysis strongly suggests another outcome: that greater delegation to the executive will replace congressional parochialism with presidential particularism.

1.1 A Tale of Two Obamas

During every administration, presidents pursue different goals. Sometimes they pursue policies as the utilitarian-in-chief with an eye toward maximizing the welfare of as many citizens as possible. In these cases, presidents are not driven by special interests (economic, issue based, geographic, or otherwise) and instead pursue policies that are in the best interests of the nation as a whole. We call this perspective the *universalistic presidency*.[6] At other times, the president will engage in decidedly particularistic behaviors that disproportionately benefit some voters more than others. Consider, for example, the following two cases from President Barack Obama's first term. In the first, President Obama appears very much the universalistic counterpart to congressional parochialism and inefficiencies, as envisioned by the conventional wisdom. In the second, however, President Obama appears to embrace particularism in ways that patently serve his electoral interests rather than the national interest.

1.1.1 *Mr. Obama Goes to Washington*

Less than two months into his first term as president, Barack Obama found himself at loggerheads with congressional leaders of his own party. The culprit was earmarks, or the line items in an appropriations bill that allocate money for specific projects in a state or district. The 110th Congress and President George W. Bush had never been able to reach agreement on nine appropriations bills to keep the federal government

---

[5] Howell and Moe (2013, forthcoming); Kagan (2001); Mann and Ornstein (2013).

[6] In applying the term *universalistic* to the presidency, we use it in a different way than most of the congressional politics literature. The universalistic president eschews parochialism and instead pursues policies that serve the national interest, rather than the more narrow interests of politically important constituencies. Within the congressional literature, universalism refers to the logrolling process through which all members see benefits in order to build a large legislative coalition (Weingast, 1979).

funded through fiscal year 2009. As a result, President Obama entered office with a government funded solely by continuing resolutions, or temporary measures that funded the government only in the short term. Without additional action, the federal government would shut down, leaving 2.7 million government employees out of work and suspending many services relied on by millions of citizens.

The administration's first priority upon taking power, however, was to pass an economic stimulus bill to buoy the failing economy, which was in a free fall. While paeans to bipartisanship filled the air in the days immediately following the new president's inauguration, as January turned into February, the prospects for bipartisan accord were fading quickly. Eventually, Obama and Democratic congressional leaders crafted an almost $800 billion stimulus bill that, despite containing a generous helping of tax cuts along with targeted spending programs, passed both chambers with only three Republican votes.

Having achieved its first major legislative success, the administration could not rest on its laurels. The continuing resolution funding the government expired on March 11, and trouble was brewing in Congress, but this time from the Democratic side of the aisle. During the 2008 campaign, then-Senator Obama had trumpeted his anti-earmark credentials during his two years in the Senate and promised to continue fighting legislative waste as president. In the first presidential debate on September 26, 2008, candidate Obama promised: "We need earmark reform, and when I'm president, I will go line by line to make sure that we are not spending money unwisely."[7] Although congressional Democrats had modestly reformed the earmark process during the 110th Congress, the version of the omnibus appropriations bill working its way through the Democratically controlled House and Senate was loaded with congressional pork. According to Taxpayers for Common Sense, the final version contained more than 8,500 earmark provisions that totaled $7.7 billion in proposed spending.

Despite Obama having campaigned in 2008 as a transformational leader who would bridge partisan divides, the administration's failure to secure even a single Republican vote for the stimulus was a harbinger of things to come. The president would need unified support among Democrats for health care reform, the signature initiative of his first term. Indeed in the Senate, where sixty votes were essential to break

---

7 http://online.wsj.com/public/resources/documents/TEXTANALYZER_TRANSCRIPT1 .xml.

a Republican-led filibuster, the administration would likely need every single Democrat to carry the day against a unified Republican opposition. Nevertheless, having railed against earmarks as serving parochial interests at the expense of the national interest, the president confronted members of his own party over the appropriations bill. However, Majority Leader Harry Reid refused to budge even in the face of pressure from a co-partisan president, and admonished his erstwhile junior Senate colleague to respect congressional prerogatives. Reid warned that crusading against earmarks, which were essential to the electoral needs of many members, would grind the legislative process to a halt.

On the other side of the aisle, many Republicans demanded the president veto the omnibus bill. These public cries against pork belied the explosive increase of earmarks under previous Republican Congresses during the Bush era. Moreover, many Republicans, including some calling for Obama to veto the omnibus because of the earmarks, had inserted their own earmarks into the legislation. Indeed, a full 40 percent of earmarked funding was requested by Republican members of Congress.[8] Rather, Republican demands for a veto were designed to embarrass the president and drive a wedge between Obama and his party.

Ultimately, President Obama backed down and signed the legislation, earmarks intact, into law. Despite losing this round, even as he signed the omnibus bill, Obama announced new guidelines for future earmarks, including greater transparency and a requirement for competitive bids for federal projects. Yet even these commonsense restrictions were met with little enthusiasm on Capitol Hill. For example, while Senate Appropriations Committee Chairman Daniel Inouye voiced basic agreement in principle with the requirement for competitive bids by private corporations for earmarked funds, he insisted that his committee would retain ultimate authority over such appropriations. Similarly, Democratic House Majority Leader Steny Hoyer showed remarkably little deference to his party's president seeking to rein in congressional pork, noting that, when it came to pork, the White house could not "tell us what to do."[9]

1.1.2 As Goes Ohio, So Goes the Nation
The 2009 budget battle aptly illustrates presidential universalism. President Obama battled parochial legislators who were more concerned with

---

[8] David Clarke, "Earmarks: Here to stay or facing extinction?" *CQ Weekly*, March 16, 2009, p. 613. Paul Krawzak and Kathleen Hunter, "Work completed on '09 omnibus," *CQ Weekly*, March 16, 2009, p. 612.

[9] Woodward (2012, 26–27).

procuring goodies for their own districts than protecting the public purse from waste and abuse. However, in other policy venues, President Obama appeared to engage in his own form of particularistic politics. Consider, for example, President Obama's varied efforts to shower residents of the Buckeye State with federal largesse.

Eight years had passed since the 2004 election, but in 2012 the political situation remained uncannily similar in at least one regard. The election appeared to hinge on Ohio. The incumbent, President Obama, faced a stiff challenge from the Republican nominee, former Massachusetts Governor Mitt Romney. The race was based largely on the president's stewardship of the economy. The country was divided, with most states either clearly blue or plainly red. Ohio again stood poised to play a deciding role in the upcoming election. In 2004, President George W. Bush narrowly won reelection by a 286–251 vote in the Electoral College. Ohio's twenty hotly contested electoral votes provided the slender margin of victory. Although Bush won the national popular vote by more than three million, if 60,000 Ohioans had switched their votes from Bush to John Kerry, the Democratic challenger would have secured the presidency.

In the spring of 2012, President Obama's advisors studied the electoral map and saw a similar scenario unfolding. Most were confident that the president, despite the sluggish economy, would continue to hold New England, the Mid-Atlantic, and the West Coast. A number of Midwestern states, including Michigan, Illinois, Wisconsin, and Minnesota, also seemed likely to end up in the president's column. Holding these states and adding New Mexico, where demographic changes continued to swing the state toward the Democrats, would put Obama at 251 electoral votes. Winning Ohio and its eighteen electoral votes would require Romney to run the table – to hold the Deep South and also carry the battlegrounds of Nevada, Colorado, and Iowa – just to force an Electoral College tie. Whereas President Obama held several paths to 270 without Ohio, a loss in Ohio would all but doom Romney's electoral fortunes.

In contrast to other swing states such as Michigan, Pennsylvania, or Illinois, Ohio had leaned Republican in recent presidential contests. Yet, the Obama campaign liked the odds. This was in large part because of the administration's politically risky bailout of General Motors and Chrysler. As the election year began, the auto bailout was hardly popular nationwide. A February 2012 Gallup poll showed only 44 percent of Americans approving "of the financial bailout for US automakers that were in danger of failing," contrasted with 51 percent disapproving of the president's action.[10] But things were different in Ohio. In rescuing the auto industry, the administration had saved more than a million jobs, many of which were located in the counties hugging Ohio's Lake Erie coast. The November election exit polls showed nearly 60 percent of Ohio voters supporting the bailouts, and of those supporters, roughly three-quarters voted to reelect the president.[11]

Yet, bailing out the automotive industry was not the only gambit made by the Obama administration to benefit Ohio voters. Throughout his first term, the president visited Ohio again and again to take credit for federal grant programs and awards that had created jobs in the Buckeye State. For example, the administration had long championed the development of alternative energy. On one tour of the state, the president highlighted the decision to award federal dollars to Ohio's own Ashlawn Energy, which would expand production of vanadium redox fuel cells thanks to an award from the Department of Energy's Smart Grid Program. In announcing the grant at a small business forum in Cleveland, President Obama also emphasized Ashlawn's commitment to retraining workers from the local community in Painesville, Ohio, for the new jobs that would be created.[12] In all, Ohio companies received more than $125 million of clean energy grants, nearly four times the national state average. Indeed, President Obama reminded voters of this fact on a 2010 trip through the state, telling the crowd that Ohio had "received more funds than just about anybody in order to build on that clean energy economy . . . almost $25 million of our investment went to a plant right here in Elyria that's helping produce the car batteries of the future. That's what we're going to keep on doing for the rest of 2010 and 2011 and 2012, until we've got this country working again."[13]

Other sectors of the Ohio economy would also benefit. When, in March 2012, the president announced plans for the creation of a new network

---

[10] Gallup/USA Today Poll, February 20–21, 2012, USAIPOUSA2012-TR0220.

[11] Keith Lang, "Road to President Obama's win in Ohio paved by support for auto bailout," *The Hill*, November 7, 2012. http://thehill.com/blogs/transportation-report/automobiles/266691-auto-bailout-paved-the-road-for-obamas-ohio-win-.

[12] Barack Obama, "Remarks at the Closing Session of the Winning the Future Forum on Small Business in Cleveland, Ohio," February 22, 2011. Online by Gerhard Peters and John T. Woolley, The American Presidency Project. www.presidency.ucsb.edu/ws/?pid=89477.

[13] Barack Obama, "Remarks at a Town Hall Meeting and a Question-and-Answer Session in Elyria, Ohio," January 22, 2010. Online by Gerhard Peters and John T. Woolley, The American Presidency Project. http://www.presidency.ucsb.edu/ws/?pid=87444.

of manufacturing centers across the country, the first grant awarded was to a group from Youngstown, Ohio. Similarly, although passenger rail service between Cincinnati and Cleveland had ended more than forty years prior, in 2010 the Obama administration sought to revive this route and others in Ohio through $400 million of transportation grant funding. Even in terms of Race to the Top education grants, the allocation of which is overseen by independent educators, Ohio emerged a clear winner, securing the fourth-highest grant total of any state.[14]

Moreover, in a campaign that would evolve into an argument over which candidate could do more for small businesses, the president was quick to emphasize to Ohio voters how new grants from the Small Business Administration (SBA) would bolster the local economy. After attending a conference on small business creation in Cleveland – the seat of Cuyahoga County, which the president would need to win heavily to carry the state in November – President Obama touted the many ways in which his administration was channeling federal dollars into projects that would benefit the local economy. One grant would bolster the Flex-Matters cluster, which aimed to make Cleveland a global leader in the development and production of flexible electronics. High tech in Ohio was not the only winner, however. Micelli Dairy Products received what was the largest SBA grant awarded to date in an effort to increase its production of ricotta cheese and to expand its product line to include mozzarella and provolone. Obama jovially proclaimed this "one of the tastiest investments the government has ever made" and noted that the grant directly led to the creation of sixty jobs at the Buckeye Road facility in Cleveland.[15] In all, in 2012 the administration approved 2,726 loans for small businesses in Ohio, a figure that well surpassed the totals secured by many states with significantly larger populations.[16]

We could present many more illustrations of presidents – Democrats and Republicans alike – pursuing policies that target benefits to key

---

[14] Jerry Markon and Alice Crites, "Obama showering Ohio with attention and money," *Washington Post*, September 25, 2012. www.washingtonpost.com/politics/decision2012/obama-showering-ohio-with-attention-and-money/2012/09/25/8ab15a68-019e-11e2-b260-32f4a8db9b7e_story.html.

[15] Barack Obama, "Remarks at the Closing Session of the Winning the Future Forum on Small Business in Cleveland, Ohio," February 22, 2011. Online by Gerhard Peters and John T. Woolley, The American Presidency Project. www.presidency.ucsb.edu/ws/?pid=89477.

[16] Jerry Markon and Alice Crites, "Obama showering Ohio with attention and money," *Washington Post*, September 25, 2012. http://www.washingtonpost.com/politics/decision2012/obama-showering-ohio-with-attention-and-money/2012/09/25/8ab15a68-019e-11e2-b260-32f4a8db9b7e_story.html.

constituencies for political gain. President Reagan famously backtracked on his free-trade rhetoric to protect the steel industry in key swing states during the lead-up to the 1984 elections. Four years later and despite solid steel profits, George H. W. Bush vowed to renew protectionist measures in pursuit of votes in steel-producing states.[17] In 1996, the *Wall Street Journal* accused Bill Clinton of "playing Santa Claus" to win reelection, for example by awarding $35 million in seed money for economic development projects with a heavy geographic bias toward swing states and California.[18] And as Pennsylvania voters prepared to head to the polls in 2004, the Bush administration dispatched the Secretary of Energy to the key swing state to announce more than $100 million worth of energy and clean coal funding; critics charged that Bush was "setting a new standard for preelection pork."[19]

However, such an approach would offer only a limited understanding of the forces driving presidential behavior. Because of the difficulties inherent in generalizing and extrapolating from a handful of cases, which are rarely picked at random, in the chapters that follow we analyze a comprehensive array of data to test whether the universalistic or particularistic paradigm best fits presidential politics. Through this data, we endeavor to show that the preceding case of President Obama consciously targeting federal resources to the pivotal battleground state of Ohio is not the exception that proves the rule, but rather the norm in contemporary politics. Presidents routinely pursue policies that disproportionately benefit their core partisan base and electorally pivotal swing constituencies. Moreover, patterns in the extent to which presidents engage in core and swing constituency targeting vary systematically with the electoral cycle. Presidents consistently pursue policies that benefit core partisan constituencies over parts of the country that back the opposition throughout their term in office. However, as the next election draws near, presidents increasingly target policy benefits toward swing constituencies as well.

The image of the president as a universalistic counterbalance to the rampant particularism of Congress is so deeply embedded in our national consciousness that we often accept it on blind faith. Yet this vision is not

---

[17] "The high cost of steel quotas," *Chicago Tribune*, February 19, 1989, http://articles
.chicagotribune.com/1989-02-19/news/8903060951_1_steel-quotas-steel-industry-
subsidized-foreign-steel.

[18] Michael Frisby, "Despite funding cuts, Clinton manages to use power of the purse to get votes," *Wall Street Journal*, October 10, 1996, A20.

[19] Michael Dobbs, "Run-up to vote is season for U.S. largesse," *Washington Post*, October 28, 2004, A23.

supported by a systematic assessment of the data. Through a series of analyses of presidential action in policy areas ranging from trade politics to disaster declarations, as well as a comprehensive analysis of the allocation of all federal grant dollars across the country from 1984 to 2008, we examine the extent to which presidents actually serve as a brake on the parochial impulses of Congress. The results of our analysis are unambiguous: the president does not serve as an equalizing, countervailing force against the particularistic pursuits of legislators. In fact, we find that presidents pursue their own brand of particularism that resembles what conventional accounts have led us to expect from Congress. Presidents systematically use their leverage over policies from base closings to budgets to target federal benefits to battleground states in search of votes; to reward their core partisan base; and to help members of their party in Congress. What sets presidents apart, rather, is their success in achieving these goals. Our data show that the inequalities arising from presidential particularism, across a number of policies, dwarf those arising from congressional parochialism. For example, in Chapter 5 we estimate that in 2008 four states – Florida, Ohio, Michigan, and Pennsylvania – received more than a billion dollars of additional grant spending simply by virtue of being swing states. Moreover, we show that states that reliably back the president's party at the polls receive hundreds of millions of dollars more in federal grants each year than do similar states that instead reliably back the opposition party in presidential elections. For red and blue states, who sits in the Oval Office can mean the difference in billions of dollars of federal spending.

In uncovering and measuring the extent of presidential particularism, we do not argue that the universalistic paradigm is baseless. Undoubtedly, presidents do pursue different interests and policies than do members of Congress. And plainly, presidents may sometimes take a more national view than do individual legislators who are tied to more narrow geographic constituencies. However, in many policy areas and particularly when it comes to the distribution of federal dollars to specific constituencies, we find that universalism routinely gives way to particularism.

1.2 Presidential Universalism

The snapshot of President Obama's first budget battle echoes what is perceived to be a larger truism in American politics. More often than not, the primary focus of individual members of Congress is the needs of their narrow geographic constituencies. By contrast, presidents take a broader view and pursue the interests of the nation as a whole rather than the parochial interests of a few. This conventional assessment of the competing interests of our political institutions is widely espoused by pundits and scholars. And presidents themselves have gone to great lengths to imprint this contrast on the nation's collective psyche.

Virtually every chief executive from George Washington to Barack Obama has publicly proclaimed that unlike members of Congress, who are so responsive to parochial concerns, presidents are, by the very construction of the office, stewards of the nation as a whole. In a 1795 letter to the Selectmen of Boston, President Washington wrote: "In every act of my administration, I have sought the happiness of my fellow citizens. My system for the attainment of this object has uniformly been to overlook all personal, local, and partial considerations; to contemplate the United States as one great whole...and to consult only the substantial and permanent interest of our country."[20] More than two centuries later, President Obama sounded a similar note while championing additional infrastructure programs in his 2013 State of the Union address. Investing in the nation's aging infrastructure was good for America. However, to heighten his proposal's appeal to reluctant members of Congress, the president playfully and a bit mockingly reminded members of the direct benefits an infrastructure program would yield for their individual constituencies. Investment in infrastructure creates jobs, Obama argued. To members of Congress he teased that "I know that you want these job-creating projects in your districts. I've seen you all at the ribbon-cuttings."[21]

This vision of a universalistic presidency also features prominently in a great deal of presidency scholarship from across academic disciplines. For example, legal scholars routinely use the assumption of universalism to justify the expansion of presidential power and influence over the administrative state. Before her appointment to the Supreme Court, Elena Kagan argued that an increased role for a president-led bureaucracy in policy formulation and implementation would lead to more normatively desirable policy outcomes that better serve the national interest. "Because the President has a national constituency," Kagan argued, "he is likely to consider, in setting the direction of administrative policy on an ongoing

<hr>

[20] Quoted in Wood (2009, 6).
[21] Barack Obama, "Address Before a Joint Session of Congress on the State of the Union," February 12, 2013. Online by Gerhard Peters and John T. Woolley, The American Presidency Project. www.presidency.ucsb.edu/ws/?pid=102826.

basis, the preferences of the general public, rather than merely parochial interests."[22] Summarizing the field, Jide Nzelibe concludes: "One of the most widespread contemporary assumptions in the discourse about the separation of powers is that while the president tends to have preferences that are more national and stable in nature, Congress is perpetually prone to parochial concerns."[23]

Within political science, many argue that presidents pursue more representative policies in part because of the very institutional structure of their office.[24] Terry Moe, in particular, has championed this view, arguing that presidents alone are held accountable for the performance of the whole government.[25] By contrast, legislators "have their eyes on their own electoral fortunes, and thus on the special (often local) interests that can bring them security and popularity." As a result, for members of Congress "politics is not about the system!" rather "it is about the pieces and about special interests."[26] Presidents, by contrast, are motivated by different, more national interests. As a result, "they think in grander terms about social problems and the public interest, and they tend to resist specialized

[22] Kagan (2001, 2335). Kagan acknowledges that such arguments can be taken too far and even suggests that in some instances presidents may be more responsive to particular interests than national ones. However, Kagan (2001, 2336) concludes: "Take the President out of the equation and what remains [particularly members of Congress on key committees] are individuals and entities with a far more tenuous connection to national majoritarian preferences and interests."

[23] Jide Nzelibe. 2006. "The fable of the national president and the parochial Congress." *UCLA Law Review* 53: 1217–1273, p. 1218. For additional legal scholarship in this vein, see: Jerry Marshaw. 1997. *Greed, Chaos, and Governance: Using Public Choice to Improve Public Law*. New Haven, CT: Yale University Press. Steven Calabresi. 1995. "Some normative arguments for the unitary executive." *Arkansas Law Review* 48: 23–104. Lawrence Lessig and Cass Sunstein. 1994. "The president and the administration." *Columbia Law Review* 94: 1–123. In his critique of this literature, Nzelibe argues that the Electoral College may compel the president to cater to an even narrower constituency than the median member of Congress does, and he argues that while individual members of Congress may be shortsighted, collectively they will often pursue policies that are more representative of the interests of the nation as a whole than any single individual would.

[24] Another branch of presidency scholarship argues that norms of behavior encourage presidents to behave in a universalistic fashion. For example, Cronin and Genovese (2004, 198) argue that "Once in office, presidents often bend over backward in their attempt to minimize the partisan appearance of their actions.... Presidents are not supposed to act with their eyes on the next election; they are not supposed to favor any particular group or party." See Wood (2009) for a full overview of this literature. For similar sentiments, see, among others, Bond and Smith (2008); Cohen and Nice (2003); Edwards et al. (2008); Patterson (1990); Pika et al. (2006).

[25] Moe and Wilson (1994).

[26] Moe and Wilson (1994, 427).

appeals." Moreover, because presidents "are held uniquely responsible by the public for virtually every aspect of national performance, and because their leadership and their legacies turn on effective governance,"[27] they have strong incentives to pursue a coherent national agenda that maximizes outcomes for the country as a whole.[28]

This basic argument is formalized in recent game theoretic research by William Howell, Saul Jackman, and Jon Rogowski. In *The Wartime President*, Howell and colleagues begin by noting that policies made in Washington have both national and local outcomes; they then model the policy implications of the relative weights that politicians attach to the national and local ramifications of public policy choices. Members of Congress, Howell and colleagues argue, are attentive to both the national and the local consequences of policy choices made in Washington. Presidents, by contrast, face a truly national electorate and thus approach policy differently. "Presidents focus on the national implications of public policies while members of Congress monitor the effects of public policy on both the nation as a whole and their local constituencies – and, crucially, often these emphases are in conflict with one another."[29]

---

[27] Moe and Wilson (1994, 428).

[28] In a similar vein, game theoretic scholarship on delegation has long argued that presidents prefer more nationally optimal policy outcomes than do legislators who pursue more narrow, particularistic interests. For example, writing on trade policy, Lohmann and O'Halloran (1994, 509) note: "The President ... has a national constituency and cares about the losses incurred by all districts. If given discretionary powers to set trade policy, the President would implement measures that trade off the marginal benefits derived from protecting industries in one district against the marginal costs imposed on all other districts."

[29] Howell et al. (2013, 31–32). Indeed, Howell et al.'s main contention is that only significant exogenous shocks, such as major, nationally unifying wars, can encourage members to place greater weight on the national component. When this happens, policy inexorably moves toward the president's preferences and away from the more inefficient, parochial policies that Congress would otherwise pursue if left to its own devices. Echoing David Lewis and Terry Moe (2010, 370), Howell and colleagues argue that presidents care only about national outcomes. At one point, the model is generalized to account for the possibility that presidents may care about both national and localized outcomes; however, it is always assumed that presidents care more about national outcomes than do members of Congress: "There is good reason to suspect that, at all times, the President is judged primarily on (and hence cares primarily about) his achievements at the national level. Local events may occasionally figure into his thinking, but in the main the President concerns himself primarily with the national implications of policy. Meanwhile, legislators feel pressure to appeal to the relatively more parochial interests of their constituent base. Therefore, when comparing a President and a Legislator, it seems natural to assume that, at all times, the President places relatively more weight on national outcomes than does the Legislator" (54–55).

Thus, Howell and colleagues' model suggests that legislators may oscillate back and forth between acting parochially and more universalistically, depending on the relative weight they place on national and local consequences at a given moment.[30] By contrast, presidents, "because they care only about national policy outcomes," are decidedly more universalistic in their orientations and pursue policies that maximize outcomes for the nation as a whole.[31] Taken to its logical conclusion, this model suggests that when Congress defers more to presidential preferences, the country benefits.

But why are presidents inherently more universalistic in orientation than are members of Congress? Political science scholarship has suggested two answers. First, presidents simply may be less influenced by electoral concerns than legislators. In *Congress: The Electoral Connection*, David Mayhew revolutionized the study of legislative politics by arguing that much of what happens in Congress – from how the House and Senate are organized to how members spend the bulk of their time to the types of policies members pursue and, conversely, eschew – can be understood by positing that members act as if they are single-minded seekers of reelection.[32] Popular appeals to constituents back home often appear more important to members than does the hard work of compromise and enacting legislation for the nation as a whole. And logically so, Mayhew argues, as the former are much more important than the latter to maximizing a member's reelection prospects. To be sure, as Richard Fenno has argued, members of Congress also desire personal power within the

---

[30] As such, Howell and colleagues argue that members of Congress routinely pursue policies and amendments that minimize the costs and maximize the benefits for their constituencies, even if the result is considerable inefficiency for the nation as a whole. For example, while the lofty objective of the Affordable Care Act was to ensure equal access to quality health care for all Americans, Senators Ben Nelson and Mary Landrieu, among others, used their clout to procure a better deal for Nebraska and Louisiana, respectively, in maneuvers popularized as the Cornhusker Kickback and the Louisiana Purchase. Even long-time universal health care advocates, such as Joe Lieberman, sought concessions – in Lieberman's case, additional protections for the insurance industry, which is largely headquartered in his home state of Connecticut. Agricultural state representatives routinely battle for the continuation of long-outdated New Deal subsidies and price supports or for ethanol subsidies, even when the result is artificially heightened food prices that must be borne by the entire nation. And many conservative members of Congress, some of whom welcomed federal aid after Hurricane Katrina in 2005, cast a vote against the "fiscally irresponsible" federal aid for the northeastern states hit hard by Hurricane Sandy in 2012.

[31] Howell et al. (2013, 58).

[32] Mayhew (1974a).

institution as well as sound public policy.[33] Yet, in an institution grounded on the seniority norm and in which influence is cultivated and developed over decades, continual reelection to the chamber is all but a prerequisite to achieving these goals.

Presidents, by contrast, enter office with vastly different power prospects and significantly shorter time horizons. In sharp contrast to a freshman member of the House, a newly elected president assumes office quite possibly at the height of his power. As a result, for presidents reelection is only loosely related to exercising power and influence in Washington. Barred at first by precedent and then by law from seeking a third term, presidents are not preoccupied with an electoral sword of Damocles constantly dangling above their heads. Their more finite time horizons in power combined with the unique characteristics and powers of their office combine to give presidents both the incentives and the tools to seek and exercise power as quickly as possible to maximize their influence on policy.[34] Power-seeking presidents are free and institutionally encouraged to eschew parochial and even electoral concerns and instead focus intently on the national consequences of policy decisions. In so doing, presidents will have the greatest long-term impact on the course of the nation and single-mindedly pursue power to build bold legacies as national leaders.[35]

Some may be skeptical of the idea that presidents are only weakly motivated by electoral calculations. Perhaps this was once true, but superficially it seems hard to believe given the rise of the permanent campaign that has transformed contemporary politics. Presidents frequently take their priorities directly to the electorate in what Samuel Kernell calls "going public."[36] Jeffrey Cohen has also detailed the increasing specialization and microtargeting of presidential messaging, a trend that he has called "going local."[37] Both of these developments reflect presidential efforts to sell their legislative initiatives in a manner indistinguishable from campaigning. With reelection battles beginning earlier and earlier, in politics today it is not uncommon to see clear signs that presidents are putting themselves on a campaign footing immediately after the midterm elections if not even before them.

However, even if we accept that presidents, like members of Congress, are significantly influenced by electoral calculations, most scholarship

---

[33] Fenno (1978).
[34] Howell and Brent (2013).
[35] Moe and Wilson (1994).
[36] Kernell (1997).
[37] Cohen (2010).

suggests that electoral pressures drive presidents and members of Congress in opposite directions. Subscribing to what Wood (2009, 19) labels a "centrist view of representation," presidency scholarship in this vein argues that electoral pressures encourage presidents to respond not to specific geographic constituencies like members of Congress, but to the national median voter.

Most immediately, these divergent expectations are derived from the different constituencies of legislators and presidents. First and foremost, members of the United States Congress are elected to serve the interests of the narrow geographic constituencies that elect them. The Speaker of the House may be third in line to the White House and among the most powerful officeholders in Washington; however, to return to the Capitol every two years, he or she must win election only from a district of approximately seven hundred thousand residents. Regardless of whether a representative views her role primarily as a Burkean trustee to act as guardian of the interests of her constituents or as a pure delegate charged with mirroring the wishes of a majority of her constituents, that member inevitably faces strong electoral incentives to prioritize the needs and wants of her constituents over those of citizens in other parts of the country.

The president, by contrast, is the only government official (besides the vice president) elected by a national constituency. Alexander Hamilton recognized the implications of this when he argued in *Federalist 68* that, while members of the House or Senate needed to appeal to a subset of their own narrow constituency to gain office, presidents had to appeal to the country as a whole. In stark contrast to parliamentary systems such as Great Britain's, in the U.S. constitutional system only by securing "the esteem and confidence of the whole Union" can a candidate gain and hold the office of chief executive. Democratic theorist Robert Dahl argues that presidents since at least Andrew Jackson have used their method of election to claim a popular mandate for their policy agendas. On Jackson, Dahl writes that "[i]n justifying his use of the veto against Congressional majorities, as the only national official who had been elected by all the people and not just by a small fraction, as were Senators and Representatives, Jackson insisted that he alone could claim to represent all the people."[38] Thus, a president seeking to maximize his electoral prospects need not pander to narrow geographic constituencies; rather, presidents

---

[38] While presidents themselves have repeatedly pointed to their national constituency as justifying their unique place in our system, Dahl (2001, 69) and other democratic theorists have expressed considerable skepticism.

need only respond to centrist opinion and pursue policies that maximize outputs for the greatest number of people.

Brandice Canes-Wrone presents a theory of presidential responsiveness that nicely combines these two perspectives.[39] Echoing Moe, Howell, and others, she argues that most presidents most of the time pursue their vision of good public policy with an eye toward bolstering their historical legacies. However, as a reelection contest nears, some presidents – specifically those with middling approval ratings – may perceive electoral pressures to deviate from the policies they consider best. Ironically, voters prefer candidates who are unlikely to pander to them, and who instead will pursue optimal policies in the best interest of the nation. However, uncertainty limits their ability to judge candidates' competence, and thus when heading to the voting booth they are often forced to rely on whether a president champions policies that voters perceive to be consistent with their preferences and interests. Thus, in the lead-up to an election, some presidents may succumb to electoral pressure and cater to the policy preferences of the national median voter. The end result is a fortuitous and virtuous cycle in which ambitious presidential office seekers are compelled by the institutional design of the presidency to pursue policies that either maximize the general welfare or that respond to the will of centrist median voters – a far cry from the parochialism lamented in Congress.

Claims of presidential universalism are more than just idle rhetoric. Rather, the universalistic paradigm also informs policy prescriptions. Specifically, it has led many to call for greater delegation to the executive branch in the belief that it will lead to more efficient policies responsive to the median American. In response to clear signs of dysfunction on Capitol Hill, a growing chorus of scholars has called for increased delegation to the executive branch. For example, Elena Kagan has written at length defending the growth of what she has termed "presidential administration."[40] Through a variety of levers, presidents since Reagan have sought to increase their control over the administrative state and policy implementation. Critics lament such developments as presidential power grabs that undermine Congress's constitutional prerogatives to insulate discretion delegated to executive agencies from presidential influence.[41] Yet, Kagan defends increased presidential authority over bureaucratic policy implementation on both constitutional and, perhaps even more

---

[39] Canes-Wrone (2006).
[40] Kagan (2001).
[41] See, e.g., Pildes and Sunstein (1995).

important, normative grounds.[42] Whereas accountability and efficiency in bureaucratic policymaking are often held to be in tension, Kagan argues that both can be achieved through enhanced presidential administrative control. "Because the public holds Presidents, and often Presidents alone, responsible for so many aspects of governmental performance, Presidents have a large stake in ensuring an administration that works, at least in the eyes of the public."[43] The end result, for Kagan, is that "presidential direction thus represents the best accommodation of democratic and efficiency values."[44] The need for greater presidential authority is only heightened in an era of highly polarized divided government. "These new circumstances," Kagan concludes, "create a need for institutional reforms that will strengthen the President's ability to provide energetic leadership in an inhospitable political environment."[45]

Similarly, congressional scholars Thomas Mann and Norman Ornstein, while more cautious in their call for greater delegation to the executive, argue that the contemporary Congress is so fundamentally broken that greater presidential initiative may provide at least a partial corrective for the present congressional malaise. While noting that presidential power has already expanded dramatically in recent decades at the expense of the legislature, Mann and Ornstein conclude that further "modest shifts to give more leeway to the executive make sense, given the current and continuing dysfunction."[46]

Presidency scholars Terry Moe and William Howell have more forcefully called for expanded presidential power to rescue the country from its institutional dysfunction. Noting the myriad problems the United States

[42] Regarding the former, Kagan (2001, 2251) argues that "statutory delegation to an executive agency official – although not to an independent agency head – usually should be read as allowing the President to assert directive authority, as Clinton did, over the exercise of the delegated discretion."

[43] Kagan (2001, 2339).

[44] Kagan (2001, 2341). Similarly, Yale University Law Professor Jerry Marshaw vigorously claims that expansive delegation of policymaking to the bureaucracy would strengthen democratic accountability because of the president's natural institutional advantages in leading the bureaucracy. In stark contrast to members of Congress, Marshaw (1985, 95) argues, "the president has no particular constituency to which he or she has special responsibility to deliver benefits." Rather, presidents will pursue policies that more closely mirror the interests of the nation as a whole through bureaucratic decision-making procedures than policies whose details were specified in the hall of Congress and its committee rooms. Moreover, Marshaw argues that bureaucratic policymaking may even be more democratically accountable than legislative policymaking precisely because presidents are elected by the nation as a whole on the basis of national, not local, issues.

[45] Kagan (2001, 2344).

[46] Mann and Ornstein (2013, 166).

faces, from climate change to skyrocketing debt and the global financial crisis to the ongoing war on terror, they ask who within our system of governance is best positioned to craft genuine solutions. Congress, they argue, is not the answer: "Truth be told, Congress is unlikely to provide the leadership needed to identify and design solutions for the nation's most trenchant social problems. Its very character as a collective decision-making body nearly guarantees that it won't. Leadership is a scarce commodity among the 535 independently elected members who make up Congress, each with radically different views about what good policy looks like. . . . It comes as no surprise, then, that the recent history of legislative activity is littered with bills that, in name, promise to confront challenges of national importance, but that in fact constitute little more than disfigured conglomerations of sectional initiatives."[47] Instead, expanded presidential power is the nation's best hope for grappling with contemporary challenges in a rational way that reflects the needs of the nation as a whole.

1.3 Presidential Particularism

When deciding on questions of war and peace, the scope and extent of gun control laws, or the optimal level of federal spending and revenues, presidents may routinely take a more holistic, national view than do many members of Congress.[48] Yet, when implementing public policy – when determining who gets what and when – we argue that presidents are also highly particularistic, systematically favoring the needs of some constituents over others. For example, when deciding whether or not to go to war presidents may well consider only the national interest rather than the war's implications for any more narrow constituency. However, once a war has begun, who will receive the contracts to feed the troops, transport gasoline and other supplies, and ultimately reconstruct the vanquished foe? Here, the door for presidential particularism is wide open. For example, many have alleged that the Bush administration repeatedly awarded federal contracts to key campaign contributors or companies

---

[47] Howell and Moe (forthcoming).
[48] For example, in game theoretic research Daren Acemoglu and James Robinson argue that presidents, because they are elected by a popular vote, "tend to represent the preferences of the median voter in society" (2006, 115). By contrast, Congress must seek to reconcile the diverse preferences of its many members, which undermines its ability to be a truly representative institution. As a result, presidential policies should more closely reflect the will of the national median voter than would those articulated and advanced in Congress.

with other ties to the administration during the reconstruction and occupation of Iraq.[49]

Similarly, Presidents Bush and Obama have championed the virtues of free trade against protectionist impulses in Congress demanding "fair trade" agreements that are contingent on labor and environmental provisions. Bush and Obama acknowledged that free trade agreements would occasionally inflict economic pain on specific industries; yet, they argued that ultimately free trade was in the best interest of the nation as a whole. However, both deviated from this norm when politically expedient. President Bush famously imposed tariffs in 2002 on imported steel to protect mills across the Rust Belt – a case we examine in detail in Chapter 3 – and President Obama followed suit when he raised tariffs in 2009 on foreign tires to defend manufacturers in Ohio and elsewhere. Recent research by economists has shown that while these tariffs may have protected a few American jobs in a handful of electorally valuable constituencies, they came at a significant cost to the overall economy and consumers nationwide.[50]

In a slightly different vein, consider President Obama's initiative to reinvest in American manufacturing. Clearly, the overall policy was designed to pursue the national interest. With manufacturing experiencing a modest rebound in the aftermath of the great recession, the administration hoped that an infusion of federal dollars might spur additional innovation and job growth and help American manufacturers further expand their market share in a post–financial crash world. The ultimate aim was to help jump-start the economy as a whole. However, it also behooves us to ask who were the specific beneficiaries of this infusion of federal dollars? The first of these manufacturing innovation centers to be announced in 2012 was awarded to Youngstown, Ohio.[51] While we cannot infer motivations from such limited data, this case does remind us that presidents may pursue ultimately universalistic ends through particularistic means.

Why are presidents incentivized to engage in particularism? We contend that the theoretical underpinnings of the universalistic presidency

[49] Accounts of cronyism and favoritism abound; among others, see Rajiv Chandrasekaran. 2006. *Imperial Life in the Emerald City: Inside Iraq's Green Zone*. New York: Alfred A. Knopf.
[50] Charnovitz and Hoekman (2013); Hufbauer and Lowry (2012); Read (2005).
[51] The president mentioned the Youngstown center in his 2014 State of the Union address, along with a second innovation center based in Raleigh, North Carolina, another swing state.

paradigm are problematic. Chapter 2 unpacks our theoretical argument concerning the forces driving presidential particularism in detail. Here, we briefly outline what we consider to be the major weaknesses in the arguments for a universalistic presidency and why we believe presidents instead have strong incentives to pursue particularistic policies, specifically those that disproportionately benefit swing state voters and channel benefits to their co-partisan base.

Are presidents driven by reelection? After all, from the start of their administrations, they already possess an innate institutional capacity to attain power as well as an intense popular expectation to use it. Moreover, they face only a single reelection campaign and a maximum of eight years in office. These factors may combine to weaken the influence of electoral incentives on presidents' behavior in office, compared to those faced by members of Congress.

Yet, it is hard to deny that electoral calculations matter considerably to presidents based on the sheer weight of contemporary experience. Presidential actions from executive orders to liberalize immigration policies to decisions concerning how fast to draw down the war in Afghanistan appear in both their content and timing to be influenced by electoral concerns.[52] Moreover, Mayhew's fundamental insight for members of Congress – that without first securing their reelection members are unable to pursue the policy and institutional power goals that also motivate them – also holds for presidents. First-term presidents inherently desire a second term to complete and consolidate their initial accomplishments and to strike out in new directions. Moreover, even in their second terms, presidents know that the best way to solidify their legacy and entrench their lasting influence on the course of public policy is to ensure the succession of a co-partisan in the White House. Presidency scholars have never given the electoral incentive as much emphasis as have congressional scholars following in Mayhew's wake. However, presidency scholarship has long acknowledged the need to build electoral coalitions.[53]

Assuming presidents are motivated by electoral pressures, how do they maximize their and their party's electoral fortunes? The universalistic paradigm argues that presidents embrace policies that maximize the national interest. Pursuing policies based on efficiency, not politics, benefits the most people, which in turn translates into the most votes.

As we argue in greater detail in the next chapter, this view fails to recognize the seeds of presidential particularism that are ingrained within

---

[52] See, e.g., Milkis (2013); Nasr (2013).
[53] See, e.g., Cohen (2006); Edwards (2000); Seligman and Covington (1989).

the constitutional structures of our electoral system. To foreshadow our argument, all voters are not of equal electoral importance to the president, as most of the scholarship positing presidential universalism either explicitly or implicitly assumes. Rather, the existence of the Electoral College, coupled with the adoption of winner-take-all apportionment of electoral votes in forty-eight states, results in some Americans having greater electoral clout than others.[54] From an electoral perspective, neither President Obama nor Governor Romney cared much about the average Massachusetts voter in 2012. It was a foregone conclusion that President Obama would capture the Bay State's eleven electoral votes. By contrast, the average voter just up I-93 in New Hampshire was heavily targeted by both camps, because the state was a hotly contested battleground state that, despite having fewer than one-fifth as many people as Massachusetts, potentially could have determined the outcome of the election.[55]

How should a president cater to these swing voters, aside from bombarding them with campaign visits and advertisements? The universalistic presidency paradigm argues that presidents do so by pursuing nationally optimal outcomes. By contrast, we argue and demonstrate empirically in the chapters that follow that voters punish or reward presidents not only for the performance of the government as a whole but also for how their policies affect voters' local geographic constituencies. Thus, voters incentivize presidents to pursue particularistic policies that channel federal dollars disproportionately to key constituencies in swing states.[56] This is a core logic and expectation of our theory of presidential particularism.

Moreover, while presidents aspire to be leaders of the nation as a whole, they are also undeniably leaders of their political parties. Pundits and scholars alike have argued that presidents have embraced this mantle more strongly than ever before in recent decades, culminating in what Charles Cameron has called the "polarized presidency."[57] As a partisan

---

[54] See, inter alia, Edwards (2004).

[55] Often lost amid the 2000 fiasco in Florida was the fact that if Vice President Gore had carried New Hampshire, he would have won a majority of votes in the Electoral College.

[56] Prior scholarship has recognized the possibility that presidents will pursue, at least on occasion, policies that are primarily aimed at securing votes for reelection. For example, George Edwards notes that there are exceptions to our common conceptions of the presidency and Congress: "Of course, members of Congress are not, at least not usually, merely parochial and selfish representatives of special interests, with no concern for the general welfare. Moreover, presidential policies may be ill considered or be designed primarily to benefit the president's electoral coalition" (Edwards, 2000, 67).

[57] Bond and Fleisher (2000); Cameron (2000); Galvin (2009); Milkis and Rhodes (2007); Skinner (2008).

leader, a president has strong incentives to pursue policies that maximize outcomes for the core partisan constituency, not policies that maximize outputs for the nation as a whole.[58] Thus, partisan forces, which are particularly strong in our contemporary, ideologically polarized, and hyperpartisan environment, may also compel presidents to pursue aggressively particularistic policies.[59]

1.4 When Goals Collide

At least since Paul Light, presidential scholars have acknowledged that presidents pursue multiple goals when seeking to put their stamp on public policy.[60] As the universalistic framework emphasizes, presidents are concerned with power, legacy, and securing policy outcomes that benefit the nation as a whole. However, to achieve any of their goals, presidents must first build and sustain an electoral coalition. Once in office, presidents rely heavily on their partisan base for support in the public and in the legislature. This creates strong incentives for presidents to pursue policies that will solidify and grow their partisan base. In some instances, these goals may be complementary. But in many others, they will necessarily be in conflict. When this happens, which goals and incentives have the greatest influence on presidential behavior?[61]

When seeking to allocate finite federal resources, particularly in an era of growing scarcity, will the president primarily seek maximum efficiency increasing the overall utility of the nation? Or will he strive to target such resources strategically, concentrating benefits in key swing states

---

[58] Wood (2009).

[59] On polarization more generally, see McCarty et al. (2006).

[60] Light (1998 [1982]).

[61] We are not the first to note this tension and speculate about its consequences for policymaking. For example, Jeffrey Cohen (2006, 541) emphasizes the competing directions in which presidents are sometimes pulled: "For instance, on the one hand the president is a symbol, representative, and leader of the entire nation. But the president is also a partisan who seeks benefits for some sectors of the polity, such as his party and those who voted for him. Presidents seek these particularized group-specific benefits as they try to build coalitions in support of their electoral and policy goals." Similarly, Sidney Milkis, Jesse Rhodes, and Emily Charnock (2012, 59) describe Barack Obama as "an ambitious politician caught between the conflicting institutional and electoral imperatives of contemporary party politics." We build on this prior research; develop precise hypotheses about how such concerns will manifest themselves in policy outcomes; and marshal an array of data, both quantitative and qualitative, across multiple policy venues to provide the most comprehensive assessment yet of the relative influence of universalistic and particularistic impulses on presidential policymaking.

and districts or channeling as many benefits as possible to core partisan constituencies?

In arguing that presidents are routinely driven to engage in their own form of particularism, we still acknowledge important and fundamental differences in the policy outlooks and priorities of presidents and members of Congress. To be sure, congressional scholarship from Mayhew onward emphasizing the importance of the electoral connection and catering to the needs of specific constituencies undoubtedly characterizes a great deal of congressional behavior. Similarly, presidents undeniably have a national constituency. The power they wield in Washington and ultimately their lasting historical legacies depend in large part on national policy outcomes; their continuance in office depends to a considerable degree on national conditions and political forces. Using Howell and colleagues' framework, we acknowledge that presidents and members of Congress may routinely differ on the relative importance they attach to the national and local consequences of governmental policy. Yet, existing scholarship arguing that presidents almost exclusively care about the national consequences of policy choices misses the strong electoral and partisan incentives they have to pursue policies that cater to the needs of politically valuable constituencies. The universalistic perspective risks blinding us to the potential adverse consequences of the erosion of checks and balances and the ascendance of presidential power that has occurred in recent decades by falsely assuring Americans that presidents pursue policies that maximize the national interest.

The material costs of presidential particularism are sizable. As we show in analyses throughout the book, a single county may lose out on tens of millions of dollars by virtue of whether it is located in an uncompetitive rather than a swing state, or whether it reliably backed the opposition party as opposed to the president. While we offer new theoretical insights into the political behavior of presidents, we also describe a phenomenon with real-world consequences. Particularistic impulses drive presidents to influence substantially the allocation of federal benefits across the country as a whole, to the tune of billions of dollars each year. And further delegation to the White House, which many analysts have proposed as a solution to our current institutional malaise, is likely to exacerbate these trends.

1.5 Road Map

In the next chapter, we lay out in detail our theory of the forces driving presidential particularism. We begin by arguing that the universalistic framework fundamentally misconstrues the nature of the electoral incentives that presidents face. Rather, the Electoral College dictates that some voters are more important to the president than are others. Moreover, voters reward or punish presidents at the polls not only for national policy performance but also for how federal policies have affected their local communities. These factors combine to give presidents strong incentives to target federal dollars to voters in battleground states. However, presidents also possess incentives to engage in other forms of particularism. Presidents are partisan leaders with strong incentives to pursue policies that reward their core partisan base. Presidents may also strategically use their influence over the budget to reward co-partisan members of Congress in an effort to build political capital for future initiatives. The chapter concludes with a precise set of hypotheses that guide our analysis of presidential particularism that follows.

We begin by looking for evidence of presidential particularism in a range of policy areas, including several where we might least expect it. In Chapter 3, we find strong evidence of electoral particularism in trade policy. Seeking to insulate trade policy from parochial impulses, Congress has delegated considerable authority to the president to decide whether to employ protectionist measures to assist domestic industries hurt by unfair foreign competition. While presidents since Franklin Roosevelt have advanced free trade in the aggregate, they have routinely deviated from their overarching principles to defend the interests of industries concentrated in electorally critical parts of the country. Within the context of closing obsolete and redundant military bases, we show that the commander-in-chief has repeatedly acted as partisan-in-chief. When given the opportunity, presidents have sought to protect bases in core co-partisan constituencies and concentrate the economic pain of closures in parts of the country that reliably back the partisan opposition.

In Chapter 4 we present startling evidence of electoral and partisan particularism in presidential natural disaster declarations. Even after controlling for actual disaster damage and objective economic need, we find that presidents disproportionately award disaster aid to parts of the country that are key to their electoral prospects or that are part of their core partisan base. We also find strong evidence of presidential targeting in a policy venue long held to be dominated not by the president but by Congress: the allocation of federal transportation dollars across the country.

We then cast a broader net and look for evidence of presidential particularism in federal spending writ large. Chapter 5 begins by describing the mechanisms through which presidents can influence budgetary outcomes.

Although Congress has the power of the purse, as head of the bureaucracy presidents possess a number of levers through which they can shape how federal dollars are geographically distributed. We then examine the allocation of more than $8 trillion in federal grant spending across the country from 1984 through 2008. In sharp contrast to the norms of universalism, we find strong evidence that presidents systematically target federal grant dollars both to battleground states and to core partisan constituencies. Swing state targeting varies with the electoral calendar, while core constituency targeting is a persistent force in presidential policymaking. We also test arguments about where presidents should target dollars within swing states to reap the maximum electoral advantage. Surprisingly, our data suggests that the inequalities that arise through presidential particularism may dwarf those produced by parochial impulses within Congress.

The analysis concludes by shifting focus to voters and how they respond to targeted spending in their local communities. Chapter 6 tests one of the core assumptions underlying our theory of electoral particularism: that voters reward or punish presidents at the polls for the share of federal spending their local communities receive. Past scholarship has almost exclusively focused on the effects of federal spending on congressional outcomes to surprisingly little effect. We argue that earlier studies have largely looked in the wrong place for evidence of an electoral linkage between local spending and electoral outcomes. In our increasingly presidentialized political system, voters logically hold presidents accountable for a full panoply of policy outcomes, including the distribution of federal spending. Marshaling election data from more than two decades, we show that presidents reap significant rewards at the ballot box in counties that experienced an infusion of election-year federal grant spending. We supplement this observational evidence from electoral returns with an original survey experiment showing conclusively that voters do indeed reward the president for federal spending in their local communities.

To conclude, Chapter 7 reflects on the broader consequences of presidential particularism for our polity. As citizens, we overlook the consequences of presidential particularism at our own peril. Political scientists, economists, legal scholars, and average Americans alike risk fundamentally misunderstanding policy processes if they assume that presidents act as a counterbalance to the particularistic impulses of members of the legislative branch. The danger of this misunderstanding is compounded by the ever-growing powers of the American presidency. If presidents pursue the national interest, then rising presidential power at the expense of Congress may – apologies to Madison – paradoxically serve the public interest. However, if growing presidential power leads to the replacement of one form of particularism with another, the erosion of our system of checks and balances is unlikely to yield any benefits in terms of policy outcomes, and instead may come at a significant cost for democratic governance.

2

The Origins of Presidential Particularism

The political scientist Harold Lasswell famously defined *politics* as who gets what, when, and how. On these questions, the universalistic presidency framework and the vision of a particularistic presidency that we offer in its place yield starkly diverging expectations. When making major policy decisions and deciding how to allocate federal resources across the country, do presidents prioritize the needs and desires of some constituencies over others? The universalistic presidency framework argues no. Presidents, alone in our system, possess a truly national constituency. As such, they are uniquely positioned to pursue nationally optimal policy outcomes. Unlike members of Congress, they know that their lasting legacy will be measured by how they served the national interest, not how they balanced such imperatives with the need to serve a more narrow geographic constituency.

We do not dispute that presidents are motivated by an intense desire to champion and implement policies that benefit the nation as a whole. However, we argue that presidents also have strong incentives to be particularistic – that is, to weigh the needs and desires of some Americans more heavily than others when forming their policy priorities. The incentives driving particularistic behaviors are multiple. For example, electoral motivations drive presidents to respond disproportionately to the interests of voters in constituencies with the most clout in the next presidential contest. Moreover, presidents are more than reelection seekers; they are also partisan leaders. As such, presidents routinely prioritize the needs of their partisan base over those of constituencies that reliably back the partisan opposition. As party leaders, presidents reliably move to channel federal benefits to constituencies that send co-partisan legislators to Washington.

The differences between the universalistic and particularistic paradigms are not merely theoretical or semantic. Rather, they have serious, tangible consequences for public policymaking in America. Left to their own devices, presidents do not simply pursue policies that maximize benefits for the entire nation. Rather, strong particularistic forces compel them to pursue policies that produce significant inequalities in federal policy that benefit constituencies of greater political importance to the president at the expense of others.

2.1 Electoral Particularism

Virtually all analysts of the presidency from the founding through to the modern day begin by emphasizing that the president is the only officeholder in our political system elected by the nation as a whole.[1] In 2012, the president's constituency numbered almost 241 million voters.[2] No elected office in the United States, or the world for that matter, has as many constituents.[3] But the fact that the presidential constituency is orders of magnitude larger than that of any member of the House or Senate does not in and of itself imply that presidents care only about national policy outcomes. Rather, the key question is what policy outcomes presidents should pursue to maximize their prospects of winning elections? Whether presidents should embrace particularistic policies to maximize their vote share depends on how voters make choices in presidential elections. For what outcomes do voters hold presidents accountable at the ballot box?

Election postmortems produce a dizzying array of factors that are alleged to have tilted the balance of victory from one candidate to the other. Many journalistic accounts focus on the personalities of the principals, single events, or the strategic decisions made by campaigns. Following President Obama's reelection in 2012, for example, pundits proffered

---

[1] The vice president is also elected by the nation as a whole but as the less prominent partner on the president's ticket.

[2] http://elections.gmu.edu/voter_turnout.htm.

[3] The next largest single constituency belongs to the Indonesian president. According to the International Institute for Democracy and Electoral Assistance, the voting aged population in the 2014 Indonesian presidential election numbered 168 million, about 70% of the American voting aged population in 2012. However, more voters turned out to vote for the Indonesian president in 2014 than the American president in 2012.

a host of explanations for Obama's victory ranging from Governor Romney's verbal gaffes – the infamous 47 percent critique and his "binders full of women" debate slip – to the Obama campaign's decision to advertise early and often on sitcoms popular among young women.[4] The ebb and flow of campaign momentum provides for dramatic political theater, and it offers steady employment for a host of modern day TV augurs who inspect daily the latest presidential tracking polls for evidence of each factor's impact on the horse race. However, as Andrew Gelman and Gary King noted two decades ago, a great puzzle of American elections is that, despite the considerable volatility in public opinion polls during the course of the campaign, American presidential election outcomes are often quite predictable in the aggregate.[5]

Among most scholars and many commentators, national factors, especially the state of the national economy, matter most. For many election cycles, political scientists have created forecast models that use only a few variables to predict with considerable accuracy the final vote share of the incumbent presidential party, usually before the general election campaigns even begin. At the core of virtually every one of these models is some measure of national economic performance.[6] The change in real disposable income, the index of consumer sentiment, growth in the gross domestic product: each scholar tweaks the specifics of his or her model, but the emphasis on the state of the national economy is constant. Armed only with a few key economic variables and usually some measure of public support for the incumbent president – itself a quantity highly influenced by economic assessments – scholars can predict with considerable accuracy how well the incumbent party will fare at the polls.[7]

Other scholarship emphasizes the power national forces and assessments have on individual voting decisions. Forecast models show that national economic indicators often yield accurate predictions of presidential vote share in the aggregate, presumably because voters hold presidents accountable for national economic outcomes. This is supported by a long tradition of scholarship emphasizing the importance of "sociotropic"

---

[4] Scott Wilson and Philip Rucker, "The strategy that paved a winning path," *Washington Post*, November 7, 2012. http://www.washingtonpost.com/politics/decision2012/the-strategy-that-paved-a-winning-path/2012/11/07/0a1201c8-2769-11e2-b2a0-ae18d6159439-story.html.

[5] Gelman and King (1993).

[6] See, e.g., Abramowitz (2008); Erikson (1989); Lewis-Beck and Tien (2008).

[7] See, e.g., Clarke and Stewart (1994); Erikson et al. (2000); MacKuen et al. (1992); Norpoth (1985).

voting among individuals: studies of how individual voters make up their minds have consistently shown that how voters view the health of the national economy is among the most important determinants of their vote choices.[8] To be sure, there are differences in emphasis. Some scholarship argues that voters are primarily retrospective; they cast the proverbial finger to the wind and reward incumbents for strong economic performance and punish those who preside over sluggish economic conditions.[9] Others contend that voters are more sophisticated and make prospective assessments of how well the economy is poised to perform in the near future.[10] Regardless of the relative weight voters give to retrospective and prospective assessments, the most important consequence for presidents is that assessments of the health of the national economy are paramount on voters' minds as they head to the polls.[11]

If this view is correct, and if voters hold presidents accountable only for the state of the nation as a whole, then presidents have scant electoral incentive to weigh the needs and interests of some voters more heavily than those of others. Because the president serves a national constituency, the utility of one voter or group of voters is of equal value to the president

---

[8] The importance of national economic assessments or "sociotropic" concerns, as they are often called in the political science literature, may surprise some, particularly given the widespread lack of political information (Delli Carpini and Keeter, 1996) and heavy reliance on simple heuristics (Popkin, 1994) that characterize the median voter. However, Diana Mutz argues that the mass media play a key role in encouraging such behavior (Mutz, 1992). By repeatedly emphasizing national economic conditions in its election coverage, the media produce a sociotropic priming effect through which they encourage voters to evaluate candidates in terms of the performance of the national economy.

[9] Alesina et al. (1993); Bartels (2008); Fiorina (1981); Key (1966).

[10] See, e.g., Erikson et al. (2000); Suzuki and Chappell (1996).

[11] See, e.g. Kinder and Kiewiet (1981). Some scholars have challenged this emphasis on national conditions, arguing that voters rely more on pocketbook considerations when voting in presidential contests. Instead, this school of thought argues that voters reward or punish incumbent presidents based on whether their personal economic fortunes have risen or sunk during the incumbent's term in office. While there is modest evidence of pocketbook voting, the bulk of the data strongly supports the preeminence of national economic conditions in voters' decision calculus (Kiewiet, 1983; Kinder et al., 1989; Kinder and Kiewiet, 1981; Lanoue, 1994; Markus, 1992); though see Kramer (1983). For example, in 1992 the Clinton-Gore campaign famously ran on the slogan, "It's the Economy, Stupid!" (a slogan that Mitt Romney reprised two decades later in 2012). But which economy mattered? In an analysis of voter decision making in 1992, Alvarez and Nagler (1995) present convincing evidence that voters gave only scant weight to their own employment prospects and financial situation when deciding whether to vote to reelect President Bush or to support Clinton or the third-party candidate, H. Ross Perot. Instead, voters' assessments of the overall economic climate in the country dominated their electoral choices.

as that of any other voter. Therefore, to compete for the greatest number of votes, presidents should pursue policies that maximize outputs for the greatest number of people.

Moreover, even if Americans in some parts of the country had disproportionate influence on the election, because voters evaluate presidents and their policies primarily on national and not local or personal terms, presidents should pursue policies that benefit the economy and country as a whole, rather than cater to the needs of specific constituencies. Whereas members of Congress may logically seek to channel as many dollars as possible to their own narrow constituencies, because voters are held to evaluate presidents primarily based on national outcomes, presidents do not have electoral incentives to target budgetary resources inefficiently. Instead, serendipitously, presidents are incentivized to pursue policies that maximize national outcomes and eschew the parochial concerns of a privileged few.

As a result, the universalistic presidency framework predicts that measures of a constituency's electoral importance to the president and his party will not be associated with the share of federal benefits that it receives. Under the universalistic framework, there is no reason to expect presidents to target funds toward some constituencies and away from others for electoral reasons.

We argue that this perspective fundamentally misconstrues the nature of the electoral incentives that presidents face. In sharp contrast to a foundational assumption of the universalistic framework, we contend that voters hold presidents accountable for *local* as well as national outcomes.

2.1.1 *All Politics Is Local*

To adapt former House Speaker Tip O'Neill's famous aphorism, all politics – even presidential politics – is, at least in part, local. To ignore the local dimension of presidential electoral politics is to risk making false assumptions about the forces motivating presidential behavior. Most prior researchers have downplayed the importance of local forces in presidential elections. The relative weight that voters place on national versus local concerns will vary across individuals and over time. However, a growing number of studies suggest that the local consequences of federal policies have significant and consistent influence on presidential elections.

Why do local conditions and experiences influence voters' decisions for a national office? First, policies made in Washington have consequences for both the nation as a whole and the communities in which voters live.

As a result, voters may logically hold presidents accountable for both national and local policy outcomes. Second, local conditions and policy outcomes may be particularly salient because most Americans are not instinctively attuned to national conditions. Rather, they see the world and the effects of government policies largely through the lens of their local communities. Particularly when trying to assess the president's policies and whether they have been good or bad for the nation, the local impacts of these policies may be more readily available and accessible for many Americans. When evaluating a president, voters may care more about whether the local steel mill was protected from foreign competition, flood victims down county received federal disaster assistance, or the military base on which the local economy heavily depends escaped the latest round of base closings than about conditions in the nation as a whole. Consequently, voters rationally use this localized information as a heuristic when evaluating the president's job performance.[12]

On most issues, even issues of major national import, the public as a whole is surprisingly uninformed. For example, research has shown that the public knows very little about objective economic conditions in the country as a whole[13] or the total number of casualties suffered in a foreign war.[14] This holds even for highly salient metrics on which we judge government performance. Consider public views about the unemployment rate, perhaps the most frequently reported and readily interpretable national economic indicator. According to the Bureau of Labor Statistics, unemployment peaked at 10.0 percent in October 2009. As late as the close of 2010, it sat at 9.4 percent, and then it declined steadily throughout 2011, reaching 8.3 percent by February 2012. That month, the Pew Research Center asked a representative sample of Americans: "In recent months, has the national unemployment rate been increasing or decreasing?" Only 58 percent correctly said that unemployment was falling, a figure not that much higher than what should have been produced by random guessing. A full 32 percent of respondents thought that unemployment was increasing.[15]

For a number of reasons, these discrepancies are not all that surprising. Average Americans do not directly experience the national gross

---

[12] For example, Cohen (2006) shows that state unemployment rates are a strong and statistically significant predictor of state-level presidential approval ratings.

[13] Conover et al. (1986, 1987).

[14] Berinsky (2007).

[15] Pew Research Center for the People and the Press Political Survey, February 8–12, 2012, USPSRA.021612.R3.

domestic product or the national unemployment rate. National statistics can be ominously portrayed in the mass media, but for millions they may have little relationship to the conditions that voters observe in their daily lives.[16]

Whereas national policy outcomes can be removed from everyday experience, the localized consequences of these policies are more directly integrated into daily life. Moreover, personal experiences with the localized consequences of federal policies are supplemented through conversations with family, friends, coworkers, and neighbors; the information about governmental performance in general and presidential stewardship of the country in particular gleaned through interpersonal networks tends to be heavily influenced by the local climate in which these networks are embedded.

Information about the local consequences of federal policies is also made more readily available by local media outlets, on which many Americans continue to rely for the bulk of their political information.[17] Local media sources pay more attention to federal policies, from taxes and spending priorities to foreign wars, when their effects hit close to home. Physical closeness is a critically important news value.[18] Consider, for example, local news coverage of federal stimulus spending. To the extent that local media covered various efforts by the Obama administration to prime the pump with federal dollars in the aggregate, local papers and TV broadcasts, like larger, more national outlets, often emphasized bickering and ugly politicking in Washington, including rampant charges that taxpayer dollars were being wasted. However, federal stimulus projects that affected local communities most often received significant and favorable coverage.

In Chapter 1, we briefly discussed the Obama administration's efforts to channel as many federal dollars as possible to support a wide array of projects in the key swing state of Ohio. Local media outlets matched

---

[16] For example, in early 2012, the unemployment rate in Virginia sat at 5.6 percent, whereas in California it was almost twice as high at 11.0 percent. Voters in the former experienced a labor market significantly better than the country as a whole, while those in the latter faced even bleaker employment prospects than the average American. Given such disparities, it would be surprising if the average Virginian did not judge President Obama's economic stewardship differently than the average Californian, all else being equal.

[17] Gilliam, Jr. and Iyengar (2000).

[18] Among others, see Behr and Iyengar (1985); Goidel and Langley (1995); Harrington (1989); Molotch and Lester (1974); Shoemaker and Reese (1996); Wilkins and Patterson (1987).

the deluge of dollars from Washington with story after story detailing the federal projects undertaken in the state and how they might translate into jobs. Large grants, such as a federal award for an airport runway extension in Toledo, received considerable attention in large city newspapers.[19] But even smaller grants received significant attention from local newspaper outlets.[20] For example, under the headline "Federal grant may restore jobs," *The Middletown Journal* in March 2012 heralded a federal firefighter staffing grant that would allow the town to rehire five laid-off workers and to hire an additional firefighter for the local station.[21] Even when jobs were not at the forefront, local coverage emphasized the direct effect of federal grant programs on the quality of life in local communities. For example, an article in *The Lima News* proclaimed that "the effort to help Allen County residents live healthier lives got a little easier, thanks in part to a $1.2 million federal grant to Activate Allen County, community leaders said this morning."[22]

Thus, local reporting encourages retrospective Americans to evaluate presidents not just in terms of national conditions and policy outcomes but also in terms of the state of affairs in their local communities and whether presidential policies have brought additional benefits or imposed costs on the places where voters live and work. Indeed, a wave of recent research from varying perspectives has found evidence that local conditions and the localized consequences of federal policies affect voters' electoral calculus in presidential contests. For example, recent studies argue that local economic conditions exert substantial influence on presidential vote choice. Local unemployment, income growth, and even factors such as local fuel prices and foreclosure rates all have been shown to be influential in presidential elections.[23]

In a different policy venue, other scholars have shown that even major wars – seemingly the most national of all public policies – can also have

[19]   David Patch, "Toledo Express wins $5.7 million runway grant," *The Blade*, August 29, 2012.
[20]   Examining the credit that members of Congress receive for local spending, Grimmer et al. (2012), in an experimental context, find that politicians are rewarded based on the number of awards, not on the amount of the reward.
[21]   Michael Pitman, "Federal Grant May Restore Jobs," *The Middletown Journal*, March 4, 2012.
[22]   Bob Blake, "Activate Allen County nets $1.2 million federal grant," *The Lima News*, September 26, 2012.
[23]   See, e.g. Abrams and Butkiewicz (1995); Books and Prysby (1999); Reeves and Gimpel (2012); Snowberg et al. (2014).

significant localized electoral consequences.[24] None of America's wars since World War II have required mass mobilization of society on a war footing; as a result, those fighting and dying in America's wars from Korea through Afghanistan have not hailed equally from all parts of the country.[25] Americans from communities that suffer high casualty rates "see" the costs of war in much sharper relief than do residents of low-casualty communities, which are relatively more insulated from the human toll of the nation's military policies. Those who see the localized costs of war disproportionately punish the incumbent president or his partisan successor at the ballot box.[26]

To some observers, the importance that voters attach to local conditions and policy consequences in presidential contests may be surprising. After all, these are commonly thought to be the stuff of congressional, not presidential, elections. However, it bears emphasizing that politics at all levels is increasingly centered around the president. More than forty years ago, Richard Neustadt warned that demands for presidential action from all corners far outstripped presidential capacity to meet them. In Neustadt's memorable phrase, "Everybody now expects the man in the White House to do something about everything."[27] If anything, the popular expectations under which presidents labor have only increased since Neustadt wrote. On virtually every issue, of grand or trivial import, the public looks to the president for leadership and solutions. Emphasizing the irrelevant, research by Andrew Healy, Neil Malhotra, and Cecilia Mo finds that support for the president increases after local college football and basketball game victories.[28] Likewise, Christopher Achen and Larry Bartels document the strange case of President Woodrow Wilson being punished for shark attacks off the southern coast of New Jersey in his 1916 bid for reelection.[29] While these are extreme cases, they underline a wider point: voters routinely hold presidents accountable for localized outcomes, even if they are beyond the president's control.

Just as important, presidential campaigns *believe* that voters in key constituencies make their decisions based in large part on local factors. For example, Bush administration officials publicly stated that they

---

[24] Kriner and Shen (2014).
[25] Kriner and Shen (2010).
[26] Karol and Miguel (2007); Kriner and Reeves (2012).
[27] Neustadt (1990 [1960], 7).
[28] Healy et al. (2010).
[29] Achen and Bartels (2004).

believed their victory in West Virginia in 2000 – which was pivotal in securing the presidency – was in large part the result of voters punishing Vice President Al Gore for the Clinton administration's failure to defend domestic steel from foreign competition.[30] President Obama made his support for the auto bailouts a centerpiece of his efforts to win Ohio in 2012. Governor Romney tried to turn the tables by launching a series of ads alleging that GM and Jeep were shipping Midwestern jobs overseas. However, David Plouffe, the president's campaign guru, argued that the Romney gambit would only backfire by reminding voters of the extraordinary efforts Obama took to rescue the industry and save jobs in the Buckeye State – see discussion above.[31] Similarly, Obama campaign officials expressed confidence that low unemployment in Virginia (5.9 percent versus just under 8.0 percent in the nation as a whole) would buoy the president's chances there, while the Romney campaign hoped that the looming specter of sequestration, which threatened massive layoffs of federal employees living in Virginia, would open the door for a Romney victory.[32]

Perceiving that they are held responsible for many local phenomena, presidents have responded in kind. In his aptly titled book *Going Local*, Jeffrey Cohen shows that presidents have adapted to major changes in the media environment by increasingly geographically targeting their public appeals.[33] As national presidential appeals have gradually lost their influence with the demise of large national audiences and the Golden Era of Presidential Television dominated by the Big Three networks, presidents have increasingly targeted their appeal to specific localities, emphasizing the connection of their initiatives to local conditions and endeavoring to dominate local news coverage.[34] In this way, presidents have further encouraged voters to hold them responsible for localized policy outcomes. Yet, we argue these incentives have done more than change the way presidents communicate with and seek to mobilize voters. They have also

---

[30] "Behind the steel-tariff curtain," *Businessweek*, March 7, 2002. http://www.business week.com/stories/2002-03-07/behind-the-steel-tariff-curtain.

[31] Gabriella Schwarz, "Axelrod: Obama closing argument 'from his loins,'" *CNN Political Ticker*. http://politicalticker.blogs.cnn.com/2012/11/02/axelrod-obama-closing-argument-from-his-loins/.

[32] Elizabeth Hartfield, "Battleground: Will Virginia stay with Obama?" *ABC News*, October 30, 2012. http://abcnews.go.com/Politics/OTUS/virginia-swing-voters/story?id=17589979.

[33] Cohen (2010).

[34] Baum and Kernell (1999).

encouraged presidents to craft policy initiatives that respond specifically to the needs of local communities.

2.1.2 The Electoral College and Political Equality

We argue that voters hold presidents accountable for local policy outcomes. However, this does not imply that presidents should deviate from the expectations of universalism. If all voters have equal weight in selecting the next president, then the best strategy for securing the most votes is to benefit the greatest number of people. This would dictate a budgetary strategy that seeks to maximize only economic efficiency; the political characteristics of a state or county should have no influence on the share of federal dollars it receives. But as even casual observers of American presidential elections know, this is not the case. Presidential elections are governed by the Electoral College, which distinguishes the presidential election contest from a popular vote in two important respects.

First, the Constitution specifies that each state receives the number of electors "equal to the whole number of Senators and Representatives to which the State may be entitled in the Congress." Therefore, the malapportionment present in the U.S. Senate is also enshrined in the Electoral College. As a result, residents of less populous states, such as Delaware or Wyoming, enjoy more representation in the Electoral College than do residents of large states, such as California or Texas.

Second, despite its affront to "one man, one vote," malapportionment of electors is less influential than how states allocate their electoral votes to the winner. The Constitution grants to each state the prerogative to determine how to award its electors. In the early nineteenth century, many states allocated their electors on a district basis, awarding electors to the candidate who carried the popular vote in a specified region of the state. However, this began to change with the advent of Jacksonian Democracy, and since 1832 only three states have deviated from the new norm of winner-take-all allocation; that is, the candidate who wins a plurality of votes in a state receives all of its electoral votes. Today, only Maine and Nebraska follow a version of the district plan.[35]

The almost universal adoption of winner-take-all allocation means that many states are firmly in the camp of one political party or the other. For instance, even though the share of the two-party vote earned by the Republican presidential candidate in Texas has ranged from 53 percent

---

[35] For historical overviews of the Electoral College, see Berdahl (1949); Dougherty (1906); Edwards (2004).

to 62 percent since 1996, there is little chance that the Republican will lose the state. Although the level of support for the Republican candidate may shift substantially, there is virtually no chance that it will fall below that of the Democratic nominee. The result is that voters in Texas and other such states are taken for granted by the favored party's candidate and systematically ignored by the other party's candidate. Swing state voters plainly wield more political clout than citizens of electorally uncompetitive states.

Critics of the Electoral College have long noted the many unintended consequences that have arisen from its design. Perhaps one of the most oft-cited and immediately obvious consequences is that presidential candidates concentrate the bulk of their time, advertising dollars, and resources reaching out to and seeking to persuade voters in swing states at the expense of voters residing in other parts of the country.[36] For instance, in 2004, California saw neither George W. Bush nor John Kerry make a campaign appearance between early September and Election Day.[37] President Barack Obama himself put it best while on the reelection trail in October 2012. The president began the day in New Hampshire, a small but critically important swing state that, with the election only four weeks away, many pundits still labeled a toss-up. After a campaign event in Manchester, Obama headed to Manhattan for the Al Smith dinner at Manhattan's glitzy Waldorf Astoria Hotel in the non-battleground state of New York.[38] In addition to offering presidential candidates the opportunity to hob-knob with top Catholic leaders, the Al Smith dinner traditionally gives candidates the chance to show off their comedic credentials. Following this protocol, after Governor Romney gave his address to the assembly, the president rose and led off with a joke: "In less than three weeks, voters in states like Ohio, Virginia, and Florida will decide this incredibly important election, which begs the question, what are we doing here?"[39] The audience roared its approval with a hearty laugh. But beneath the chuckles, the joke reminded listeners of a fundamental truth about our electoral system: because of its institutional

[36] Among others, see Banzhaff (1968); Bartels (1985); Brams and Davis (1974); Nagler and Leighley (1992).
[37] Shaw (2006, table 4.3).
[38] For the president's schedule that day, see http://www.whitehouse.gov/schedule/president/2012-10-18.
[39] Barack Obama, "Remarks at the Alfred E. Smith Memorial Foundation Dinner in New York City," October 18, 2012. Online by Gerhard Peters and John T. Woolley, The American Presidency Project. http://www.presidency.ucsb.edu/ws/?pid=102391.

structure, presidential candidates are all but compelled to value and vie for the votes of some Americans more than others.

If all the Electoral College and winner-take-all apportionment did was to encourage presidential candidates to spend the bulk of their time and campaign dollars in swing states or even to focus on the issues and concerns of swing state voters, perhaps the ramifications for American democracy would be modest. However, because voters hold presidents accountable for local phenomena, presidents have strong incentives to pursue policies that advance the interests of swing states in the hopes of maximizing their and their co-partisan successors' chances at winning the next election.[40] Voters reward presidents for increased federal largesse in their local communities and punish them for failing to be responsive to their needs.[41] Thus, presidents should pursue policies that allocate federal dollars disproportionately to swing states with the most electoral leverage.

We readily acknowledge that the universalistic and particularistic conceptions of the presidency are not mutually exclusive. The president is undoubtedly a universalistic actor concerned about the national welfare. However, the structure of our electoral system coupled with voters holding presidents accountable for local policy outcomes combine to incentivize the president to trade an efficient pursuit of the national good for policies that disproportionately benefit electorally important constituents. Through this mechanism, political inequality in presidential elections is translated into inequality in concrete policy outcomes.

2.2 Partisan Particularism

While presidents are representatives of the American people as a whole, they are also the leaders of their political party. Scholars have long recognized that presidents of different political parties enter office with different agendas and competing ideological visions concerning the types of

---

[40] See also Hudak (2014).

[41] Not all voters will reward presidents for increased spending in their local communities equally – and some may not even reward the president at all. For example, the demand for federal benefits, even for benefits specifically targeted to voters' local communities, may vary by ideology, with liberals rewarding presidents more than conservatives do (Lazarus and Reilly, 2010). Indeed, we have explored some of this variation in our earlier research (Kriner and Reeves, 2012). While understanding this variation is undoubtedly important, the central implication of this alternative vision of American electoral behavior is that geographic targeting of federal grants stands to benefit the president and his party at the polls within the targeted constituencies.

policies that best serve the national interest. However, much of the research in the universalistic framework fails to consider the extent to which partisan imperatives cause presidents to prioritize the needs of some members of their national constituency over those of others.

In *The Myth of Presidential Representation*, B. Dan Wood challenges the idea that presidents respond to centrist opinion and instead argues that presidents are first and foremost partisan leaders responsive to the needs and wants of the constituency that put them in office. "Having achieved electoral success," Wood argues, "presidents are anxious to pursue their most favored policies and reward core supporters with benefits that accrue from election outcomes."[42] In a similar vein, Daniel Galvin's *Presidential Party Building* emphasizes the important role that many modern presidents, particularly Republicans, have played in building their party's resources and enhancing its electoral competitiveness. The ever-increasing polarization of our political system in recent decades has only exacerbated matters, with some scholars decrying the emergence of a "partisan presidency."[43] The hallmark of this new vision of presidential leadership, according to Sidney Milkis and colleagues, is "an emergent style of partisan presidential leadership featuring vigorous efforts to accomplish party objectives."[44]

This scholarship reminds us that presidents are both national leaders and partisan leaders. The latter role motivates another form of presidential particularism: presidents may be more responsive to the needs of their core partisan base than to those of less reliable partisan voters. As a result, rather than targeting federal benefits only in swing states, constituencies that are highly populated with presidential co-partisans – which we label *core states* – might also reap disproportionate shares of federal largesse.

Presidents could pursue policies that disproportionately reward core states for several reasons. First, presidents could target core states for electoral purposes. Risk-averse presidents may be wise to take nothing for granted. A state may be "core" today but gone tomorrow. For example, throughout the 1990s and early 2000s, Indiana was a solidly Republican state; yet, in 2008, Indiana voters sent shock waves through the political system by narrowly voting for Barack Obama over John McCain. Pursuing policies that channel federal resources to core states

---

[42] Wood (2009, 36).

[43] See Cameron (2002); Cohen et al. (2008); Galvin (2013); Milkis and Rhodes (2007); Newman and Siegle (2010); Skinner (2008).

[44] Milkis et al. (2012, 58).

may serve an important role in shoring up the party's electoral foundation. However, such a strategy comes at a cost, as resources that are spent in core constituencies are then unavailable to help bolster a president's cause in swing states, the most electorally valuable constituencies.

Second, as Dan Wood has argued, presidents may face strong incentives to reward their partisan base. As partisans-in-chief, presidents may pursue policies consciously designed to channel benefits disproportionately to core partisan constituencies. For example, Democratic presidents owe their election in significant part to strong levels of support in many of the nation's cities. By championing large expansions of federal housing, community development, and other grant programs that overwhelmingly benefit urban communities, Democratic presidents can reward a key component of their party base. By contrast, Republican presidents may pursue an expanded program of agricultural grants, the benefits of which will accrue disproportionately to rural areas that tend to be bastions of Republicanism. Geographic targeting is not the conscious aim – rather, benefiting specific groups is – but it is the end result of pursuing such priorities.[45]

Third, it is possible that core state targeting – the concentration of federal policy benefits in parts of the country that solidly back the president and his party – could be an unintended though no less tangible result of presidents of different parties possessing different ideas of how best to serve the needs of the nation and pursuing different programmatic agendas accordingly. In this framework, Democratic presidents may pursue mass transit and expanded welfare programs not to reward co-partisan voters but because they believe such policies best serve the needs of the nation. Republican presidents, by contrast, may believe that the national interest is better served through other projects, like agricultural subsidies or additional defense spending, which tend to concentrate benefits in Republican-leaning districts. Thus, presidents may pursue universalistic ends through particularistic means.

In many policy venues, discerning between the partisan reward and competing visions of the national interest hypotheses is exceedingly difficult because they both yield the same observable prediction: core

---

[45] This logic is consistent with the Congress-centric literature on federal spending, which argues that the distribution of federal spending across the country varies significantly depending on whether Democrats or Republicans control Congress because the two parties pursue different programmatic agendas and priorities. See, inter alia, Albouy (2013); Stein and Bickers (1995).

partisan constituencies receiving a disproportionate share of federal benefits. Consider tax policy. Few would be surprised if a Democratic president championed increased tax rates on the rich and an expansion of the earned income tax credit to assist the working poor. By contrast, most Republican presidents reliably support reduction in tax rates, particularly at the top end of the distribution, and other policies such as reduced capital gains tax rates and the elimination of the estate tax that disproportionately benefit the wealthy. If enacted, such policies concentrate their benefits on each party's core constituency. The poor, even in red states, overwhelmingly vote Democratic, while the rich, particularly in the red states, solidly back Republicans.[46] The resulting inequality in the allocation of policy benefits along political lines is partisan particularism. However, in this case geographic targeting to core constituencies may not be the primary aim. Rather, Democratic presidents believe that a tax code benefiting the poor best serves the national interest, particularly in an age of stark income inequality, while Republican presidents believe that lessening the tax burden on the wealthy will create more jobs and increase opportunity for all. Whether presidents are consciously seeking to reward fellow partisans or merely pursuing different visions of how best to serve the national interest is difficult to determine.

However, through a pair of carefully chosen case studies on military base closings and natural disaster declarations, we are able to gain leverage on the question. In these narrow cases, objective economics alone should drive presidential decisions. Democratic presidents cannot credibly claim that the national interest is better served by closing a base in a Republican rather than a Democratic district, all else being equal. Similarly, how could a Republican president truthfully argue that responding to a natural disaster in a Republican district is in the national interest, but ignoring a disaster that caused equivalent levels of damage in a Democratic district is not? Thus, if we find evidence of partisan particularism in these cases, it would testify to the paramount importance of partisan motives and imperatives.

2.3 Coalitional Particularism

Partisan incentives and a desire to bolster the strength of their legislative coalitions can combine to induce another form of presidential particularism: presidents may target benefits to parts of the country that

---

[46] Gelman (2008).

elect co-partisans to Congress. In one of the only other political science analyses of presidential targeting, Christopher Berry, Barry Burden, and William Howell find that presidents engage in precisely this behavior.[47]

Targeting grant dollars to the constituencies of co-partisan members can serve a number of goals. First, contemporary presidents face strong demands from all corners to be a strong party leader. Core constituency targeting is one way to respond to such pressures. Shifting more federal resources toward districts represented by co-partisan members can also help satisfy these demands. Second, co-partisan targeting provides presidents with valuable political currency on Capitol Hill. Members of Congress value specific federal benefits such as grants for their districts. By helping co-partisans procure them, presidents seek to win political favors that they can call on for support of their major priorities. Indeed, solidifying support among their co-partisans on Capitol Hill has long been recognized as a key legislative coalition-building strategy.[48] Third, presidents may target federal dollars to co-partisan members' constituencies with an eye toward the future in the hopes of bolstering their party's ranks in succeeding Congresses. While political pundits often emphasize various sources of presidential power, such as the president's eloquence, his arm-twisting ability in private negotiations, or his standing among the public, decades of research show that the strength of the president's party in the legislature is the most important factor influencing the president's success in Congress.[49] As a result, through this type of particularistic targeting, presidents can pursue a mix of partisan and legislative goals.

2.4 Presidential Particularism and the Political Business Cycle

Thus far, we have focused on the *who* of the particularistic president. That is, we have identified three types of constituencies that presidents might endeavor to target with additional federal resources: swing states, core states, and constituencies represented by co-partisans in Congress. Yet, the logic of the particularistic president also suggests differences in

---

[47] Berry et al. (2010). For a similar logic concerning the distribution of campaign fundraising efforts, see Jacobson et al. (2004). For other studies examining the role of the president in the allocation of federal spending, see Bertelli and Grose (2009); Frisch and Kelly (2011); Gimpel et al. (2012); Hudak (2012); Larcinese et al. (2006); Shor (2006). For a different interpretation of the empirical evidence for this type of targeting, see Dynes and Huber (2015).

[48] Cohen (2006); Edwards (2000).

[49] See, e.g., Barrett and Eshbaugh-Soha (2007); Beckman (2010); Canes-Wrone and De Marchi (2002); Marshall and Prins (2007); Rivers and Rose (1985).

when presidents should target these types of constituencies. To this end, we outline a further testable implication of our theory. If presidents are actively targeting federal dollars to swing states for reelection purposes, they should be especially incentivized to do so during an election year.

One of our central claims is that presidents respond to electoral incentives to target federal dollars to swing states. This behavior, we argue, is motivated by voters who reward the commander-in-chief for federal spending in their local communities. Because swing states have disproportionate influence over the next presidential contest, presidents should logically direct as many federal resources as possible to communities within battleground states. But should presidents pursue such swing state targeting with the same vigor throughout their term in office? Or does the incentive to target federal grants for electoral gain increase as the next election nears?

Political scientists have long searched for evidence of a political business cycle in presidential politics. If voters focus on factors in the immediate runup to an election instead of evaluating performance over an entire four-year term, then politicians have incentives to pursue short-term improvements of the election-year economy.[50] Edward Tufte was one of the first to present evidence of this behavior.[51] Among the anecdotal evidence he offers was that in 1972, an election year, Richard Nixon notified Social Security recipients that the Congress had passed and he had signed into law a 20 percent increase in their benefits. To ensure that the message was not lost on voters, Nixon had it printed on the envelope.[52] In a study of presidential elections from 1948 to 2005, Larry Bartels finds evidence of a broader trend. Republican presidents see exceptionally high income growth during election years (perhaps a result of explicit policy choices), which may be a reason for their success in presidential elections despite weaker income growth over the entirety of their administrations.[53] Though the logic of retrospective voting suggests that voters' evaluations of presidents should be based on economic performance over their entire tenure in office, virtually every study linking economic outcomes to presidential vote share has focused exclusively on economic performance during the election year itself.[54] The data is unambiguous: short-term economic conditions have much greater

---

[50] On voter myopia see Healy and Lenz (2014); Huber et al. (2012); Kramer (1971).
[51] Tufte (1978).
[52] Tufte (1978, 32).
[53] Bartels (2008, 106).
[54] Bartels (2008, 100).

influence on electoral outcomes than do more temporally distant economic data.

Presidents may always favor swing states; however, if our theory of electoral particularism is correct, the incentives to do so are even greater in election years. Thus, a further observable implication of our theory is that the evidence of swing state targeting should be even stronger in election years than in the first three years of a president's term.

We can also use the electoral calendar to gain greater insight into the mechanisms driving core state targeting. If presidents target core states primarily for electoral purposes, then core state targeting should be more prominent in election years. However, as we argued, core state targeting is not as efficient for electoral purposes as targeting swing states. Instead, core state targeting may be better explained by presidents' desire to pursue policies that cater to the needs of their fellow partisans in the mass public. If core state targeting primarily serves non-electoral goals, we should not expect levels of core state targeting to fluctuate with the electoral calendar.

2.5 Whither Congress?

Many of the policy areas we examine in the chapters that follow involve varying aspects of divide-the-dollar politics. Given this emphasis on distributive politics, some will undoubtedly be surprised that our discussion focuses on the president and not on Congress. After all, Article I of the Constitution entrusts the power of the purse to the legislature. As a result, with a few notable exceptions, the vast majority of studies examining the distribution of federal resources treats Congress as the main (or even the only) political player.

The president is just one of many politicians who influence the distribution of federal spending. Governors, mayors, and bureaucrats also undoubtedly shape the allocation of federal resources. We acknowledge that legislators play a key role in shaping budgetary outcomes; however, we warn that analysts of budgetary politics ignore the presidency at their peril. We do not claim that presidents unilaterally control the geographic allocation of the bulk of federal spending (though in Chapters 3 and 4 we examine several important cases in which presidents *do* wield such unilateral control). Nevertheless, through a variety of levers employed both during the legislative process itself and in the policy implementation phase, we argue that presidents have the capacity to influence the distribution of federal dollars across the country. As we have shown, presidents

TABLE 2.1. *Summary of Hypotheses*

	Universalism
Null Hypothesis	The allocation of federal policy benefits across constituencies should not be correlated with a state's or county's political characteristics.
	Particularism
	Electoral
Swing State Hypothesis	All else being equal, counties in swing states should receive more federal benefits than counties in uncompetitive states in the upcoming presidential election.
Election Year Hypothesis	Counties in swing states should receive an even greater share of federal dollars in presidential election years than in off years. Effect will be even stronger when president is running for reelection.
	Partisan
Core State Hypothesis	All else being equal, core states that strongly support the president's party should receive more federal dollars than other states.
	Coalitional
Co-Partisan Hypothesis	Presidents should also target federal dollars to constituencies represented by their fellow partisans in Congress.

have incentives to pursue a different distribution of federal dollars than legislators pursue. The ability of presidents to influence spending is most often akin to a thumb on the scale. It is a bias, and the magnitude of the bias can be examined only through systematic analyses such as those we present in the chapters that follow. If there is no bias, then the political variables discussed earlier, such as whether a state is a swing state or a core state and the stage in the political business cycle, should not predict the share of federal spending that a constituency receives.

Ultimately, the relative influence of presidents and Congress over the geographic distribution of federal dollars is an empirical question. Our analysis of federal grant allocation at the county level explicitly tests for the influence of both branches of government by examining which constituencies receive the most federal funds – those that are of critical importance to the president or those that are championed by key members of Congress. Through these analyses, we endeavor to show that many features of the allocation of grants across the country reflect the interests and desires of the president and would not arise under a system dominated exclusively by legislators at the other end of Pennsylvania Avenue.

2.6 Recap

The two views of presidential electoral politics we discuss in this chapter produce two distinct sets of hypotheses about the types of policies presidents should pursue. In the chapters that follow, we test these predictions empirically. The hypotheses are summarized for quick reference in Table 2.1. The first framework, based on the assumption that voters hold incumbent administrations accountable primarily for national conditions, posits presidential universalism. Presidents maximize their and their party's electoral fortunes by pursuing policies that best serve the national interest. This leads to the expectation that presidents will not target federal benefits to specific constituencies based on their political characteristics. By contrast, recent scholarship arguing that voters also vote for president based on local policy outcomes suggests a different set of incentives for presidents. Rather than pursuing universalism, presidents have incentives to target federal resources disproportionately toward some constituencies and away from others. Electoral incentives encourage swing state targeting. Partisan imperatives incentivize presidents to disproportionately reward core partisan constituencies. A combination of partisan and coalitional incentives also motivate presidents to channel benefits toward constituencies represented by co-partisan members of Congress.

3

Base Closings and Trade

As an initial inquiry into the scope of presidential particularism, we examine the politics driving presidential behavior in the cases of foreign trade policy and military base closings. These policies are of national importance and affect communities directly. Decisions to grant an industry protection are an economic boon for the communities where that industry is concentrated – but they simultaneously impose an economic cost on the country as a whole. Similarly, decisions concerning military base closings involve the allocation of billions of tax dollars and can mean the difference between economic decay and rejuvenation for the affected communities.

We focus on trade and base closures for two reasons. First, in both policy areas presidents have enjoyed considerable independent authority to act without congressional approval. With respect to trade, Congress has delegated authority to the president on multiple fronts, particularly in dealing with domestic demands for protection from foreign competition. Presidents possess great discretion when deciding whether to help an industry adversely affected by free trade. As a result, when trying to understand why some industries are granted relief while others are denied, we look to the president and the incentives he faces. In the military realm, there have been significant shifts in the unilateral power of presidents to select military bases for closure over time. As a result, by comparing and contrasting the politics of base closings and where they occur across the country in times of unilateral presidential control versus when the president is constrained by statute, we can isolate the influence of presidential particularism on policy.

Second, these policies each present multiple avenues for presidents to act on their particularistic impulses. In trade policy, we see evidence of all three forms of particularism described in Chapter 2, with an emphasis on the pursuit of targeted policies to bolster the president's electoral fortunes. In the case of base closings, we find the strongest evidence for partisan particularism. Presidents seek to concentrate the economic pain of base closures in opposition party strongholds and insulate their core co-partisan constituencies from losses.

A final advantage of studying base closings is the insight this case affords into the motivations driving partisan particularism. In many realms, presidents could pursue policies that disproportionately benefit their co-partisans either because they desire to reward their political base or because they believe that these policies are genuinely in the national interest. In the base closure scenario, determining what is in the national interest is much more a function of straightforward economics. Thus, to the extent that we see evidence of partisan particularism in base closings, we find support for presidents acting routinely as partisan leaders who prioritize the needs and wants of their co-partisans in the mass public over those of the nation as a whole.

For each policy area, we begin with an overview of the origins and development of presidential authority and a discussion of how particularistic forces have played out more broadly. Then, for each policy venue we focus more intently on a single important case: President Bush's 2002 decision to raise tariffs to protect the steel industry, and the dramatic shift in the Department of Defense's proposed list of base closures from 1990 to 1991. In these detailed case studies, we fully unpack the particularistic forces producing presidential policy decisions.

3.1 Particularistic Trade Policies

At first blush, trade policy might appear a strange venue in which to look for evidence of presidential particularism. Article I, Section 8 of the Constitution plainly vests in Congress the power to regulate foreign commerce. However, Article II grants the president several vantage points from which he can influence America's relations with other nations. Moreover, while Congress largely dominated trade policy for the first 150 years of our nation's history, presidents since the New Deal have played an increasingly important role in shaping this critical component of national economic policy.

Most prior scholarship on trade politics argues that structural differences between Congress and the presidency lead each branch to pursue
different balances of protectionism and free trade. Power in the contemporary Congress is heavily decentralized. It is fragmented across scores of
committee and subcommittee chairs, and even members with no formal
influence can gain leverage on issues about which they care intensely.
As a result, the legislature affords multiple points of access for powerful
special interests seeking protection from foreign competition. Moreover,
because members of Congress represent relatively narrow geographic constituencies, it is easy for adversely affected industries to find allies that
will advocate their interests in the legislature as a whole. Given the way
power is distributed and the necessity of building coalitions across issues,
public choice theorists argue that members of Congress should routinely
prioritize powerful special interests over the more diffuse interests of the
nation.[1]

The president, by contrast, is insulated from narrow, geographically
based pressures and free to pursue policies that maximize outcomes for
the nation and not a single district. The pressures to respond to specialized
lobbying are tempered by a more general responsiveness to the needs of
the nation as a whole.[2] While free trade imposes costs narrowly on certain
industries and constituencies, it is held to maximize economic outcomes
for the country in the aggregate. Thus, on balance, presidents have strong
incentives to defend free trade against protectionist demands.

3.2 Presidential Protectionism

In 1930, Congress enacted the most austere tariff bill in our nation's
history, the Smoot-Hawley Tariff, with disastrous consequences for the
American and world economies.[3] After President Hoover's defeat in
1932, President Roosevelt and the Democratic Congress sought a dramatic overhaul of the nation's trade policy. The centerpiece of their
initial response was the Reciprocal Trade Agreements Act of 1934, which

---

[1] See, inter alia, Epstein and O'Halloran (1999).
[2] Rowley et al. (1995).
[3] It is interesting to note President Hoover's role in the passage of the tariff bill. Hoover
campaigned on the need for increased tariffs, and he signed the bill, despite clear threats
by more than 30 countries of retaliatory tariffs and a letter signed by more than 1,000
economists urging him to veto the legislation. In the assessment of Rowley et al. (1995,
159), "Thus, when brokering or allowing protection, one could argue that he was responding to his constituency with a keen eye on the Electoral College, and seeking to get
reelected."

authorized the president to negotiate and implement international agreements with other nations to reduce tariffs. This act, bolstered by subsequent extensions and refinements, marked a watershed in American trade policy that delegated considerable authority from the legislature to the executive branch. At least one scholar of trade policy has argued that the move was a conscious effort by Congress, understanding the economic perils of protectionism, to insulate itself from such pressures by delegating authority to the president. Essentially, Congress "legislated itself out of the business of making product-specific law."[4] True to form, presidents of both parties have consistently proclaimed greater support for free trade than many members of Congress have, particularly those who represent districts with sectors threatened by cheap foreign imports.

However, presidents have also routinely provided relief from foreign competition for select industries, particularly those with considerable political clout. As former Director of Studies at the Council of Foreign Relations Gary Hufbauer argues, "With bipartisan regularity, American presidents since Franklin Delano Roosevelt have proclaimed the virtues of free trade. They have inaugurated bold international programs to reduce tariff and nontariff barriers. But almost in the same breath, most presidents have advocated or accepted special measures to protect problem industries."[5]

Presidents have a variety of mechanisms at their disposal to assist industries adversely affected by foreign competition. Some of these tools were explicitly created by congressional statute and delegated to the president, such as the escape clause provisions of Section 201 of the Trade Act of 1974 or other provisions allowing specific tariffs or quotas to protect victims of unfair competition. Presidents also enjoy significant unilateral authority to negotiate "voluntary" agreements with other countries to limit imports in exchange for avoiding the formal imposition of tariffs or quotas. Many economists decry such voluntary export restraint (VER) agreements as even less efficient than quotas or tariffs. Yet, for presidents seeking to balance political imperatives for protection against a larger philosophical commitment to free trade, they have proven to be "a highly valuable protectionist tool precisely because they skirt around policy incoherence, addressing powerful political demands without inflicting high political or economic costs."[6]

---

[4] Destler (2005, 13).
[5] Hufbauer et al. (1986, 1).
[6] Rowley et al. (1995, 215).

Yet, just because presidents have the means at their disposal to assist industries facing stiff foreign competition does not mean that presidents uniformly do so. Rather, presidential use of these tools has been uneven, though one pattern is clear: presidents are highly responsive to demands for protectionism from industries with the greatest electoral clout.[7] As Hufbauer and colleagues argue, "Special protection is highly inequitable as between industries. Large industries with political clout – dairy, apparel, automobiles – are able to shake the U.S. political system for massive benefits. Small industries with only regional influence – footwear, copper, CB radios – at best get escape clause relief and often get nothing. Unfairness may be a fact of political life, but it is not an attractive fact."[8]

For example, in 1960 the Democratic nominee John F. Kennedy worried about his electoral strength in the South. Indignation over President Truman's integration of the military and support for more aggressive action in civil rights had broken the "solid South" in 1948 by giving rise to the Dixiecrat candidacy of South Carolina's Strom Thurmond. While most of the former Confederacy returned to the Democratic voting base in 1952 and 1956, Eisenhower carried Tennessee, Virginia, and Florida in both races, and in North Carolina the race was extraordinarily close. Eisenhower had won Texas both times, first by 7 percent and then by almost 12 percent. In 1960 the former architect of the Normandy invasion would no longer be at the top of the Republican ticket; but Kennedy worried that his liberalism on civil rights and his Roman Catholicism could be serious liabilities in both Texas and the rest of the South.

Offering the vice presidency to Lyndon Johnson was Kennedy's first gambit to locking down the South.[9] In another overture to Southern voters, Kennedy also campaigned on his determination to aid the textile industry and its workers. Indeed, Kennedy highlighted the plight

---

[7] For example, see the formal model and empirical analysis in Muûls and Petropoulou (2013), showing how the concentration of an industry in swing states significantly increased the level of protectionist non-tariff barriers it received in 1983. See also Busch and Reinhardt (2005).

[8] Hufbauer et al. (1986, 22). These inequalities serve as a reminder that even in a policy venue where presidents are explicitly held to be a counterweight to the parochial impulses of Congress, presidents routinely engage in their own brand of particularistic policies, pursuing their own electoral and political gain at the expense of maximally efficient economic policies.

[9] Kennedy adviser Kenneth O'Donnell first learned of the decision when he heard from Pierre Salinger that Robert Kennedy had asked him "to add up the electoral votes in the states we're sure of and to add Texas," Dallek (2003, 271).

of unemployed textile workers in his speech accepting the Democratic nomination.[10] Kennedy received the endorsement of the Textile Union shortly thereafter. In its statement, the union reminded its workers that this election gave them a "a genuine opportunity to change the negative attitude which has prevailed in the White House for the last seven and a half years."[11] While it is impossible to discern how important Kennedy's pledge of assistance was, he was able to stem the party's bleeding and secure enough electoral votes in the deep South to win the presidency.

In office, Kennedy pursued significant trade liberalization, culminating in the Trade Expansion Act of 1962 and the initiation of the Kennedy Round talks that resulted in significant tariff reductions. Yet, even as it began to lay the groundwork for its push for trade liberalization, the administration sought to make good on its campaign pledge to textiles manufacturers. In May 1961 the president announced a seven-point plan to provide assistance to the textile industry.[12] By March 1962, the administration had delivered on all seven of its promises.[13] Reflecting on the curious juxtaposition of free trade rhetoric and naked protectionism, the *New York Times* concluded: "In short, this was to be the most liberal American trade policy ever set to parchment.... But in performance the administration has already invited questions of whether it means what it says."[14]

As part of his own Southern strategy, Richard Nixon during the 1968 campaign pledged to go even further to defend the textile industry if

[10] "But we are not merely running against Mr. Nixon. Our task is not merely one of itemizing Republican failures. Nor is that wholly necessary. For the families forced from the farm will know how to vote without our telling them. The unemployed miners and textile workers will know how to vote. The old people without medical care – the families without a decent home – the parents of children without adequate food or schools – they all know that it's time for a change." http://millercenter.org/president/speeches/detail/3362.

[11] "Kennedy favored: Textile Union board urges support for candidate," *New York Times*, July 28, 1960, p. 16.

[12] John F. Kennedy, "Statement by the President Announcing a Program of Assistance to the Textile Industry," May 2, 1961. Online by Gerhard Peters and John T. Woolley, The American Presidency Project. www.presidency.ucsb.edu/ws/?pid=8102.

[13] While such actions were a direct response to Kennedy's 1960 campaign promise to the industry and the voters across the South who depended directly or indirectly on textiles, Kennedy's actions were also critically important to securing enough votes from southern House members as well as from New England members with strong woolen textile interests in their districts for the Trade Expansion Act. See Finger and Harrison (1996).

[14] Richard Mooney, "Trade plan's conflicts: Liberal trade policy may not be so liberal when the special exemptions are taken into account," *New York Times*, December 10, 1962, p. 13.

elected. Seeking Southern votes in what promised to be an exceedingly tight race with Vice President Hubert Humphrey – a race whose complexion in that region was severely complicated by the third-party candidacy of Alabama governor George Wallace – Nixon promised to expand the scope of existing agreements to further protect woolen textiles as well as synthetics. Nixon won the presidency by less than half a percentage point. Once in office, he made good on his campaign pledge by renegotiating Kennedy's long-term import restraint agreement with the Multi-Fiber Arrangement.

As many sectors of the American economy began to lose the global dominance they held in the 1950s and 1960s, the pressures for protectionist interventions grew. Ardent self-proclaimed free trader Ronald Reagan – who once listed among his heroes Richard Cobden and John Bright, the free trade–expounding founders of Britain's Anti-Corn Law League – engaged in protectionist actions to such an extent that I. M. Destler has summarized Reagan's record as "liberal words, protectionist deeds."[15] During his first term, Reagan granted protection to multiple industries, including sugar, automobiles, textiles, and steel.[16] We focus here briefly on the latter two.

Seeking votes in President Carter's backyard, Reagan pledged himself in 1980 to protect the textile industry in a public letter to South Carolina's senior Senator Strom Thurmond. "The fiber-textile-apparel manufacturing complex provides 2.3 million vitally needed American jobs . . . as president, I shall make sure that these jobs remain in this country."[17] Reagan narrowly defeated Carter in North Carolina, South Carolina, Alabama, and Mississippi by an average of less than 1.5 percent. Seeking to solidify his electoral prospects in the region, Reagan took a number of steps to further insulate the textile industry from foreign competition. In the assessment of the CATO Institute, the end result was that under Reagan, "textile import quotas have been negotiated or imposed in record numbers and with unprecedented degrees of restraint [on free trade]."[18]

[15] Destler (2005). For a scathing critique of Reagan's rhetoric and actions on trade, see Sheldon Richman. 1988. "The Reagan record on trade: Rhetoric vs. reality." *Cato Policy Analysis* 107. http://www.cato.org/pubs/pas/pa107.html.

[16] Hufbauer et al. (1986, 2).

[17] Steven Pressman, "Pressure mounts on protectionist bills," *Congressional Quarterly Weekly Report*, August 4, 1984, pp. 1896–1899.

[18] Sheldon Richman. 1988. "The Reagan record on trade: Rhetoric vs. reality." *Cato Policy Analysis* 107. http://www.cato.org/pubs/pas/pa107.html. During his second term, Reagan would veto legislation that would provide additional protection to the textile industry.

But perhaps nowhere was President Reagan more aggressive than in moving in an election year to protect the American steel industry. Seeking to capitalize on the administration's reelection imperative, the steel industry waited until 1984 to petition the International Trade Commission (ITC) for an investigation into unfair trading practices. The ITC heard the case in May 1984 and recommended action in June to protect the industry from unfair competition; it forwarded its recommendations to the administration in July, giving the president sixty days to decide whether to accept the ITC's recommendations, take alternative actions, or take no action. Although it can be difficult to remember given the eventual landslide won by Reagan in 1984, for much of the year most experts predicted a hotly contested battle. As a result, Reagan's response to the steel case was of considerable political importance. As described by *Congressional Quarterly*,

> The steel debate, in particular, is fraught with political ramifications. Five of the largest steel-producing states – Illinois, Indiana, Michigan, Ohio, and Pennsylvania – also are rich in electoral votes and are likely to be pivotal states in the campaign between Reagan and former Vice President Walter F. Mondale.

The steel companies knew this and tried to capitalize on it when filing their complaint. "'If I were a steel company or the union I would say that's a darn good strategy,' said Rep. Bill Frenzel, R-Minn., one of Congress' leading free trade advocates. 'If I were the administration, I'd call it cruel and unusual punishment.'"[19]

Ultimately the administration announced that it would move aggressively to negotiate a series of VER agreements with foreign exporters to reduce the total volume of steel exports by about 30 percent, lowering their volume to less than 20 percent of the domestic market. Steel executives publicly backed the move.[20]

Through such actions to protect politically important industries, protectionism increased significantly during Reagan's first term. The percentage of manufactured imports that were subject to quantitative restrictions more than doubled from 1981 to 1983.[21]

---

[19] Steven Pressman, "Pressure mounts on protectionist bills," *Congressional Quarterly Weekly Report*, August 4, 1984, pp. 1896–1899.

[20] Clyde Farnsworth, "Reagan seeks cut in steel imports through accords," *New York Times*, September 18, 1984, A1; Stuart Auerbach, "Steel imports to be cut 30%, White House announces," *Washington Post*, December 20, 1984, D1.

[21] As of 1980, the relevant figure was 6.2%. From 1981 to 1983, another 6.52 percent became subject to quantitative restraints. Bela Belassa and Carol Belassa. 1984. "Industrial protection in developed countries." *The World Economy* 7: 179–196.

3.2.1 *President Bush and the 2002 Steel Tariffs*

When Americans think about the 2000 presidential election, visions of Florida, butterfly ballots, hanging chads, and a 5–4 ruling from the U.S. Supreme Court spring to mind. However, while Florida was clearly the epicenter of the political battle after Election Day, equally critical to George W. Bush's electoral victory was West Virginia, a state that had solidly backed the Democratic candidate in five of the preceding six presidential elections. West Virginia twice awarded its electoral votes to Jimmy Carter, and Michael Dukakis carried the state by almost 5 percent over George H. W. Bush in 1988. Only four years before the 2000 race, Bill Clinton trounced Bob Dole in West Virginia, winning the state by roughly fifteen percentage points. However, George W. Bush turned the tide and captured West Virginia. Without its critically important five electoral votes, Bush would have lost the Electoral College (in addition to the popular vote) to Al Gore, even with his disputed victory in Florida.

Undoubtedly, Bush's victory was due in part to gradual ideological change and partisan realignment within the Mountain State. However, many within the Bush-Cheney team saw their victory as being in part attributable to a strategic error by the Clinton administration. By failing to act aggressively enough in 1998–1999 to protect the flagging steel industry, Clinton had missed an important opportunity to boost the Democratic ticket's fortunes in West Virginia and other steel-producing states. This was a mistake that the Bush campaign had exploited and that the new Bush administration vowed not to repeat.

In late 1998, a consortium of major steel corporations and the United Steelworkers launched the Stand up for Steel campaign to pressure Washington to enact protective tariffs and anti-dumping measures. These actions would prop up a crumbling steel industry besieged by foreign competition and low-priced imports from overseas.[22] Responding to political pressure, the Republican-controlled House of Representatives easily passed legislation that would have established quotas for foreign steel imports. The Clinton administration, however, believed that the measure violated international trade agreements and so opposed the House bill. After an extensive lobbying campaign in the Senate, Clinton succeeded in killing the bill in the upper chamber.[23] In its place, the president

---

[22] Leslie Wayne, "American steel at the barricades; With prices low, companies and labor unions unite in a campaign to limit imports," *New York Times*, December 10, 1998, C1.

[23] Lori Nitschke, "Trade: White House, farm groups stave off Senate vote on steel import quotas," *CQ Weekly*, June 26, 1999, p. 1563.

championed a more modest package of $300 million in tax breaks and anti-dumping measures to provide the industry with some relief; however, the end result was far less than what the industry demanded.[24] This is not to say that Clinton was unresponsive to the electoral imperatives in play. Rather, *Congressional Quarterly* described the administration as seeking a middle ground because it "feared political repercussions for Vice President Al Gore if President Clinton were forced to choose between free-trade interests, which opposed the bill, and unions, which supported it."[25]

In the assessment of Bob Zoellick, U.S. Trade Representative under Bush, disaffected steelworkers and voters living in steel communities in West Virginia abandoned Gore as a result and likely provided Bush's margin of victory in the state.[26] Indeed, the Bush-Cheney campaign sensed an opening created by Clinton's hesitance to back strong protective tariffs. To highlight their differences, Dick Cheney hit the campaign trail promising voters that, if elected, he and Bush would take strong and decisive action to protect the steel industry. Many steelworkers admitted feeling a sense of betrayal by Clinton.[27] Seeking to capitalize on this voter disillusionment, Cheney pledged before a crowd in Weirton: "We will never lie to you. If our trading partners violate our trading laws, we will respond swiftly and firmly."[28] The campaign's efforts to reach out to traditional Democratic constituencies bore fruit, and Bush became the first nonincumbent Republican presidential candidate to carry West Virginia since Herbert Hoover in 1928.

The steel industry would not wait long to test whether the Bush-Cheney promises of assistance were genuine. On June 5, 2001, President Bush, in response to strong pressure from steel companies, directed the ITC to begin an investigation into whether foreign producers were engaging in predatory pricing and dumping steel onto the U.S. market.[29] By December 2001, the ITC concluded that the steel industry was the victim of

[24] "Throwing sand in the gears," *The Economist*, January 28, 1999. www.economist.com/node/184376.
[25] Lori Nitschke, "Trade: White House, farm groups stave off Senate vote on steel import quotas," *CQ Weekly*, June 26, 1999, p. 1563.
[26] "Behind the steel-tariff curtain," *Businessweek*, March 7, 2002. www.businessweek.com/stories/2002-03-07/behind-the-steel-tariff-curtain.
[27] David Sanger and Joseph Kahn, "Bush weighs raising steel tariffs but exempting most poor nations," *New York Times*, March 4, 2002, A1.
[28] Quoted in Robert Byrd, *Congressional Record*, December 9, 2003, p. 323–24.
[29] Stephen Cooney, "Steel: key issues for Congress," *Congressional Research Service*, RS21152, May 30, 2002.

unfair trade practices; however, the members of the commission differed substantially in terms of their proposed remedies.

Many others disagreed with the ITC and did not recommend imposing protective tariffs. Within the White House, director of the National Economic Council Larry Lindsay (who would later be fired for publicly estimating that the costs of the Iraq War could be as high as $100 billion or even $200 billion) strongly opposed protectionist remedies on classical economic grounds. Higher tariffs might help steel producers in the short run, but they would also make U.S. manufactured goods that use steel less competitive on the global market. Secretary of State Colin Powell also opposed protectionist tariffs and warned that such a move could alienate key European allies in the War on Terror. Many former trade officials also criticized protectionist measures.[30] In addition to questioning the administration's economic rationale for imposing the tariffs, virtually all analysts questioned their legality.[31]

Ultimately, the administration was left with a choice between abiding by its free trade principles or selectively abandoning them to pursue political gain in key Rust Belt states, including West Virginia, Pennsylvania, Ohio, and Indiana. In addition to bolstering the president's own reelection prospects in 2004, helping steel was widely viewed as critical to keeping the Republican majority in the upcoming House midterm elections, as a number of Republicans won marginal races in steel-heavy districts in 2000. For example, one midterm race where steel loomed large was in Pennsylvania's 15th district, home to Bethlehem Steel. Republican incumbent Patrick Toomey faced a strident challenge from Democrat Ed O'Brien, a former United Steeelworkers Union official who worked at Bethlehem Steel. Toomey had narrowly defeated O'Brien 53 percent to 47 percent in 2000. Yet, Al Gore also narrowly carried the district, which gave hope to many Democrats that O'Brien could unseat Toomey in a rematch.[32] Presidential action to protect steel could defend Toomey,

[30] For example, former U.S. Trade Representative William Eberle suggested that a 5% to 10% tariff might have been reasonable but concluded that ultimately the problems with U.S. steel industry were internal, not a result of unfair foreign competition (Ho, 2003). Other analysts noted that there was little evidence of active dumping; indeed, domestic overproduction was perhaps an even greater problem, with 15 million tons of excess capacity.

[31] Center for Strategic And International Studies, "Trade policy challenges in 2002: Six former U.S. Trade Representatives discuss WTO, China, EU relations, FTAA, Fastrack, and the steel and lumber cases," 49, February 12, 2002.

[32] Daphne Retter, "Counting on trade issues' impact in Pennsylvania union country," *CQ Weekly*, August 10, 2002, pp. 2172–2173.

a free trader who had voted to renew the president's fast-track trade authority, and give him valuable political cover.[33]

On March 5, 2002, President Bush unilaterally imposed a range of tariffs, averaging approximately 30 percent, on imported steel products.[34] Interestingly, in almost every case, Bush's tariffs exceeded those recommended by the ITC.[35] The director of the Cato Institute's trade policy center, Brink Lindsey, decried the action as "the triumph of politics over principle and policy" and a "surrender to special interests." Similarly, Senator Phil Gramm, a fellow Texas Republican and free trader, lamented: "The president helped steel because they have got lots of political power in important states in the union. If Enron had been a steel company, they never would have gone broke. I can assure you of that."[36] President Bush's chief political strategist, Karl Rove, was widely believed to have been a driving force behind the decision. For example, Rove engaged in a public confrontation with free trade backers in New Orleans, a major port city, and articulated the administration's rationale for the decision. In the assessment of *Businessweek*: "The White House characterized the decision as being driven solely by economics and international trade law. But that Bush's chief political strategist found himself so enmeshed in the minutiae of trade policy – and so many of the administration's economic lieutenants found themselves arguing about politics – shows how the decision became a struggle of economics vs. politics."[37]

Further testifying to the key role played by politics, the tariffs themselves varied significantly across different types of imported steel products. The harshest tariffs were imposed on tin steel, precisely the type

---

[33] Buoyed by the administration's help for steel, Toomey more than doubled his 2000 margin of victory in 2002, defeating O'Brien 57% to 43%.

[34] The president could have pursued alternative legislative remedies to assist the steel industry and those affected by its contraction. For example, the House introduced a bill to assist the steel industry with nearly $13 billion in retirement liabilities, and the Senate considered a bill to establish a steelworker health care trust fund. These were the true costs saddling the industry (Ho, 2003). Both, however, were anathema to the administration's ideology.

[35] Steel Products Proclamation, 65 Fed. Reg. 10,593, March 5, 2002. Robert Read. 2005. "The political economy of trade protection: The determinants and welfare impact of the 2002 U.S. emergency steel safeguard measures." *The World Economy* 28: 1119–1137.

[36] Gebe Martinez, "Bush breaks with position, moves to protect steel industry," *CQ Weekly*, March 9, 2002, pp. 655–657.

[37] "Behind the steel-tariff curtain," *Businessweek*, March 7, 2002. www.businessweek .com/stories/2002-03-07/behind-the-steel-tariff-curtain.

made by Weirton Steel in West Virginia, the state's biggest employer, and the site of Dick Cheney's October 2000 campaign promise.[38] Ultimately, the president's own U.S. Trade Representative, Bob Zoellick, admitted that politics, not principle, drove the decision: "We are committed to moving forward with free trade...[but] we have to manage political support for free trade at home. We have to create coalitions."[39] Responding to such claims of political necessity, *The Economist* inveighed: "The steel-tariff plan, it is important to remember, lies well outside the ordinary run of bad economic policy; it is so wrong that it makes other kinds of wealth-destroying intervention feel inadequate." But was it politically inescapable? "What a depressingly feeble excuse from a president who has promised, and shown, strong leadership in other respects, and who claimed, by the way, to be a champion of liberal trade. Mr. Bush and his advisers should be ashamed."[40]

The European Union, the main target of the sanctions (exporters in many other countries, including Canada, Mexico, Brazil, and Russia, were granted exceptions by the administration), clearly believed the decision was primarily about politics – presidential electoral politics. Within days, the EU launched a formal complaint concerning the U.S. tariffs with the World Trade Organization and announced plans for retaliatory sanctions of up to $2.2 billion, including tariffs of up to 100 percent on certain American-made goods. The products targeted for countermeasures were hardly chosen at random. Rather, EU commissioners carefully selected a range of products manufactured in swing states that would be decisive in the 2004 presidential election. The resulting "smart sanctions" would hit, among others, Harley-Davidson motorcycles (made in both Pennsylvania and Wisconsin) and Tropicana orange juice (headquartered in Florida).[41] In the assessment of Paul Brenton, senior research fellow at the Centre for European Policy Studies: "They certainly are trying to up the

[38] James Cox, "Bush slaps tariffs on steel imports," *USA Today*, March 6, 2002. http://usatoday30.usatoday.com/money/covers/2002-03-06-steel.htm.

[39] Jennifer Rich, "U.S. admits that politics was behind steel tariffs," *New York Times*, March 14, 2002. www.nytimes.com/2002/03/14/business/us-admits-that-politics-was-behind-steel-tariffs.html.

[40] *The Economist*. "George Bush, Protectionist." March 7, 2002. www.economist.com/node/1021395.

[41] Interestingly, President Reagan singled out Harley-Davidson for special tariff protection in 1983. Echoing the EU's reasoning in 2002, many analysts concluded that electoral concerns drove Reagan's decision to afford Harley-Davidson protection. See Daniel Klein. 1984. "Taking America for a ride: The politics of motorcycle tariffs." *Cato Policy Analysis* 32. http://www.cato.org/pubs/pas/pa032.html.

political ante . . . if they're trying to have an impact, that's the best way to do it."[42]

More than a year later, in July 2003, the WTO ruled that the Bush administration's steel tariffs were illegal. The administration appealed the ruling, which was upheld in November 2003 by the WTO's appellate body. A week before the EU's retaliatory actions were legally permitted to go into effect, President Bush reversed course, rescinded the steel tariffs, and declared that they had served their purpose of giving the domestic steel industry time to recover. In the final analysis, the steel tariffs appear to have done little to accomplish their economic aims. Most studies concluded that the number of jobs saved in the steel industry were outweighed by those lost in other, steel-consuming sectors.[43] Instead, their primary goal appears to have been electoral.[44] Lambasting what he called an "unprecedented contempt for international rules," Paul Krugman argued that only politics could explain the president's decision. "If you believe this is about the national interest, I've got a terrorist threat against the Brooklyn Bridge you might be willing to buy." Krugman concluded, "In the case of steel, Karl Rove weighed three electoral votes in West Virginia against the world trading system built up over 60 years, and the answer was apparently obvious."[45]

---

[42] Inquirer Wire Services, "EU plans to counter U.S. steel tariffs," March 23, 2002. Similarly, Pascal Lamy, the EU trade commissioner, argued that this specific blend of targeted tariffs should maximize political leverage: "Counter measures are there to leverage a change of decision. You have to do that in sectors and places where you can build a coalition." Mark Tran, "EU plans retaliation for U.S. steel tariffs," *The Guardian*, March 22, 2002.

[43] See, inter alia, Joseph Francois and Laura Baughman. 2003. *The Unintended Consequences of U.S. Steel Import Tariffs: A Quantification of Impact During 2002*. Washington, DC: CITAC Foundation. Gary Hufbauer and Ben Goodrich. 2003. *Steel Protection and Job Dislocation*. Washington, DC: CITAC Foundation. In the assessment of Robert Read, "The Safeguards did not address long-term structural problems of the steel sector – a lack of investment and competitiveness – but were rather a politically expedient strategy that appeared to assist the industry and appeased its protectionist sentiments." Robert Read. 2005. "The political economy of trade protection: The determinants and welfare impact of the 2002 U.S. emergency steel safeguard measures." *The World Economy* 28: 1119–1137.

[44] As Kevin Ho concluded, "Bush and Rove appeared to have applied a political rule to the steel gut problem based on their understandings, expectations and solutions with regards to winning elections . . . reelection concerns gained more weight than they were due, while international concerns and the practicality of the tariff policy were given diminished weight" (Ho, 2003, 842).

[45] Paul Krugman, "America the scofflaw," *New York Times*, May 24, 2002. West Virginia had five electoral votes in both 2000 and 2004. However, a loss of only three electoral votes would have cost Bush his Electoral College majority in 2000.

The tariffs were in place for the 2002 midterms and potentially benefited Republican candidates in affected states. Moreover, their imposition
allowed President Bush to publicly claim that he had followed through
on his campaign promise to help steel-producing states. Reminiscent of
David Mayhew's argument that for members of Congress position taking
can be more important than the actual end result, the decision to impose
the tariffs likely paid considerable political dividends, even if they were
ultimately lifted before the 2004 presidential contest.[46] President Bush
increased his vote share from 2000 to 2004 across the steel states, including Pennsylvania, Ohio, West Virginia, Indiana, and Illinois. While the
latter two were not in play, the first three were all key targets for the Bush-
Cheney reelection team. Looking at changing vote patterns at the county
level within these three battleground states also offers at least sugges-
tive evidence that the steel tariffs may have paid off. Figure 3.1 maps the
change in vote share received by President Bush in each county from 2000
to 2004. It is not clear what we should expect to see if the steel tariffs
bolstered the president's electoral fortunes. The tariffs received significant
media coverage, particularly in local media outlets in the affected states.
All Pennsylvanians, not just those in the Pittsburgh area, might have been
more sympathetic to President Bush after learning of his actions to protect
an industry vital to the state. Nevertheless, the effects could be strongest
in regions most dependent on the steel industry. Turning to Figure 3.1, we
see considerable variance in President Bush's changing electoral fortunes
across all three states. Some of this variation, such as Bush's solid gains
in southwestern West Virginia along the Kentucky border, is unlikely
to be a result of his actions to defend American steel. But other results,
such as Bush's strong gains in the major steel-producing area in west-
ern Pennsylvania, the northern tip of West Virginia, and eastern Ohio,
are consistent with the hypothesis that Bush reaped direct electoral gains
from his particularistic actions in trade policy.

[46] Mayhew (1974a). Mark Lewis at *Forbes* predicted in March 2002 that President Bush
knew the tariffs were illegal and that they would almost certainly be struck down by
the WTO; however, Bush pushed forward because he wanted to be able to say "Hey,
I tried" to his steel supporters. Reflecting on the steel battle in December 2003, Lewis
concluded: "So Bush has bowed to political realities by giving the steel protectionists
much – though not all of what they asked for. Whether that will keep Ohio and West
Virginia in the Republican column in 2004 remains to be decided. But even if the WTO
decision has gone against the U.S. in the meantime, Bush will be able to claim credit for
at least trying to help the domestic steel producers." Mark Lewis, "Bush to WTO: Save
me from myself," *Forbes*, March 6, 2002.

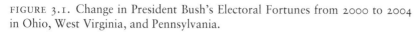

FIGURE 3.1. Change in President Bush's Electoral Fortunes from 2000 to 2004 in Ohio, West Virginia, and Pennsylvania.

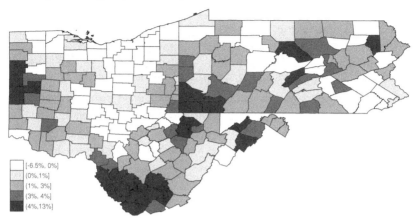

Moreover, Bush's actions may have also bolstered the electoral fortunes of Republicans in the 2002 midterms. Republicans successfully defended the seats they picked up in Pennsylvania and West Virginia in 2000, and Republicans picked up five more congressional seats in Pennsylvania, Indiana, and Ohio in 2002. Of course, any of a myriad of factors (the aftermath of 9/11 not being least among them) could have produced these positive results at the polls; however, the results are consistent with long-held beliefs in the political world that targeted, particularistic trade policies can produce tangible political gains at the ballot box.

3.2.2 *Summary*

In the more than eighty years since the Smoot-Hawley Tariff, which helped fuel the Great Depression, the United States has witnessed an extraordinary expansion of trade liberalization. Congress has provided much of the impetus for this transformation through a series of legislative acts breaking down trade barriers; and it has also sought more nationally efficient economic policies by delegating much authority over trade barriers and protectionist measures to the president. To be sure, American trade policy on the whole may be more resistant to special-interest demands for protection under the current system than it would be if Congress retained primacy over trade policy.[47] However, it is patently not

---

[47] However, it is important not to overlook the efforts of many in Congress, particularly Wilbur Mills and the Ways and Means Committee, to keep protectionist special-interest legislation from the floor. See Destler (2005).

the case that delegation has removed political calculations and parochialism from trade politics. Rather than interests represented by powerful committee chairs possessing disproportionate influence over trade policy, industries of the greatest importance to the president's and his party's electoral fortunes have gained the most leverage.

Modern presidents have routinely used their delegated and inherent constitutional powers not only to pursue trade liberalization but also to assiduously protect industries when it is in their political interest to do so. As candidates on the campaign trail, presidents have promised action to defend industries located in key constituencies, and they have largely kept these promises in office. The evidence for electoral particularism is strong.

3.3 The Particularistic Politics of Base Closings

Since the end of World War II, the United States has consistently spent more on its military than has any other nation. With the end of the Cold War, the disparities in military spending between the United States and its closest rival grew exponentially. However, the defense needs of the United States have changed dramatically over the past forty years. As the nation's defense posture has evolved, Washington has grappled with the challenge of how to allocate defense resources efficiently. For example, in the early Cold War period, bases in high latitudes, such as Maine's Loring Air Force Base, played a key role in positioning American bombers where they could best strike the Soviet Union. As land- and submarine-based ballistic missile systems came online, bases that operated in extreme weather conditions at great cost became superfluous. A basic cost-benefit analysis would dictate closing such bases and either saving the money or reallocating the resources to other, more pivotal programs. With the collapse of the Soviet Union and the end of the Cold War, many U.S. politicians from across the ideological spectrum spoke glowingly of the benefits of a "peace dividend" that would allow the nation to address its budgetary woes by reducing wasteful defense spending. However, deciding where to trim defense expenditures posed an exceedingly difficult political challenge.

While many members of Congress praised the idea of reductions and savings in the abstract, few were eager to see reductions made to facilities within their own districts. As former Majority Leader Dick Armey (R-TX) said, "many members look on the Defense bill the way Jimmy Dean looks on a hog, as a giant piece of pork to be carved up and sent to the folks back home."[48] Less colorfully, Kenneth Mayer described the politics of base closures as a classic example of the collective dilemma.[49] Closing inefficient bases is in the national interest and benefits everyone, but the benefits are diffuse. The costs, by contrast, are borne acutely by those members of Congress who represent constituencies that suffer closures. As a result, those threatened with base closures are considerably more motivated to fight closures than other members are to pursue nebulous savings.

In the case of base closings, the president's national constituency is best served by closing inefficient, redundant, and obsolete military outposts. Moreover, both Democrats and Republicans readily concede the need to reduce waste. Unlike other policy areas, such as food stamps, federal housing, or aid to education, there are no strong ideological cleavages on such an issue that could lead Democratic presidents to pursue one type of policy solution and Republicans another, both in the name of the national good. Democratic and Republican presidents alike agree on the need to eliminate extraneous military bases. As such, decisions about base closures are precisely the type of policy choice in which the universalistic presidency framework predicts we should see presidents apolitically pursuing the most economically efficient policy outcomes.

However, even within national security policymaking in a context where the economic imperatives are clear, we find strong evidence of presidents behaving particularistically. When given the opportunity, presidents have repeatedly responded as partisans-in-chief and sought to concentrate the economic pain of base closings in constituencies represented by the partisan opposition in Congress. Critics of congressional logrolls and pork-laden military spending bills have long denounced Congress's prioritization of parochial concerns over national security. With respect to base closings, we demonstrate that when left to their own devices, presidents engage in their own brand of parochialism and seek to shield their partisan allies from painful cutbacks by concentrating cuts in opposition party strongholds.

3.3.1 *From McNamara to BRAC*
Throughout the 1960s, millions of Americans watched the space race unfold on the nightly news. Receiving less coverage was a similar revolution in military technology that changed the nature of the strategic

[48] Armey (1988, 71).
[49] Mayer (1995).

conflict between the United States and the Soviet Union. As new weapons systems came on board and American capabilities evolved, many older military bases became obsolete. To address this transformation, at President Kennedy's behest, Secretary of Defense Robert McNamara undertook the first significant round of post–World War II base closings in 1961.

McNamara did so almost completely unfettered by statutory restrictions. Rather, Kennedy and McNamara interpreted base closures as an executive function, and they identified and closed bases of their own accord with virtually no input from Congress. Indeed, members of Congress complained that the Department of Defense's (DOD) actions were often kept secret or even that military officials outright misled them. For example, during the March 1961 closings, Peter Frelinghuysen (R-NJ) desperately sought information about whether Raritan Arsenal was under consideration for closure so that he could try to rally support to keep the base open. The Army informed him that there were no plans to close the arsenal. Yet, Raritan was on McNamara's list, and the decision to add it had been made months before Frelinghuysen's inquiry.[50] Such cases gave rise to widespread congressional suspicions that the executive branch was deliberately withholding information from Congress to gain the upper hand in political struggles over closures and to ensure that its preferences, not those of the legislature, would prevail.

Secretary McNamara closed seventy-three bases in 1961, thirty-three bases in 1963, sixty-three bases in 1964, and another ninety-five bases in November 1964. The last round of closings, initiated two weeks after the 1964 elections, angered many in Congress and even prompted congressional Democrats to pass legislation curbing the president's power to close military installations unilaterally. However, President Johnson vetoed the bill, calling its restrictions on his authority "repugnant to the Constitution" and "a fundamental encroachment on one of the great principles of the American constitutional system – the separation of powers between the legislative and executive branches."[51] There were also

---

[50] Twight (1989, 87–88).

[51] President Johnson defended his interpretation: "By the Constitution, the executive power is vested in the president. The president is the commander in chief of the armed forces. The president cannot sign into law a bill which substantially inhibits him from performing his duty. He cannot sign into law a measure which deprives him of power for eight months of the year even to propose a reduction of mission or the closing of any military installation, and which prohibits him from closing, abandoning or substantially reducing in mission any military facility in the country for what could be a year or more and must be 120 days. The times do not permit it. The Constitution prohibits it." Lyndon B. Johnson, "Veto of

accusations that the Johnson administration was using base closures, or the threat thereof, as a political weapon. For example, in his home state of Texas Johnson is alleged to have threatened voters and local politicians around Amarillo that if he failed to carry the region, the local Air Force base could find itself on the chopping block in the next round of closures. Amarillo voted for Goldwater, and shortly thereafter, Amarillo Air Force Base was judged "un-economical" and closed.[52]

Allegations that base closures were being used to punish constituencies that supported the opposition party increased significantly during the Nixon administration. For example, in 1973 President Nixon began a new round of base closures concentrated in the two most Democratic states in America at the time, Massachusetts and Rhode Island.[53] In the heart of Kennedy country, Nixon decided to close the Boston Navy Yard, which eliminated 5,213 jobs and $90.5 million a year from the local economy. Rhode Island was even harder hit when Nixon decided to move the Atlantic Cruiser-Destroyer Force, U.S. Atlantic Fleet from Newport and to close the Naval Air Station at Quonset Point. These and related closures stripped 17,000 jobs from Rhode Island, versus only 16,000 from the rest of the country combined.[54] Statewide unemployment tripled overnight from 6 percent to 18 percent, and local unemployment rates in the communities most directly affected by the closures surged to 30 percent. Adding insult to injury, the Navy had just completed new housing units in the area that now stood vacant, and the state of Rhode Island was still paying off millions of dollars in bonds that were issued to raise the height of the Newport Bridge, at the Navy's behest, to accommodate port calls from the next generation of aircraft carriers slated to be built.[55]

the Military Authorization Bill," August 21, 1965. Online by Gerhard Peters and John T. Woolley, The American Presidency Project. www.presidency.ucsb.edu/ws/?pid=27175. Interestingly, this language presages arguments later used by President George W. Bush to defend a broad interpretation of executive power within the context of the war on terror.

[52] Armey (1988, 73).

[53] Massachusetts and Rhode Island gave Nixon the lowest percentage of the vote of any states in the union in both 1968 and 1972. The decision to close the Massachusetts bases appears to have been made before the 1972 election; however, this did little to assuage the belief of many Massachusetts politicians that the Nixon administration was indifferent to their Democratic state's plight. John Finney, "Richardson faces a storm over move to close bases," *New York Times*, April 14, 1973, p. 1.

[54] John Kifner, "Military cuts jar New England," *New York Times*, December 25, 1976, p. 1.

[55] Mayer (1982).

Democratic New England continued to bear the brunt of base closures under the Ford administration, leading to more accusations that partisan politics were producing an unfair allocation of budgetary pain. In 1976, Loring Air Force Base in Maine and Fort Devens in Massachusetts were added to Ford's list of major proposed closures. James Scheuer (D-NY) denounced the move as emblematic of a larger, systemic bias against the Northeast, calling it "just another example of the federal government's massive discrimination against our declining regions – the Northeast and north-central industrial corridors. If all regions in the United States were starting out on equal footing with respect to military and civilian personnel, then we in the Northeast and Midwest would not be so sensitive to unchecked closings of military bases."[56] To rectify the situation, Scheuer and many other congressional Democrats demanded new legislation that would force the DOD to consider and justify the economic consequences of its actions before closing more bases.

Immediately after the 1976 closures, Congress tried to impose a one-year delay on any further military base closings initiated by the executive branch. Arguing for the legislation, Dominic Daniels (D-NJ) warned: "Mr. Speaker, more is at stake than merely the desire of the Congress to have some advance warning of military base closures. At stake once again is the issue of whether the executive branch of government may reserve for itself alone an absolute power to make decisions critical to the national welfare." But is not the president best positioned to pursue the national interest and reject the parochial impulses that dominate congressional politics, as the universalistic framework suggests? Daniels explicitly rejected this notion, retorting, "The history of decisions made exclusively within the executive branch of the government is one too littered with arbitrariness, parochialism, and caprice."[57] Ford vetoed the measure (HR 12384). The veto was overridden in the House but sustained in the Senate. However, congressional Democrats were undeterred. Three months later they passed a new bill, HR 14846, which reduced the moratorium on base closings to sixty days, but also added a host of other delaying measures and procedural hurdles to the base-closing process. Ford reluctantly signed the bill into law.

With the new strictures in place, no major base was closed between 1977 and 1988, despite the DOD recommending hundreds of closures and realignments during the period. The Reagan administration was

---

[56] James Scheuer, *Congressional Record*, July 22, 1976, 23,432–23,433.
[57] Dominic Daniels, *Congressional Record*, July 22, 1976, 23,431.

particularly aggressive in threatening base closures to gain political leverage with key members of Congress. Ironically, members alleged that Reagan and his Secretary of Defense Caspar Weinberger were threatening base closings to solicit votes for dramatic expansions in defense spending. For example, in 1986 Weinberger proposed three bases for closing: one each in the districts of high-profile critics Speaker Tip O'Neill (D-MA), William Gray (D-PA), and Patricia Schroeder (D-CO). From her perch on the House Armed Services Committee, Schroeder had previously railed against Reagan's base-closing initiatives proposed by the Grace Commission, denouncing the process as fundamentally flawed: "My frustration with this issue is that the Pentagon seems to change the criteria for closing bases every time it proposes new closings. The lists which come out of the Pentagon seem to be more based on politics than on military utility."[58]

In the assessment of Senator Gary Hart (D-CO), "by selecting bases in the home districts of [these three members], Secretary Weinberger is trying to put his most effective critics on the defensive."[59] While Weinberger's spokesman insisted that "this is a nonpartisan decision by the secretary... it has nothing to do with politics," Democrats were less than persuaded. According to Gray's spokesman, such claims failed even a prima facie test. "It is simply inconceivable that out of all the military bases in the entire country, the only three that Weinberger feels it necessary to mention happen to be in Philadelphia, Massachusetts, and Denver."[60]

Even Republicans were not immune from such pressures. As moderate Pennsylvania Republican Arlen Specter described, "[It is] not a matter of coincidence that, at the time the Department of Defense issues come before the country and at the time we are considering the budget, there are a series of releases from the Department of Defense about the prospects for reduction in forces, layoffs and base closings."[61]

---

[58] Report of the Committee on Armed Services, US House, on H.R. 1872, H. Rept. 99-81. May 10, 1985. Page 452.

[59] Joyce Germperlein, "Weinberger targets Philadelphia hospital in proposal to cut military spending," *Philadelphia Inquirer*, February 13, 1986.

[60] Fred Kaplan, "Weinberger lists three facilities to shut," *Boston Globe*, February 13, 1986, p. 3.

[61] Weinberger allegedly told Republican members that if they voted against a Democratic-sponsored freeze on DOD spending, he would instead seek to close bases in other districts. Ralph Z. Hallow, "Back the budget or lose bases Weinberger warns Republicans," *Washington Times*, May 2, 1985, p. 1. Democratic Senator Alan Dixon also charged that Secretary Weinberger was strategically using the threat of closure for political gain. "Nobody understands better than the Secretary of Defense of this country that 'politics

While congressional opponents succeeded time and again in block-ing proposed closures, as the Cold War waned, a consensus began to emerge that closing obsolete and redundant bases was essential to trim-ming defense spending. Yet, Congress was wary of going back to the "untrammeled executive authority" that governed closure decisions in the 1960s and 1970s.[62] Gradually, momentum built around a legislative solution championed by Texas Republican Dick Armey, who proposed creating an independent commission to oversee the closure process. The commission would both allow members to avoid direct blame for making tough decisions about which bases would be closed, and alleviate con-cerns about political abuses from the executive branch, particularly the use of base closures as an instrument of partisan retribution. The proposal eventually became the Defense Authorization Amendments and Base Clo-sure and Realignment Act of 1988, which established the Commission on Base Realignment and Closure (BRAC).

The BRAC commission was given until December 31, 1988, to make recommendations to the Secretary of Defense and Congress of which bases should be closed. The DOD was then required to either approve the list in its entirety or reject it; the administration could not amend the list devised by the independent commission. If approved, Congress could still reject the list of closures by passing a joint resolution. However, Congress must reject the list in its entirety.[63] The final process met both of Congress's goals: it created a mechanism to break the logjam and allow inefficient bases to be closed, but it also provided individual members with a means to insulate themselves from the resulting political fallout. Phil Gramm (R-TX) colorfully described the "out" the commission approach afforded members:

> So I can come up here and I say 'God have mercy. Don't close this base in Texas. We can get attacked from the south. The Russians are going to go after our leadership and you know they are going to attack Texas. We need this base.' Then I can go out and lie down in the street and the bulldozers are coming and I have a trusty aide there just as it gets there to drag me out

ain't bean bag.' And if there has ever been a man in the history of the United States of America that ever came out of a precinct or a ward that could play tougher hardball than the man in charge of the defense of this great Nation, I submit to you, Mr. President, I have never in all of my professional career met that man. This is hardball. And in general, if you look at the bases that are on the 22-base hit list, you will see who they affect." Alan Dixon, *Congressional Record*, May 23, 1985, S6912.

[62] Armey (1988).

[63] David Lockwood and George Siehl, "Military base closures: A historical review from 1988 to 1995," *CRS Report* 97-305F, October 18, 2004.

of the way. All the people in Muleshoe, or wherever this base is, will say, 'You know, Phil Gramm got whipped, but it was like the Alamo. He was with us until the last second.'[64]

Ultimately, the 1988 BRAC round resulted in the closure or realignment of 145 bases with minimum partisan discord.[65]

3.3.2 *The 1990 Cheney List*

Two years later, a new secretary ran the Defense Department: former Wyoming Congressman and White House Chief of Staff under Gerald Ford, Richard Cheney. As vice president in the 2000s, Cheney would become famous as one of the most ardent proponents of the unitary executive theory. However, his inclinations in this direction were already evident during his tenure as Secretary of Defense in the 1990s. Although the 1988 BRAC commission succeeded in securing the first significant round of base closings in more than a decade with minimum partisan rancor, Cheney believed that selecting which military bases to close was essentially an executive function. Thus, rather than seek congressional action to establish a new commission, in early 1990 Cheney presented Congress with a list of thirty-five proposed closures devised solely by the Defense Department.

The reaction on Capitol Hill from congressional Democrats ranged from skepticism to outrage. Of the thirty-five bases proposed for closure, twenty-nine (or 83 percent) were located in districts represented by House Democrats.[66] The partisan disparity was even starker when focusing only on the largest bases on the list; of the twenty-one major base closings, nineteen (or 91 percent) were in Democratic districts. In her opening statement at a House Armed Services Committee hearing on Cheney's proposal, Pat Schroeder was diplomatic but firm: "Unlike the Commission's [i.e., the 1988 BRAC commission] list, the Cheney list looks a little unbalanced to some of us, and I think we all need to know

[64] This quotation refers to an earlier attempt to create an independent mechanism for closures to resume, but the logic holds for the 1988 BRAC round as well. U.S. Senate Committee on Armed Services, *Base Closures Hearings*, 99th Congress, 1st session, 1985, p. 17.

[65] However, the 2005 BRAC commission report notes that some critics of the process felt that the final list still targeted closures in the districts of administration opponents. Critics desired clearer, more explicit, and more transparent criteria through which the commission would identify bases to be closed. These experiences informed subsequent legislation creating the next rounds of the BRAC process. *2005 Defense Base Closure and Realignment Committee Report*, p. 311.

[66] Mayer 1995.

what went into the idea behind all these base closures. It is not that we are against it, but we certainly want it to look balanced and non-partisan."[67] The Democratic Study Group went considerably further and in a report titled "The Great Base Closings Ploy" charged that the administration had engaged in rank particularism, punishing congressional Democrats and insulating Republican constituencies from closures.[68]

Cheney denied that the list was the product of political machinations: "My former colleagues need to know – and I think most of them do in fact believe – that . . . I didn't come down and say hit Democrats or hit liberal Democrats, not conservative Democrats. I think if you look at the list, you'll find that it is in fact the best judgment of the services of what their requirements are."[69] President Bush also insisted that politics played no role in the selection of bases: "These suggested closings were made without political favor. . . . I've got to convince these folks that we are not doing this in some vindictive political way."[70]

But if partisan politics did not influence Bush's and Cheney's calculations, why did there appear to be such a stark partisan gap, at least in the aggregate? The House Armed Services Committee's ranking Republican David Martin argued it was a product of the distribution of bases. "The point that more of these were in Democratic districts than Republican districts doesn't necessarily surprise me. Since I've been here in 1981, I have counted on any number of occasions, and note with alarm on a regular basis, that there are generally 75 more Democrats than Republicans in the House, and it has been that way since I was in the first grade. So that doesn't surprise me an awful lot."[71] Some Southern Democrats in particular had reputations for aggressively pursuing military resources for their districts. As a testament to Mendel Rivers's (D-SC) tireless efforts to bolster the military presence in Charleston, for years a joke in Washington was: "If you put another base into Charleston, it'll sink."[72]

---

[67] Hearing before the Military Installations and Facilities Subcommittee of the Committee on Armed Services, House of Representatives. March 14, 1990. HASC 101-52, page 1.

[68] Democratic Study Group, "The great base closing ploy: Creating a political tempest to shield a bloated defense budget," March 24, 1990, No. 101-29.

[69] Mike Mills, "Cheney's plan for shutdowns a new salvo in a long fight," *CQ Weekly*, February 3, 1990, p. 340.

[70] George H.W. Bush, "The President's News Conference," February 12, 1990. Online by Gerhard Peters and John T. Woolley, The American Presidency Project. www.presidency .ucsb.edu/ws/?pid=18147.

[71] Hearing before the Military Installations and Facilities Subcommittee of the Committee on Armed Services, House of Representatives. March 14, 1990. HASC 101-52. page 1.

[72] For a more nuanced view of Rivers as a procurer of defense investments par excellence, see Arnold (1979, 122–124).

TABLE 3.1. *Punishing Democratic Districts in the 1990 Cheney List.*
Logistic and least squares regression models. Democratic districts were
disproportionately targeted for base closures and military and civilian job
losses, even after controlling for the number of bases in a district.
Robust standard errors are in parentheses.

	Closure	Jobs Lost
Democratic member	1.233	378.2
	(0.474)	(144.9)
Military installations in district	0.252	141.9
	(0.0773)	(74.13)
Constant	−3.732	−96.77
	(0.433)	(76.48)
Observations	435	435
R^2		0.029

Can the uneven distribution of bases across partisan constituencies explain what at first blush appears to be strong evidence of presidential particularism in base closures? To assess this argument, we conducted a statistical analysis. By combining base closure data with information on the distribution of bases across the country, we can examine the influence of whether a district was represented by a Democrat on the probability of it containing a base designated for closure on the Cheney list while controlling for the number of military installations within that district.[73] The results are presented in Column 1 of Table 3.1.[74] As we would expect,

[73] Data on the distribution of bases across congressional districts is taken from Scott Adler. "Congressional District Data File, 101st and 102nd Congresses." University of Colorado, Boulder, CO. The Adler data also contained counts of the number of *major* military bases located in a district, as well as the number of military personnel residing in a district. The total number of military installations in a district was the strongest predictor of whether it was targeted for a base closure, and so this is the control variable included in the models reported. However, replicating our analysis using any of the district military measures in the Adler data yields virtually identical results. Thirty-two districts contained bases targeted for closures; twenty-nine districts contained one base, while three districts contained two. We use a logistic regression to ease interpretation of the model's results; doing so allows us to estimate the effect of a district being represented by a Democrat on the probability of there being a base targeted for closing within that district. To do so, districts with one or two proposed base closures were coded as 1, and districts with no closures were coded 0. Alternately, estimating a negative binomial event count model of whether a district contained 0, 1, or 2 bases targeted for closure yields virtually identical results.

[74] As a robustness check, we reestimated the parsimonious models in Table 3.1 including a host of district-level demographic control variables (e.g., percentage of the population that is black, urban, veteran, etc.). In every specification, the results are virtually identical to those presented in Table 3.1.

as the number of military installations in a district increases, so too does the probability that the district will have a base targeted for closure. Yet, even after controlling for this we find very strong evidence that Democratic districts were systematically targeted to bear the base-closing pain. For the average district, the probability of a district represented by a Republican possessing a base targeted for closure by the Bush administration was approximately .03. However, if that district was represented by a Democrat in the House, the predicted probability of it having a base targeted for closure triples to .10. Thus, the data does not support Congressman Martin's assertion that the Democratic skew of the Cheney list is due to the greater number of Democrats in Congress and military bases in Democratic districts. After controlling for the number of bases in a district, we find clear and unambiguous evidence of partisan targeting in the Cheney base closures list.[75]

Yet, all bases on the Cheney list are not created equal. For example, closing the South Weymouth Naval Air Station in Massachusetts would entail the loss of 450 military jobs and 200 civilian jobs. By contrast, closing Fort Ord in California would mean the loss of 14,849 military jobs and another 2,294 civilian jobs in California's 16th district. It is therefore at least possible that while a greater number of base closures are disproportionately concentrated in Democratic districts, the job losses such closures would entail could be more evenly and apolitically spread across Democratic and Republican constituencies. We look for evidence of this possibility in two ways. First, we constructed an ordinary least squares regression model assessing the influence of whether a district is represented by a Democrat in the House on the number of job losses it stood to sustain, controlling for the number of military bases in the district. Column 2 of Table 3.1 presents the results.[76] Again, we see strong and statistically significant evidence of presidential particularism to serve partisan purposes. The average Democratic district lost almost 400 more jobs than did the average Republican district, all else being equal.

---

[75] Cutting the data further, there is also evidence that within Democratic ranks, base closures were targeted in the districts of the most liberal Democrats. We refer interested readers to Appendix A for full model results and additional discussion. While our discussion in the chapter focuses on partisan particularism, in Appendix A we also find evidence of electoral particularism; specifically, districts in swing states appear to have been insulated from base closure pain.

[76] Alternately, controlling for the number of military personnel in the district yields virtually identical results.

This disparity appears artificially small because the vast majority of districts did not have a base targeted for closure and therefore did not stand to lose any jobs if the Cheney list was implemented. As an alternate test, we can compare the average number of jobs lost in the twenty-eight Cheney-list bases located in Democratic districts to the five in Republican districts.[77] When analyzing the data in this way, we see that the average Democratic base targeted for closure was much larger than the average Republican base. The average Democratic base closure would cost the local community more than 3,800 military and civilian jobs, versus only 1,700 lost jobs in the average base closure in a Republican district. Regardless of how we cut the data, the evidence strongly suggests that President Bush and Secretary Cheney consciously crafted a list to concentrate the pain of base closings in Democratic constituencies.

To this point, we have limited the scope of our inquiry to the bases targeted for closure by Secretary of Defense Cheney. While the closures were perhaps the most publicly salient part of the Cheney plan, the secretary also proposed a large number of base realignments that would shuffle military personnel from facility to facility across the country, presumably in the name of greater efficiency. Examining the employment consequences of these realignments, we see that a remarkable 96 percent of the 29,428 military job losses would be borne by bases in Democratic constituencies. Bases slated for realignment in Democratic districts would also suffer 84 percent of the 18,089 civilian job losses resulting from the proposed shifts. Finally, several bases would actually gain personnel under the Cheney proposal. All 1,988 military job gains were located in bases residing in Republican districts. Similarly, 277 of the total 317 civilian job gains would occur in bases located in Republican constituencies.[78]

Freed from the strictures of the 1988 BRAC process, President Bush and Secretary Cheney enjoyed unfettered discretion in proposing a list of bases for closure. However, rather than selecting these installations on the basis of maximum economic efficiency, the data strongly suggest that the Bush administration instead pursued partisan political gain by proposing a skewed list of bases that would concentrate the economic pain of closures in Democratic constituencies.

---

[77] Job loss estimates were not provided for two bases (the Detroit and Lima Army tank plants), one of which was located in a Democratic district and the other in a Republican district.

[78] Democratic Study Group, "The great base closing ploy: Creating a political tempest to shield a bloated defense budget," March 24, 1990, No. 101-29.

3.4 The Congressional Response and the 1991 DOD List

Congressional Democrats mobilized to block the highly partisan 1990 Cheney plan, and later that year they succeeded in passing new legislation that would resurrect the BRAC process under modified rules. Under the new protocols, the Secretary of Defense would prepare a list of proposed base closings identified via the application of a set list of criteria emphasizing military efficiency, economic costs, and environmental impact. The DOD list would then be reviewed by the BRAC commission, which could add to or subtract from the list.[79] The BRAC commission's recommendations would then go to the president for his approval.[80] Congress could again block the list of closures from going into effect by passing a joint resolution of disapproval within forty-five days of receiving the commission's report.

Critical features of the process were the establishment of firm criteria through which the list of proposed closures was to be compiled and the institutionalization of General Accounting Office (GAO) monitoring and analysis of closure decisions and the logics employed in arriving at the list of bases. In the assessment of Kenneth Mayer, "given such a high level of monitoring, any substantial deviation from the criteria would have been discovered."[81]

Secretary of Defense Cheney had insisted in 1990 that his proposed list was based solely on the grounds of military efficiency. Confronted with the new criteria and procedures enshrined in the Defense Base Closure and Realignment Act of 1990, including formal GAO review, would the DOD's proposed list of closings in 1991 look similar to or very different from the list proposed in 1990?

At first blush, the partisan character of the 1991 DOD list appears to be significantly less skewed than the 1990 list. The revised list of DOD base closings affected twenty-four Democratic districts and seventeen Republican districts.[82]

---

[79] The law also gave Congress significant influence over the composition of the BRAC commission through mandated consultation between the president and House and Senate leaders.

[80] Technically, the president could request changes in the commission's list, but no president in any of the subsequent rounds (1991, 1993, 1995, or 2005) requested changes.

[81] Mayer (1995, 400).

[82] The DOD report lists forty-four bases in all; however, three of the installations involved zero military job losses (and only small numbers of civilian job losses) and are therefore excluded from the analysis. *Congressional Quarterly* identified thirty-one of the proposed bases as "major." Limiting our analysis only to this subset of the DOD closure list

TABLE 3.2. *Lack of Particularism in the 1991 DOD List. Logistic and least squares regression models. After Congress reinstituted the BRAC and GAO oversight of the closure process, the new 1991 DOD list did not disproportionately concentrate losses in Democratic districts after controlling for the number of military installations in each district. Robust standard errors are in parentheses.*

	Closure	Jobs Lost
Democratic member	−0.140	18.75
	(0.351)	(162.8)
Military installations in district	0.301	209.3
	(0.0781)	(85.89)
Constant	−2.612	153.3
	(0.275)	(110.5)
Observations	435	435
R^2		0.042

House Armed Services Committee chair Les Aspin reacted positively to the DOD proposal, saying that it "appears fair."[83] An empirical analysis confirms Aspin's assessment. Replicating the analysis described earlier in the chapter for the new 1991 DOD list shows no evidence of closures or job losses being concentrated disproportionately in Democratic constituencies. The results of parallel statistical models constructed using the 1991 data are presented in Table 3.2. Indeed, after controlling for the number of military bases in a district, the estimated effect of a district being represented by a Democrat on its probability of having a base closure is actually negative, although the relationship is substantively very small and not statistically significant.

As shown in Column 2 of Table 3.2, after controlling for the number of bases in a district, Democratic constituencies did not suffer significantly greater job losses under the 1991 DOD plan than did Republican constituencies. If we compare the average job loss in bases located in Democratic districts to the average loss in Republican districts, we again see no evidence of a significant difference. In sharp contrast to the 1990 Cheney list, under the 1991 DOD plan the average base closure in a

produces virtually identical results to those discussed in the text. For example, in the aggregate the thirty-one major base closes affected nineteen Democratic districts and fourteen Republican districts (two bases spanned two districts each).

[83] David Lockwood and George Siehl, "Military base closures: A historical review from 1988 to 1995," *CRS Report* 97-305F, October 18, 2004, p. 7. Not all Democrats shared Aspin's assessment. Joe Moakley of Massachusetts, for example, concluded, "It almost looks like the Democratic strongholds have been hit the worst."

Democratic district would result in the loss of 4,870 jobs versus roughly 4,190 jobs from a closure in a Republican constituency.[84]

3.4.1 *Summary*

Perhaps nowhere does the universalistic presidency framework better resonate with many of us than within foreign policy. In the realm of military procurement, members of Congress are routinely cast as parochial players seeking only to bring home as much pork as possible to their districts, while presidents are the only stewards of efficiency and the interests of the nation as a whole. However, even in the military realm we see strong evidence of presidential particularism. The early rounds of base closings during the Cold War were accompanied by numerous charges that presidents were using their unilateral control over selecting which bases to close for political purposes. Time and again, presidents appear to have used that discretion to concentrate the costs of base closings in constituencies that vote for the partisan opposition and to insulate their core co-partisan base from cuts as much as possible.

The evidence for such partisan particularism is most clear in the 1990 list of proposed cuts by the DOD. Freed from the independent commission process instituted in the late 1980s, the Bush administration proposed a list of closures in 1990 that unabashedly targeted losses in Democratic constituencies, despite the administration's protestations to the contrary. Tellingly, after Congress intervened by passing new legislation specifying the precise economic criteria that must be used to select bases, creating a new independent base-closings commission, and mandating GAO oversight, the DOD's list of proposed bases that would maximize efficiency changed dramatically in only a year. In this new list, devised in 1991 under the auspices of the new law, partisan particularism disappeared.

Critics may object that delegating considerable governing authority to independent commissions such as the BRAC commission may undermine democratic accountability and, in the long run, be disadvantageous for the health of American democracy.[85] We do not necessarily disagree.

---

[84] For the two bases that straddled two congressional districts, the job losses were divided evenly between the two districts. In sharp contrast to the 1990 Cheney list, other researchers have also found that the BRAC process has largely insulated base closings from partisan politics. Beaulier et al. (2011) found no evidence of political influences on the 2005 BRAC round, and Flora and Parker (2007) found only limited evidence that political factors mattered in an assessment of the 1991, 1993, and 2005 rounds.

[85] However, for an analysis of the value independent commissions afford in national security policymaking, see Tama (2011).

However, this case plainly shows the danger of delegating additional authority to the executive branch under the belief that doing so will lead to normatively positive policy outcomes based solely, or even primarily, on the grounds of maximizing efficiency. Rather, empowering the executive may merely result in the substitution of presidential for congressional parochialism.

4

Disaster Declarations and Transportation Grants

In the previous chapter, we searched for evidence of presidential particularism in military base closings and trade policy. In both cases, we found that presidents favored the interests of some Americans over others. In some cases, presidents sought to court key swing voters; in others, they endeavored to protect their partisan allies from economic pain and instead concentrate it in constituencies that backed the partisan opposition. This stands in stark contrast to the conventional wisdom of presidential universalism, where presidents eschew parochialism and instead pursue policies that maximize outcomes for the nation as a whole. In this chapter, we look for further evidence of presidential particularism by analyzing presidential disaster declarations and executive influence over the allocation of transportation grants.

Presidential decisions concerning whether or not to issue a federal disaster declaration present an ideal venue to examine presidential motivations because the stimulus (severe weather) is determined outside the political system and creates a direct need for relief. As a result, we can assess whether – after controlling for storm damage and objective economic need – political factors influence the allocation of federal disaster aid. Although need is the preeminent determinant of presidential disaster declarations, our data unambiguously show that these presidential directives are also influenced by whether the affected area is in a battleground state or a core partisan constituency.

Shifting focus to the politics of transportation grants affords us an opportunity to look for evidence of presidential particularism in a realm where presidents do not have unilateral authority over policymaking. Indeed, transportation funding is a policy realm long held to be dominated not by the president but by Congress. As a result, transportation grants serve as a critical test for our argument; if we find evidence of presidential particularism here, there are strong reasons to expect to find it in a myriad of other policy realms as well.

4.1 Presidential Disaster Declarations

Disaster declarations are opportunities for presidents to make unilateral decisions about distributive politics. Moreover, in this policy realm we are able to measure accurately and objectively economic need – the dollar amount of damage caused by the severe weather. As a result, disaster declarations provide a powerful lens through which to examine presidential particularism. If presidents are universalistic, they should assess the severity of weather damage and then decide whether to issue a declaration. By contrast, our theory of presidential particularism argues that the political characteristics of the state requesting aid will influence the president's calculations. To be sure, the severity of the damage should still be (and in fact is) the most important factor influencing the particularistic president's decision. However, our theory argues that particularistic political calculations shade presidential decisions to initiate the federal disaster response.

A president's handling of a natural disaster may be as consequential as major decisions about war and peace. At President George W. Bush's final White House press conference, he was asked about mistakes he made during his presidency. Presidents do not like to admit mistakes, and this was perhaps especially true of President Bush. But on that day of his waning administration, he was willing to reflect on his failings. Among his regrets was the federal response to Hurricane Katrina, the catastrophic storm that devastated states along the Gulf of Mexico in late August 2005. In the immediate aftermath of the storm, Bush's favorability suffered markedly, falling to, at the time, the lowest level of his presidency.[1] His support even among Republicans dropped 12 points according to a *Washington Post* poll.[2] Although he never campaigned on his abilities to confront natural disasters, Katrina had become, as the president was well aware, an indelible part of his legacy.

Though few events match the scope of Katrina, natural disasters commonly inflict significant losses of property and human life on communities

---

[1] Michael A. Fletcher and Richard Morin, "Bush's approval rating drops to new low in wake of storm," *Washington Post*, September 13, 2005.
[2] Ibid.

across the United States. While most severe weather events do not become national stories, the political decisions surrounding relief have significant meaning for the communities that are affected. As President Clinton put it, "[V]oters don't choose a president based on how he'll handle disasters, but if they're faced with one, it quickly becomes the most important issue of their lives."[3] To the stricken community, even relatively minor damage may represent a major local event covered by newspapers, discussed by neighbors, and remembered long after repairs are finished. Consider a windstorm suffered in and around Belleville, Illinois, just outside of Saint Louis. The damage was relatively minimal. About 2,500 people lost power and a steeple at a local church was blown over. The *Belleville New Democrat* featured the story including a picture of the damaged church and a number of interviews with residents without power and facing bitterly cold conditions.[4] As President Clinton noted, even if a natural disaster is limited in scope, it may dominate the lives of those individuals who are affected. Even those not directly affected will likely read about the travails of their neighbors and the destruction of schools, churches, or local infrastructure.

Before 1950, when a major natural disaster or other catastrophe befell a state, Congress was forced to pass an individual piece of legislation for relief on an ad hoc basis. One analysis shows that 128 individual pieces of legislation were passed by Congress before 1950 to provide relief for disasters.[5] These efforts were susceptible to both delay and regional division as members from less affected districts sometimes used the opportunity to extract resources for their own constituents. One commentator characterizes the congressional response thusly: "[T]hese appropriations proved erratic. Regional rivalries, political pettiness, economic gyrations and racial prejudice could sink a disaster relief bill."[6] To cope with these inefficiencies, Congress frequently delegated decision-making power to the president. For example, during the aftermath of the War of 1812, Congress established a presidential commission to distribute relief.[7]

---

3 Clinton (2004, 428).
4 "Wind storm causes power outages, church damage," *Belleville News Democrat*, January 27, 2014.
5 *Congressional Record*, 1950, 81st Cong., 2d sess., vol. 96, p. 11,900.
6 Marian Moser Jones, "Haggling over Hurricane Sandy relief: The unraveling of a rational disaster relief policy," *Congress Blog*, January 29, 2013. http://thehill.com/blogs/congress-blog/economy-a-budget/279587-haggling-over-hurricane-sandy-relief-the-unraveling-of-a-rational-disaster-relief-policy.
7 Landis (1998, 985).

Though some members of Congress scolded the delegation of the decision to the president, it came to typify the federal response to catastrophic events in the United States. The Federal Disaster Relief Act of 1950 codified the president's power in this sphere, giving him the authority to initiate or decline to initiate a federal response to a catastrophe.

Today, the Robert T. Stafford Act governs the disaster declaration process. Formally, the process leaves the definition of who qualifies for aid to the president. A major disaster is defined by the statute as "any natural catastrophe...in any part of the United States, which *in the determination of the President* causes damage of sufficient severity and magnitude to warrant major disaster assistance." Once a declaration is made, the president can, among other things, "direct any federal agency, with or without reimbursement . . . in support of state and local assistance response and recovery efforts."[8] Phil Kuntz of *Congressional Quarterly* observed that the Stafford Act "gives [the president] more power than he's ever likely to use."[9] A national response to a disaster requires quick action in a context where the expertise of executive agencies is crucial in assessing the needs of the affected areas.[10]

4.1.1 Electoral Particularism: Rewarding Swing States

Each year, the Atlantic hurricane season extends from the beginning of June to the end of November. Every four years it coincides with the frenetic height of presidential campaigns culminating in the general election in November. For example, Hurricane Andrew, at its time the costliest and most powerful hurricane in American history, struck in late August 1992 causing $26 billion in damage as President George H. W. Bush and Governor Bill Clinton were campaigning for president.[11] In the months leading up to the 2004 election, the Atlantic produced Hurricanes Charley, Frances, Ivan, and Jeanne, which caused a total of $45 billion in destruction.[12] In 2012, Superstorm Sandy struck just days before the election, causing $65 billion in damage in states across the entire Eastern

---

[8] Stafford Act, Sec. 102. Definitions (42 U.S.C. 5t122). Emphasis added. www.fema.gov/media-library-data/20130726-1646-20490-1658/stafford_act_booklet_042213_508d.pdf. 26.

[9] Phil Kuntz, "President, agencies have wide latitude in providing aid in wake of disasters," *CQ Weekly*, October 28, 1989, p. 2854–2855.

[10] From a theoretical perspective, the federal response to disasters meet several of the criteria for broad congressional delegation described by Moe and Howell (1999).

[11] www.srh.noaa.gov/mfl/?n=andrew.

[12] www.nhc.noaa.gov/outreach/history/.

seaboard.[13] In each of these cases in this incomplete list, critics claimed that the president was using disaster relief as part of his campaign.

Presidents (or at least members of their campaign staff) are occasionally willing to lend credence to this notion. Commenting on Hurricane Charley, David Johnson, a political consultant and former executive director of the Florida Republican Party, noted that the storm's path had "cut through a lot of good Republican turf, and then I-4 – that's a lot of swing voters."[14] The consultant suggested that, because of Charley, President Bush would have an opportunity to direct resources to both swing voters and those already part of his base in order to win reelection. Another such remark came after Hurricane Andrew in 1992 when a campaign aid to George H. W. Bush "joked that it wouldn't be so bad if Andrew blew on up 'to Kentucky and the rust-belt states' where Bush was behind in the polls."[15] Although Bush was ultimately criticized for his handling of Andrew, it appeared at the time that the disaster could potentially bolster his chances for reelection.

While there was little doubt that the federal government would provide aid after disasters of the magnitude of Hurricanes Andrew and Charley, we can examine cases where the disasters were far less severe. For example, the National Climatic Data Center reports that there were more than 1,200 tornadoes annually from 1991 to 2010, yet only a fraction of these received presidential disaster declarations.[16] Why did some see disaster declarations while others did not? Did the political pressures on the president have any effect on which locales were selected to receive aid? Did factors above and beyond objective economic need influence the president's determination?

The political benefit of disaster aid is more than consultant folklore. The opportunities for electoral payoffs are many. Disaster declarations provide benefits that are ideal for presidential "credit-claiming" and "advertising" – the same reelection activities in which members of Congress engage.[17] Indeed, disaster declarations provide multiple platforms from which to woo voters, and a number of studies have considered

---

[13] www.ncdc.noaa.gov/billions/.
[14] http://articles.latimes.com/print/2004/aug/15/nation/na-charleybush15.
[15] Tom Mathews, Peter Katel, Todd Barrett, Douglas Waller, Clara Bingham, Melinda Liu, Steven Waldman, and Ginny Carrol, "What went wrong," *Newsweek*, September 7, 1992, p. 22.
[16] www.ncdc.noaa.gov/climate-information/extreme-events/us-tornado-climatology.
[17] Mayhew (1974b).

the political determinants of disaster aid.[18] For example, one study finds that, while voters punish presidents for the mere occurrence of natural disaster damage, they reward them at much higher levels when they respond with federal aid in the form of a disaster declaration.[19] Though presidents are subject to Mother Nature's fortune, they are ultimately held responsible for how they react toward destruction.

In addition to providing a test of leadership, natural disasters afford the president several opportunities to strengthen his support among the electorate. For instance, the president may court voters in electorally important states by directly distributing funds. Federal disaster relief is a substantial part of the federal budget, with one study estimating that Congress spent at least $136 billion from 2011 to 2013, or about $400 per household per year.[20] Included in this spending is direct assistance for individuals. Voters may receive direct payments to provide for temporary housing, housing repair, new housing, replacement of personal property, small business loans, unemployment assistance, legal services, and crises counseling, among other services.[21] Indeed, one study of voting in Florida in 2004 finds that these direct benefits increased turnout among Republican voters (i.e., the party of the incumbent president) and decreased turnout among Democrats.[22]

While some voters receive checks from the federal government, many more voters may witness the leadership of the president as he tours ravaged areas and comforts vulnerable victims. Disasters represent major news events that attract viewers who are both inherently interested in the news story and in need of information.[23] In August 2004, the White House website posted a photo essay of President George W. Bush embracing voters and First Lady Laura Bush delivering supplies in Florida in response to the hurricanes leading up to the 2004 election.[24] The logic behind using disasters to spotlight leadership and to court popular

---

[18] Chen (2013); Daniels (2013); Garrett and Sobel (2003); Gasper and Reeves (2011); Healy and Malhotra (2009); Reeves (2011); Salkowe and Chakraborty (2009); Sylves and Búzás (2007).

[19] Gasper and Reeves (2011).

[20] Weiss and Weidman (2013).

[21] Federal Emergency Management Agency, U.S. Department of Homeland Security. 2011. *A Guide to the Disaster Declaration Process and Federal Disaster Assistance.* Washington, DC.

[22] Chen (2013).

[23] Sood et al. (1987).

[24] http://georgewbush-whitehouse.archives.gov/infocus/hurricane/photoessays/.

sentiment was articulated in the sixteenth century by Machiavelli, who advised that leaders must react to and shape fortune, the things beyond their control, in order to achieve success.[25] As Rahm Emanuel said while serving as Chief of Staff to President Obama, "Never let a serious crisis go to waste."[26] When politicians hesitate after fortune delivers a *force majeure*, the result can be swift defeat. For example, incumbent Mayor of Chicago Michael Bilandic's loss of the Democratic primary to Jane Byrne is still attributed to his handling of the city's blizzard of 1979.[27] Others have speculated that President George W. Bush drew lessons from the failure of his father's handling of Hurricane Andrew. During the 2004 presidential campaign, Peter Wallsten of the *Los Angeles Times* drew parallels between President H. W. Bush's handling of Andrew and President W. Bush's handling of Charley. The elder, Wallsten suggested, had lost votes because of his handling of the disaster, while the younger Bush acted swiftly to assist the storm-ravaged Florida gulf coast in 2004.[28] Yet the Bush administration's swift response in the election year of 2004 stands in stark contrast to the image of an aloof commander-in-chief looking distantly at Katrina-ravaged New Orleans in 2005.

It is not just leadership failures that rile political nerves. Days before the 2012 election, in the aftermath of Superstorm Sandy, the teamwork of President Obama and New Jersey Governor Chris Christie, a Republican, frayed nerves among GOP elites. With voters on their way to the polls, President Obama was presented an opportunity to act as comforter-in-chief. In one widely circulated Associated Press photo, the president was shown with his arms wrapped around a visibly distraught Donna Vanzant, a business owner in Brigantine, New Jersey, whose marina was destroyed by the storm.[29] Ms. Vanzant was not the only New Jerseyan to share an embrace with President Obama in the aftermath of Sandy. As reported by Mark Halperin and John Heileman in their chronicle of the 2012 presidential election, the Romney campaign was furious over what they saw as Christie's excessive praise of President Obama's handling

[25] Machiavelli (1998 [1532], XXV).

[26] "A 40-year wish list: You won't believe what's in that stimulus bill," *The Wall Street Journal*, January 28, 2009. http://online.wsj.com/news/articles/SB123310466514522 309.

[27] Whet Moser, "Snowpocalypse then: How the blizzard of 1979 cost the election for Michael Bilandic," *Chicago*, February 2, 2011. www.chicagomag.com/Chicago-Magazine/The-312/February-2011/Snowpocalypse-Then-How-the-Blizzard-of-1979-Cost-the-Electionfor-Michael-Bilandic/.

[28] Peter Wallsten, "On storm, Bush aims to be unlike dad," *Los Angeles Times*, August 15, 2004. http://articles.latimes.com/print/2004/aug/15/nation/na-charleybush15.

[29] http://bigstory.ap.org/photo/barack-obama-donna-vanzant-1.

of the disaster. Halperin and Heileman note, "Watching Christie wrap Obama in a bear hug left most of the Romneyites somewhere between annoyed and irate."[30] The reporters capture the ability of a president to use a disaster declaration to his electoral advantage, writing that Romney was

> dealt the cruelest fate imaginable for a presidential challenger: an effective news blackout in the election's last week. [Romney advisor Stuart Stevens] feared that the storm had halted Romney's momentum, allowing Obama to project both leaderly strength and (with Christie's help) a bipartisan aura. Stevens confided to his boss that...if we lose, Sandy will be why.[31]

At least one academic study lends some credence to this conclusion about Sandy, finding that "Virginia would likely have been won by Romney were it not hit [by Sandy] at all, whereas North Carolina would likely have gone for Obama had it been directly in the storm's path."[32]

Anecdotes aside, do presidents systematically engage in electoral particularism and grant disaster declarations disproportionately to counties in swing states? Presidential responses to disasters are clear opportunities to court voters. The incentives are stark: a single swing state can determine victory or defeat in the quest for the nation's highest office. The public policy ramifications are unnerving in that presidents are biased toward political favorites in a case where need should be the only determinant.

4.1.2 *Partisan Particularism: Rewarding Core Constituencies*

Given the significant sums in play, we also examine whether presidents might be tempted to use their unilateral control over disaster declarations to disproportionately reward core partisan constituencies. Members of Congress routinely look after their own in battles over disaster funding. For example, while Congress normally acts with alacrity to designate the requested funds after a presidential declaration, individual members frequently strive to secure extra funds for their constituents. Such was the case in the aftermath of the 1989 Loma Prieta earthquake, when members of the California delegation requested $3.84 million more than

---

[30] Mark Halperin and John Heilemann. 2013. *Double Down: Game Change 2012*. New York: The Penguin Press. p. 455.

[31] Ibid, p. 456. See also, Michael Barbaro, "After Obama, Christie wants a GOP hug," New York Times, November 19, 2012. www.nytimes.com/2012/11/20/us/politics/after-embrace-of-obama-chris-christie-woos-a-wary-gop.html?partner=rss&emc=rss&_r=0 &pagewanted=all.

[32] Velez and Martin (2013, 313).

either the Bush administration or the House Appropriations Committee had signaled.[33]

The universalistic paradigm reminds us that all Americans are presidential constituents. However, partisan forces may encourage the president to disproportionately reward Americans who are reliable members of his partisan base. In Chapter 2 we discuss several mechanisms that might drive core constituency targeting. For instance, presidents may consciously channel federal dollars to core states as an explicit reward for support in recent elections. Alternatively, inequalities in the allocation of federal resources along partisan lines may naturally arise when presidents of different parties pursue different policy agendas formed by competing views of the natural interest. In many policy venues, discerning between these possibilities is exceedingly difficult.

Within the context of disaster declarations, the interpretation of any evidence of core state targeting is much clearer. Is it reasonable to think that Democratic presidents genuinely believe responding to disasters in Democratic states is in the national interest, but responding to disasters producing equivalent destruction in Republican states is not (and vice versa for Republican presidents)? No – if we find evidence of core state targeting in disaster response, the only compelling explanation is that presidents prioritize the needs of core co-partisan constituencies over the needs of constituencies that reliably back the opposition party at the polls.[34]

---

[33] David Johnston, "The California quake; House panel votes $2.85 billion in quake relief," *New York Times*, October 24, 1989.

[34] Core targeting may also reflect the concentrated pressure of mass and elite campaign supporters all requesting assistance after a tornado, earthquake, severe storm, or other weather event. For instance, core states are likely to have governors, representatives, and senators who may pick up the phone and pressure the president to declare a disaster declaration in a case where he otherwise might not. As then-Governor Mitt Romney noted, having a Republican president in office meant that "For Republican governors... we have an ear in the White House, we have a number we can call, we have access that we wouldn't have otherwise had, and that's of course helpful." Dan Balz, "GOP governors want a seat at the table," *Washington Post*, November 22, 2004, A2. Presidents may find requests from co-partisan politicians for assistance more persuasive than those from equally hard-hit members of the partisan opposition. Core states may also be home to more campaign contributors eager to be rewarded for their electoral support. For example, one study found that campaign contributors were more likely to receive government contracts to clean up and reconstruct the Gulf Coast after Hurricane Katrina (Hogan et al., 2010). (We note, however, that the study does not distinguish to whom the contributions are made.) A precondition for these contributors to receive contracts is, of course, that the president must issue a disaster declaration to allow federal dollars to flow.

4.1.3   Coalitional Particularism: Targeting Congressional Co-partisans

Last, we consider the possibility that presidents may target congressional co-partisans in order to augment their influence in Congress by earning loyalty from lawmakers that is badly needed to pass their legislative agendas. Logically, presidents might be more responsive to pleas for assistance from co-partisans in the House than to those from members of the opposition party. Moreover, disproportionately assisting constituencies represented by co-partisans is another way for the president to strengthen party bonds and bolster his credentials as party leader.

4.1.4   An Assessment

To examine the influence of particularistic forces on presidential decision making, we construct a logistic regression model of the forces driving whether each county received a natural disaster declaration in each year from 1984 to 2008.[35] We focus on weather-related disasters and exclude those rare declarations issued to address non-weather emergencies, such as the Oklahoma City bombing in 1995 or the World Trade Center bombing in 1993.[36] From 1984 to 2008, 98 percent of counties saw at least one disaster declaration, and all counties experienced at least one year where they saw none. Some counties saw several declarations in a single year. For instance, in 2007, many counties in Oklahoma saw multiple disaster declarations after experiencing severe winter storms in February and December and tornadoes in June, July, and August. The map in Figure 4.1 presents the total number of natural disaster declarations that each county received from 1984 to 2008.

Given its importance, our models include three measures of objective need. Indeed, presidential universalism suggests that need should be the only significant predictor of aid. First, to measure storm damage we rely on the University of South Carolina's Spatial Hazard Events and Losses Database for the United States (SHELDUS), which records in constant 2005 dollars the amount of weather-related damaged sustained

---

[35] We employ this operationalization of the dependent variable for ease of interpretation. In Appendix B, we operationalize our dependent variable as a count of the number of disaster declarations in a county in a given year and use a poisson regression model to estimate the effects. The substantive results are the same, and we present them in their entirety in Appendix B. We obtained data on county-level disaster declarations from https://explore.data.gov/Other/FEMA-Disaster-Declarations-Summary/uihf-be6u, accessed September 26, 2013.

[36] The number of non-weather-related disaster declarations is small, at just over one-tenth of a percent of total declarations.

FIGURE 4.1. Presidential Disaster Declarations, 1984 to 2008. While our analysis considers the number of yearly disaster declarations, this figure shows the total number of presidential disaster declarations each county received from 1984 to 2008.

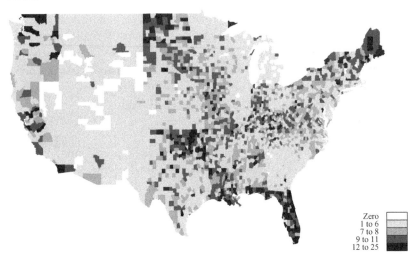

Zero
1 to 6
7 to 8
9 to 11
12 to 25

by each county in each year. The distribution of damage across counties is presented in Figure 4.2.[37] Second, we control for the number of severe weather events each county sees. For each county in each year, we record the number of weather events experienced that fall above the seventy-fifth percentile of severity, which is approximately $340,000 in property damage.[38] We also control for each county's per capita income. This provides a measure of the capacity of the locale to respond to the event without assistance from the federal government. The wealthier the county, the greater its capacity to handle the disaster unassisted.

If presidents engage in electoral particularism, the structure of presidential elections offers clear expectations about which voters they should target. Because of the Electoral College and winner-take-all apportionment of electors, presidents are motivated to direct resources toward battleground states that are likely to be the most competitive in the next electoral contest. By contrast, the null hypothesis generated by the universalistic presidency suggests that swing states will not receive any

---

[37] SHELDUS is a data source relied on by several other studies, including Healy and Malhotra (2009) and Gasper and Reeves (2011).

[38] The median amount of damage caused at the county level by an event is about $48,000. Similarly, Reeves (2011) relies on private insurance designations of "catastrophes" in order to proxy for extreme single weather events.

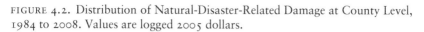

FIGURE 4.2. Distribution of Natural-Disaster-Related Damage at County Level, 1984 to 2008. Values are logged 2005 dollars.

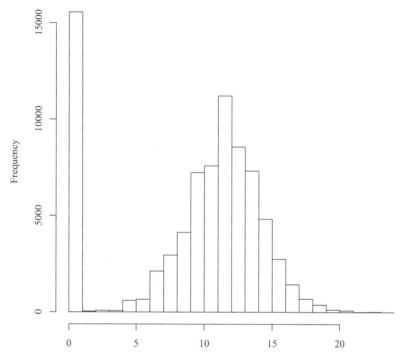

Estimates of Damage Caused by Natural Disasters (logged 2005 dollars)

additional resources, all else being equal. Need alone should predict when presidents issue disaster declarations.

To identify which states are most important in the next election, we measure electoral competitiveness as the average share of the two-party vote that the losing candidate received over the three preceding presidential elections. This creates a measure theoretically anchored at zero, which would occur if one party won 100 percent of the vote in that state in the past three elections. The maximum value of the scale is fifty, which would be observed if the Democratic and Republican candidates averaged the exact same share of the vote over the past three contests. The greater the share of the vote seized by the losing candidate in recent elections, the more competitive that state is expected to be in the next presidential race.[39] From this continuous measure, we designate states as either

---

[39] This measure is also used in measuring competitiveness for presidential (Kriner and Reeves, 2012; Reeves, 2011; Shaw, 1999b) and congressional elections (Bartels, 1991; Jacobson, 2004; Mayhew, 1974b).

competitive or uncompetitive. We define swing states as those in which the losing candidate has averaged 45 percent or more of the two-party vote over the preceding three elections. This categorization reflects how campaigns see states as either swing state or not.[40] For example, while a state in which the losing party has averaged 40 percent of the vote in the last three elections is more competitive than one in which the losing party has averaged only 30 percent of the vote over the past three contests, neither is anticipated to be a key swing state in the upcoming election. Both states are solidly in one partisan camp, albeit to slightly varying degrees. Rather, campaigns focus their energies very narrowly on the small group of states that are most likely to be in play in the next electoral contest.

As a prima facie test of our measure's validity, we examine whether our list of competitive states matches those compiled by political experts in recent elections. For instance, the five least competitive states in 2008 according to our metric were Utah, Wyoming, Idaho, Massachusetts, and Rhode Island. Each of these states was also listed by political pundits and campaign experts as being firmly in the camp of one of the two candidates; the first three were solidly in the Republican column, and the latter pair was all but certain to vote overwhelmingly for the Democrat. The five most competitive states on our metric in 2008 were Nevada, New Mexico, Florida, Wisconsin, and Iowa, with Ohio and Pennsylvania not far behind. In each of these five states, the losing candidate averaged 47.9 percent or more of the two-party vote in the 1996, 2000, and 2004 presidential contests. Our ranking corresponds with the professional assessment of the *Washington Post*, which listed all of these states as "battlegrounds" in their June 8, 2008 analysis of the presidential race.[41] In the most recent 2012 election, this metric captured all of the states commonly listed by major news outlets to be tossups during the fall campaign (e.g., Nevada, Florida, Ohio, Iowa, Colorado, Pennsylvania, New Hampshire, Virginia, New Mexico) save one; in North Carolina, the loser had averaged 44.92 percent of the two-party vote in the last three elections, causing it to miss narrowly our chosen threshold. Armed with this measure, we can test the main expectation of electoral particularism. When a state is uncompetitive, particularistic presidents lack incentives to target resources to its counties.

---

[40] See, for example, Shaw (2006).

[41] www.washingtonpost.com/wp-dyn/content/graphic/2008/06/08/GR2008060800566 .html. See also Susan Page, "New swing states pop up in '08," *USA Today*, May 28, 2008. http://usatoday30.usatoday.com/news/politics/election2008/2008-05-27-Newmap_N .htm.

When they have an opportunity to court voters in battleground states, we expect them to do so.

We also argue that partisan motivations may encourage presidents to target grants to a different type of constituency. Presidents as partisans-in-chief may pursue policies that reward members of their voting coalition. As a result, our theory predicts that those counties in states that are firmly in the partisan camp of the president will receive additional disaster declarations. To test this core state hypothesis, our analysis includes an additional variable identifying whether or not a county is located in a core state – that is, whether a significant majority of voters in the state consistently back the president or his party's candidate. We identify core states as those in which the incumbent presidential party's candidate has earned more than 55 percent of the two-party vote share in the preceding three presidential elections.

We also consider whether a county is represented by a member of the president's political party. If presidents engage in targeting in order to strengthen their influence in the legislature, then counties situated in districts of co-partisan members of the House may by more likely to receive disaster declarations.

To test each of these hypotheses, we include indicator variables for whether a county sits in a competitive state, a core state, or a district represented in Congress by a member of the president's party. To the extent that presidents engage in particularism, these characteristics will be related to the number of disaster declarations that a county receives.

Last, in addition to the previously listed variables, we also control for total county-level population. We include year and county fixed effects to account for unusual trends in a given year and to account for all time-invariant characteristics of the counties in our model.

Column 1 of Table 4.1 presents the estimates for our base model of presidential disaster declarations. As expected, we find strong evidence that objective measures of need predict disaster declarations. Disaster damage and severe weather events are both strongly related to the probability of a county receiving a presidential disaster declaration. Moreover, wealthier counties are better able to cope with storm damage and are less likely to receive disaster assistance than are poorer counties.

Nevertheless, even after controlling for need, we find strong evidence of electoral, partisan, and coalitional particularism. All three coefficients are positive and statistically significant. The effects of particularism are stark. Even after controlling for multiple measures of storm damage and objective need, counties in swing states, core states, and districts represented

FIGURE 4.3. Presidential Particularism and Disaster Declarations across All Years. The estimated effects of electoral, partisan, and coalitional particularism on disaster declarations. Each point represents the increased probability of a disaster declaration a county can expect if it is located in a swing state, core state, or district represented by a member of Congress from the president's party. For instance, the probability of a county seeing a disaster declaration is about .1 higher than the baseline of .25 if it is located in a core state.

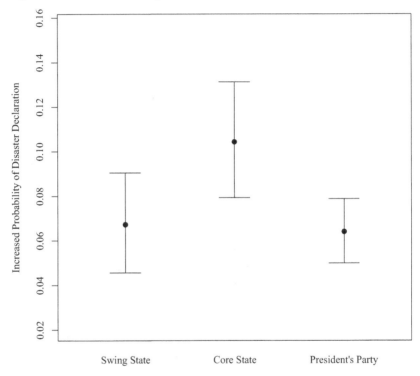

by members of Congress from the president's party have a higher probability of receiving a disaster declaration.

Figure 4.3 presents a substantive interpretation of the coefficients in Column 1 of Table 4.1.[42] The figure presents the estimated effects of particularism on the probability that a county in a given year receives a disaster declaration. Each point indicates the increased probability of a disaster declaration for a county in a swing state, core state, or district

[42] Throughout the book, we base our analyses on statistical models and illustrate the substantive interpretations of models through the interpretations of figures. We also present the results from the statistical models in the main text with alternative specifications referred to and presented in appendices.

TABLE 4.1. *A Model of County-Level Presidential Disaster Declarations, 1984 to 2008, Logistic Regression Model. All models include county and year fixed effects. Standard errors are in parentheses.*

	(1)	(2)
Swing state	0.238	0.077
	(0.036)	(0.040)
Core state	0.349	0.191
	(0.037)	(0.042)
Member of Congress from presidential party	0.228	0.227
	(0.023)	(0.024)
Swing state × Election year		0.639
		(0.069)
Core state × Election year		0.616
		(0.078)
Severe disaster events	0.119	0.121
	(0.008)	(0.008)
Disaster damage (logged 2005 dollars)	0.180	0.180
	(0.005)	(0.005)
Personal income (logged 2005 dollars)	−0.893	−0.902
	(0.184)	(0.184)
County population (logged, in millions)	−0.303	−0.306
	(0.214)	(0.215)
Observations	63,175	63,175
Number of counties	2,999	2,999

that is represented by a member of Congress from the president's political party. The I-bars around the point represent the statistical uncertainty around our estimates based on 95 percent confidence intervals. These differences are based on counties that see identical amounts of damage and that possess identical capacities to respond.

All types of particularism are associated with increased disaster declarations while holding objective need constant. Consider that the baseline probability of a county in a non-swing, non-core state receiving a disaster declaration is about .25. If that county was instead located in a swing or core state, the likelihood of that county receiving a disaster declaration increases to .31 and .35, respectively, all else being equal. If a county in a non-swing, non-core state is, however, represented by a member of the president's party in the house, then the probability of it receiving a disaster declaration also increases significantly, from .25 to .31.

We do find that measures of objective need are the strongest predictors of a disaster declarations; universalism is undoubtedly at work in the decision-making process. Yet we also find that electoral, partisan, and coalitional particularism are influential forces in determining this profoundly need-based decision. Such increases in the probability of receiving a declaration can translate into millions of dollars of federal aid.

4.1.5 Electoral and Partisan Particularism and the Political Business Cycle

We now adapt our model to explore the temporal dynamics of the disaster declaration process and consider whether presidents are influenced by a political business cycle when declaring disasters. Given voters' relatively short time horizons, presidents should feel increasing pressure to reward constituencies in swing states with disaster declarations as the next general election approaches. Whether core state targeting should vary with the electoral cycle is less clear. On one hand, the election-year dynamics for core targeting may be attenuated by a constant need to maintain and reward core partisan support. In this sense, partisan targeting should not necessarily be any more pronounced during an election year. On the other hand, presidents may feel pressure to maintain their base in the face of electoral vicissitudes. For instance, from 1960 to 1996, West Virginia elected only Democrats to the Senate and the governor's mansion. Only twice during this period did the state vote for a Republican presidential candidate. However, after Bill Clinton won the state by fifteen points in 1996, the state has gone Republican in every presidential election since.[43] This realistic fear of a slipping base may cause presidents to doggedly court even their most loyal supporters, particularly in election years, in pursuit of securing reelection.

To examine whether swing and core state targeting varies with the electoral cycle, we replicate our base models but include the interaction between the core state and swing state variables and another variable indicating election years.[44] We present these findings in Column 2 of Table 4.1 and present the substantive effects in Figure 4.4. The results suggest that both swing state and core state targeting is significantly stronger in election years than non-election years. When the next presidential contest is far off, counties in swing states receive only a modest increase in the probability of a disaster declaration, all else being equal. We also find

[43] Karen Tumulty, "A blue state's road to red," *Washington Post*, October 26, 2013. www.washingtonpost.com/sf/national/2013/10/26/a-blue-states-road-to-red/.

[44] The election-year variable itself is not included in the model because it is subsumed in the year fixed effects.

FIGURE 4.4. Presidential Particularism and Disaster Declarations in Election Years. Each point represents the increased probability of a disaster declaration that a county can expect if it is located in a swing state or core state, versus a state that is neither swing nor core. The figure also distinguishes between these effects in election and non-election years. For instance, given a baseline probability of .25, a county in a swing state during an election year can expect an increase by .23 in the probability of a disaster declaration, for a total probability of .48.

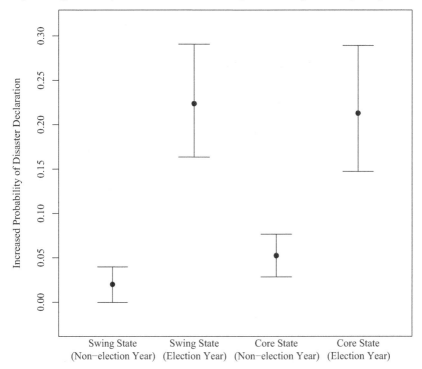

significant, if modest, evidence of core state targeting in non-election years. When presidential elections are distant, being in a core state increases a county's probability of receiving a disaster declaration by .05. Though the effect is modest, the data show that presidents systematically reward their partisan base even when the election is distant.

The effects of particularism are dramatically larger in election years. The probability of a county in a swing state seeing an election year disaster declaration increases by .23 compared to a non-swing, non-core state county, all else being equal. Remembering that the baseline probability is .25, this means the chance of an election-year swing state disaster declaration for a county nearly doubles. This is precisely what we would expect given presidential incentives based on voters' short memories; presidents get the most bang for their buck by assisting swing states in election years. Consider a tornado that killed 6, injured 28, and destroyed almost 100 homes and businesses in Oklahoma in April 2012.[45] Despite the significant damage, when the governor of this decidedly Republican state requested aid, the request was denied. When New Hampshire experienced heavy rains that led to flash flooding and serious damage to roads and bridges, the governor of this swing state asked for and received a disaster declaration. According to one report by Daniel Vock and Jim Malewitz of *Stateline*, "experts in the field say the disaster standards are unclear – and often ignored. The result is that disaster decisions can seem arbitrary or politically motivated."[46] We suggest that particularism is one potential mechanism behind the sometimes confusing outcomes of these processes. Even after controlling for multiple measures of objective need, we find that political factors influence the probability of a county receiving a disaster declaration, particularly in election years.

Counties in core states in election years are also much more likely to receive a presidential disaster declaration than are counties in states that are neither swing nor core. Indeed, the data suggest that in election years presidents reward co-partisan constituencies with disaster aid to almost the same extent that they reward constituencies in swing states. This suggests that presidents may use disaster aid to play electoral politics, both by courting swing state voters and by shoring up their core partisan base. Additionally it suggests that the biggest losers are those counties residing in enemy territory of electorally minded presidents. Those locales may expect to see disasters go unaided despite a need comparable to that of their swing and core state neighbors.

Our analysis of disaster declarations provides further insight into how presidential particularism operates. First, it shows that, in a context where presidents have a high degree of unilateral authority, electoral particularism is most prevalent during the run-up to an election. This provides yet another piece of evidence that presidential particularism is not a statistical fluke. Additionally, the presence of an electoral cycle with respect to disaster declarations is further evidence that the behavior is originating with the president himself and that swing state targeting is an electoral strategy designed to net the president and his party additional votes. Meanwhile, partisan particularism operates throughout the term with an

---

[45] "Governor requests federal disaster assistance for Woodward," *News9.com*, April 18, 2012. www.news9.com/story/17526306/governor-requests-federal-disaster-assistance for-woodward.

[46] Vock and Malewitz (2013).

increase during an election year. That we observe partisan targeting in disaster declarations – a policy decision that normatively, we would hope, would be apolitical and based solely on objective measures of economic need – is strong evidence that partisan particularism is not an incidental by-product of presidents of different parties pursuing competing broader policy goals, but rather the product of a systematic effort to reward the partisan faithful.[47] At least in the context of disasters, this dynamic is particularly strong in election years, suggesting that core constituency targeting can serve both electoral and broader partisan goals.

4.2 Transportation Grants

Past scholars have argued that transportation grants are the "quintessential example of a geographically targetable form of public expenditure."[48] As a result, they should be particularly fertile ground for particularistic politics. However, unlike with disaster declarations, the president's capacity to influence the allocation of transportation dollars across the country is anything but absolute. Indeed, the vast majority of prior research on the allocation of federal transportation grants has argued for the primacy of Congress in this policy venue. In *Congress: The Electoral Connection*, David Mayhew argues that members of Congress, seeking to impress voters, have strong incentives to pursue policies that are "of a scale that allows individual members of Congress to be recognized as the claimant for the benefit" and that provide for benefits that are "given out in apparently ad hoc fashion (unlike, say, social security checks), with a congressman apparently having a hand in the allocation."[49] A bevy of studies has shown that transportation projects meet these criteria and that members of Congress jockey to bring as many of these projects as possible to their districts.[50]

Academic studies aside, the role of Congress in allocating transportation pork would become clear to anyone flying into the John Murtha Johnstown-Cambria County Airport in Pennsylvania. However, few people will ever have such an experience, since there are only three flights a day into this airport, despite it being the beneficiary of more than

---

[47] One could imagine that when a president is faced with accepting or rejecting a request for a borderline case for federal disaster aid, the pressure brought to bear by numerous supporters from a core state could potentially be enough to tip the balance.

[48] Hauk and Wacziarg (2007).

[49] Mayhew (1974a, 54).

[50] See, e.g., Evans (2004); Lee (2003).

$150 million in taxpayer funding thanks to the airport's namesake, a member of Congress until his death in 2010.[51] The importance of transportation projects to many members is also nicely encapsulated in the illustrious career of Senator Robert Byrd of West Virginia. Having risen to power on the Senate Appropriations Committee, Byrd saw it as his duty to use his position to channel as many federal dollars as possible to support projects in his largely rural home state, one of the poorest in the nation.[52] It is difficult to not be reminded of Senator Byrd's legacy of procuring federal transportation dollars as one travels through the state on the Robert C. Byrd Appalachian Highway System, drives over the Robert C. Byrd Bridge in Huntington, or perhaps visits the fishing pier off the Robert C. Byrd Locks and Dam over the Ohio River at Gallipolis Ferry.[53] One could also park in the Robert C. Byrd Intermodal Transportation Center as she visits the Wheeling National Heritage Area. Byrd, commenting on his devotion to his state, noted, "West Virginia has always had four friends: God Almighty, Sears Roebuck, Carter's Liver Pills and Robert C. Byrd."[54]

Senator Byrd is far from alone in seeking pork barrel transportation projects for his constituency. The 2005 Highway Bill's infamous "Bridge to Nowhere," a pet project of Alaska Republican Don Young, is perhaps the most indelible contemporary symbol of pork barrel politics. Congressman Young succeeded in winning almost $400 million for a pair of bridges that would service a mere fifty permanent residents on the remote Ketchikan Island in Alaska.[55] Given the priority that most members place on influencing the distribution of federal transportation dollars and securing funds for their own constituencies, finding evidence of significant presidential targeting in a policy realm long held to be dominated by congressional politicking would constitute especially strong evidence for our theory of a particularistic presidency. If presidents can succeed

[51] Jonathan Karl, "Welcome to the airport for nobody," *ABCNews.com*, April 23, 2009. http://abcnews.go.com/Business/Politics/story?id=7412160.

[52] In 2008, West Virginia ranked 49th of 50 states in per capita income. www.census.gov/statab/ranks/rank29.html.

[53] There is even a Wikipedia page for places named after the Senator. http://en.wikipedia.org/wiki/List_of_places_named_after_Robert_Byrd.

[54] Greg Moore, "U.S. Senator Robert C. Byrd dies at 92," *Charleston Gazette*, June 28, 2010.

[55] While outrage over such perceived government waste led to the money being stripped in 2005, the project remains funded through the Surface Transportation Extension Act of 2011. See Billy House, "Dems decry continued funding for 'Bridges to Nowhere'," *National Journal*, March 3, 2011. www.nationaljournal.com/daily/dems-decry-continued-funding-for-bridges-to-nowhere-20110302.

in skewing policy outcomes to favor constituencies of great political importance to them in this realm so dear to members of Congress, then it would suggest that few policy venues are immune from presidential influence.

An additional advantage of looking for evidence of presidential particularism in transportation grants is that, as in the analysis of disaster declarations, we can roughly control for need. While measuring a constituency's demand for transportation funds is much less straightforward than accounting for the amount of storm damage it has sustained, accounting for lane mileage in our statistical models affords an important measure of control for need. Also, transportation grants are another policy venue where interpreting evidence of core constituency targeting is easier. As Frances Lee has argued, "No one claims that liberals and conservatives in the United States have different positions on how a fixed sum of money for infrastructure grants should be distributed among the states."[56] As a result, ideological differences about how best to meet the transportation needs of the nation are unlikely to lead to core constituencies receiving a disproportionate share of infrastructure dollars. Rather, such inequalities in the allocation of transportation dollars would be strong evidence of partisan motivations.

4.2.1 *Presidential Particularism and Transportation Grants*

In 2008, the Consolidated Federal Funds Report showed that the federal government allocated almost $54 billion in grant funding for transportation projects across the country. In 2007, transportation grant spending exceeded the $80 billion mark. To examine whether presidents skew the distribution of these funds across the country, we model the factors shaping the amount of transportation grant spending received by each county in each year.[57]

As in the analysis of disaster declarations, our three main explanatory variables of interest are indicators of whether a county is located within a swing or core state, as well as an indicator for whether a county is represented by a member of the president's party in the House.[58] Electoral incentives should compel the president to target transportation grant

---

[56] Lee (2009, 50).

[57] Because transportation grant spending at the county level is heavily skewed by a small number of counties that received very large grant hauls, our dependent variable is the natural log of transportation grant spending.

[58] An alternative measure of the degree to which the state is a core state is simply the average margin of victory of the president's party in that state over the last three elections. Using

dollars to battleground states with the greatest potential influence over the next presidential race. Partisan incentives may encourage the president to channel federal dollars disproportionately to communities that are key components of his core partisan constituency. Last, targeting transportation grants to constituencies represented by co-partisans in Congress could serve a number of political goals for the president, including bolstering his credentials as a party leader and buying him leverage with the core of his co-partisan coalition in Congress.

However, given the long-held scholarly consensus that Congress dominates the process by which transportation projects are distributed across the country, we must also account for Congress's capacity to influence the allocation of transportation grant dollars across the country. Which members should be best positioned to secure disproportionate shares of transportation dollars for their districts? Past researchers offer several hypotheses. First, congressional scholars have long speculated that committee members have advantages in seizing a larger piece of the budgetary pie for programs within their purview. For example, in the specific context of transportation spending, Frances Lee has shown that members of the Transportation and Infrastructure Committee were more successful in securing earmarks, and earmarks with large dollar values, in the 1998 Transportation Reauthorization than were House members not on the committee.[59] As a result, in our models we control for whether or not a county was represented by a member of the Transportation and Infrastructure Committee.

Alternatively, a number of researchers have suggested that members of the majority party in Congress are able to secure greater shares of federal spending than are members of the congressional minority.[60] Past scholars have also observed this dynamic specifically in some transportation spending programs.[61] Accordingly, we also control for whether each county is represented by a member of the majority party in the House.

While our emphasis is on the political forces driving variation in the distribution of transportation dollars across the country, undoubtedly varying levels of need across states and counties also influence the distribution of transportation grants. To control at least partially for geographic

this measure instead of the core state indicator variable yields strong evidence of core state targeting. For full results and additional discussion, see Appendix B.

[59] Lee (2003).
[60] Inter alia Albouy (2013), Balla et al. (2002), Cox and McCubbins (2007), Levitt and Snyder (1995), Martin (2003).
[61] Lee (2000).

variation in need, we include a measure of the total number of lane miles in each state's road system in each year as reported by the Department of Transportation.[62]

The model also includes a series of demographic controls including each county's population, its annual real per capita income, and its unemployment rate. Finally, the model includes both county and year fixed effects. County fixed effects allow us to determine a different base level of grant funding for each state that is a product of a myriad of other factors we cannot explicitly control for in the model. Year fixed effects allow us to account for annual fluctuations in the overall level of transportation grant spending.

Table 4.2 presents the results of our regression model. Even in this quintessential policy venue for congressional pork barrel politics, we continue to find strong evidence of *presidential* particularism. Interestingly, we found no evidence that members of the majority party in Congress or members of the Transportation and Infrastructure Committee were able to skew the distribution of federal grants to benefit their constituencies.[63] To be sure, individual members of Congress in specific cases can exert enormous influence over the allocation of transportation grants. The $286.4 billion 2005 Highway Bill included earmarked funds for horseback riding trails in Virginia, a Vermont snowmobiling path, expanded parking at New York's Harlem Hospital, and, of course, the eponymous Bridge to Nowhere, among hundreds of others. While it is easy to identify the transportation pet projects of members of Congress, which provide little benefit to those outside of district contractors, when we examine trends in all of the projects from 1984 to 2008, it is the president who seems to have the greatest influence over how federal dollars are distributed. Swing states and constituencies represented by his co-partisans reap significant rewards, while many other counties with less electoral or political importance to the president receive systematically smaller shares of federal transportation dollars.

Figure 4.5 illustrates the effects of being in a swing or core state or being represented by a presidential co-partisan for the median county. The population-weighted median county received just over $47 million in

---

[62] This data can be obtained from the Office of Highway Policy Information's Highway Statistics Series' Table HM-60.

[63] In Appendix B, we estimate additional models that show the chair and ranking member of the Transportation and Infrastructure Committee appear able to secure disproportionate shares of transportation dollars for their districts; however, we find no evidence that rank-and-file members of the committee are able to do so.

TABLE 4.2. *Federal Grant Spending and Presidential Particularism within States. A county-level model of federal transportation grant spending, 1984 to 2008. Counties in swing states and those represented by members of the president's party in the House receive disproportionately large shares of transportation dollars. The model is a least squares regression with fixed effects for county and year. Robust standard errors clustered on county are in parentheses.*

Swing state	0.154
	(0.054)
Core state	0.067
	(0.051)
Member of Congress from presidential party	0.142
	(0.035)
Member of Congress from majority party	0.033
	(0.037)
Member of Congress Transportation Committee	0.007
	(0.051)
Lane mileage (in 1000s)	0.008
	(0.002)
County population (logged)	−0.154
	(0.184)
Per capita income	0.001
	(0.008)
Unemployment rate	−0.018
	(0.011)
Constant	14.768
	(1.945)
Observations	76,930
Number of counties	3,083
R^2	0.040

federal transportation grants in 2008.[64] As shown in Figure 4.5, our model estimates that the median county in a swing state receives an additional 17 percent, or about $7.8 million in transportation grants than does an identical county located in a state that is neither swing nor core. To put this figure in comparison, in 2013 the Department of Transportation awarded a $1.4 million grant to repair 42 miles of railroad tracks between Rollinsford and Ossipee, New Hampshire. Another $5 million

[64] In other words, half of Americans lived in counties that received more than $47 million in transportation grant funding, and half of Americans lived in counties that received less than this sum.

FIGURE 4.5. Presidential Particularism and Transportation Grants (County-Level Effects). I-bars represent 90% confidence intervals around estimates.

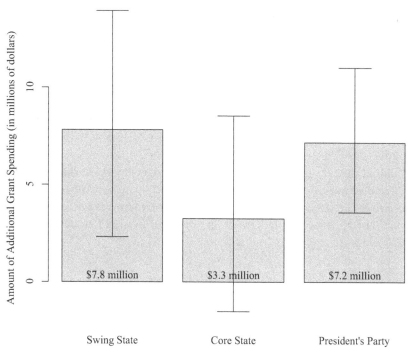

was awarded to Arkansas to resurface a section of Highway 92 running through Conway, van Buren, and Cleburne counties and to replace two aging, weight-restricted bridges. A third project devoted $8.2 million in federal cash to help replace a 110-year-old bridge in Greene County, Indiana, critical to the operations of two freight rail lines. Thus, the swing state advantage reaped by the median county in a competitive state could fund at least one additional major project within that county in a given year.

We also find evidence of other forms of presidential particularism. We find that counties represented by members of the president's party in Congress – not members of the majority party – also receive disproportionately high levels of federal transportation funding. This is strong evidence of presidential particularism. Presidents may target federal dollars to such constituencies in an effort to reward their fellow partisans and gain more leverage in Congress by bolstering the ranks of their co-partisans. Our model suggests that, all else being equal, counties represented by presidential co-partisans in the House receive 15 percent more in transportation grant spending than counties represented by a member of the opposition party. For the median county in 2008, this translates into an infusion of more than $7 million.

Finally, we find modest evidence consistent with core state targeting. Counties in core states received almost 6 percent more, on average, than do counties in states that are neither swing nor core. In the median county in 2008, this would translate into an additional $2.7 million in transportation grant spending. As the error bars in Figure 4.5 demonstrate, there is considerable uncertainty around this estimate. Nevertheless, using alternative measures of whether a state is a core constituency, such as the share of the two-party vote won by the president's party in the preceding three elections, reveals a strong and statistically significant relationship between the strength of electoral support for the president's party in a state and the share of federal grants received by counties within it. See Appendix B for additional discussion and analysis.[65]

4.3 Summary

Disaster declarations and transportation grants are two policy areas where we might not have expected to find evidence of presidential particularism. After all, we hope that decisions concerning federal disaster aid are driven solely by the scope of a disaster. By contrast, few would suspect that politics do not enter into decisions about how transportation dollars are allocated. Yet, members of Congress are routinely held to dominate in the realm of transportation pork. From the Bud Shuster Highway in Pennsylvania to the Norman Y. Mineta San Jose International Airport, from sea to shining sea, the influence of individual members of Congress in transportation projects is notorious.

Nevertheless, in both cases we find significant empirical evidence of presidential particularism. The decision of whether to declare a disaster and dispense federal aid to affected communities is the president's alone to make. Here, the president's authority is uncluttered by competing claims of other actors. Despite the relatively straightforward, apolitical factors

---

[65] We also examine whether presidential particularism in transportation grant spending ebbed and flowed with the electoral cycle. Following the same methods employed in the analysis of disaster declarations, we find modest evidence that both swing state and core state targeting increase in election years. The coefficients on both election-year interaction terms are positive; however, both fail to reach conventional thresholds of statistical significance.

that drive the need for disaster relief, we see significant evidence of presidential particularism. Even after controlling for the amount of damage that a constituency has sustained, we find that presidents target disaster aid disproportionately to counties in swing and core states, especially in election years. This is particularly stark evidence for the full extent of presidential particularism and how it skews policy outcomes.

Similarly, in sharp contrast to the conventional wisdom emphasizing pork-hungry legislators battling to bring transportation projects home to their districts, our results suggest that presidents exert considerable influence over the distribution of federal transportation grant dollars. We find strong evidence of swing state targeting. Far from being unconcerned with reelection, presidents appear to go to great lengths to channel billions of transportation dollars per year to the most electorally important states in the hopes of bolstering their fortunes at the ballot box. We also find strong evidence of presidential co-partisan targeting. Counties represented not by members of the majority party in the House but by members of the president's party reap disproportionate shares of federal transportation dollars. Finally, we found more modest but still considerable evidence of core state targeting within federal transportation grant spending.[66]

In a diverse range of settings ranging from those where presidents have complete unilateral authority to those where presidents must battle with Congress and other actors for influence, presidents have succeeded in skewing policy outcomes to serve their political objectives and not the unbiased needs of the nation as a whole.

---

[66] For additional evidence of core state targeting, see Appendix B.

5

Federal Grants and Presidential Particularism

In 1909, President William H. Taft began his public appeal for a massive expansion and improvement of American waterways with a flotilla down the Mississippi River. The convoy included nearly one hundred members of Congress and was, in part, an early twentieth-century publicity stunt designed to garner support for infrastructure improvements legislation. But the president also used the public spectacle as a powerful platform from which to warn Congress not to treat the initiative as pork barrel legislation. Taft "caused a sensation" among members, especially Speaker of the House Joe Cannon, for criticizing Congress for doing what was politically expedient to the detriment of the general welfare.[1] If the local interests of members of Congress caused them to invest in strengthening already solid riverbanks and deepening untraveled waterways in their districts, the collective aims of the nation would suffer. Taft demanded that funds be allocated based on objective need and not the wants of powerful members of Congress.[2]

---

[1] "Taft leads flotilla down Mississippi," *New York Times*, October 26, 1909, p. 7.

[2] Presidential-congressional tensions over alleged pork barrel spending in water infrastructure projects emerged again in the Carter administration. As President Carter remembers in his diary, "We began to notify members of Congress that I was deleting 19 water resources projects that had been previously approved by Congress, the Corps of Engineers, and the Department of Interior. I know this is going to create a political furor, but it's something that I am committed to accomplish. These projects ultimately would cost at least $5.1 billion, and the country would be better off if none of them were built. It's going to be a pretty touchy legislative fight to get these projects removed permanently." Jimmy Carter. 2010. *White House Diary*. New York: Farrar, Straus and Giroux, p. 23. See also Frisch and Kelly (2011).

More than a century later, modern presidents still echo Taft's warnings. Presidents continue to rail against pork barrel spending and to champion the office of the presidency as the defender of the national interest from petty and parochial politics. At times, members of Congress seem to acknowledge their own failings and look to the president to save them from themselves. Witness the Line Item Veto Act of 1996, which gave presidents the power to strike certain types of provisions from legislation individually rather than veto the entire bill.[3] While the Supreme Court struck down the line item veto as unconstitutional in 1998, both George W. Bush and Barack Obama have called for its reintroduction in a form that might pass constitutional muster. Most recently, in 2010 the Obama administration submitted a new proposal to Congress, the Reduce Unnecessary Spending Act, which the president claimed would help his administration cut billions of dollars of federal waste inserted into appropriations bills by spendthrift members of Congress each year.[4]

Yet, presidents do not always provide the universalistic counterbalance to congressional particularism as is so often claimed. Rather, presidents bring their own political imperatives and biases to the budgetary process and, in so doing, inject new forms of politicized inequities into the allocation of federal spending. Consider, again, President Obama's efforts to court voters in Ohio in the lead-up to the 2012 election. More than one hundred years after Taft's denunciation of congressional efforts to lard up national improvement legislation with inefficient pork, President Obama embraced a different view of the utility of particularized federal spending. In more than twenty visits to Ohio, a battleground state that saw more presidential visits than any other during the 2012 campaign, the president highlighted the exceptional benefits that Ohio had received from federal coffers. At campaign stops in places such as Bowling Green, President Obama trumpeted this support for the new federal spending projects brought to Ohio under his watch; the administration even invited many grant recipients to the rallies that he and the vice president held. In September 2012, the *Washington Post* took note of the amount of federal

---

[3] The act allowed the president to strike specific items of discretionary budget authority, any new direct spending item, and any limited tax benefit. For an overview of the legislation and the debate over its constitutionality, see Thomas Nicola, "Line Item Veto Act Unconstitutional: *Clinton v. City of New York*." CRS Report, 98-690A, August 18, 1998.

[4] Eamon Javers, "Barack Obama seeks line-item veto," *Politico*, May 24, 2010. www.politico.com/news/stories/0510/37711.html.

money that had flown into the state, including hundreds of millions of dollars in energy tax credits, money for high-speed rail, and $30 million for a pilot program for innovation in manufacturing.[5] But rather than shrink from such seemingly rampant particularism, the president touted what his administration had done for the state on the campaign trail.

President Obama is far from the only president to engage in such electoral calculations. For example, many would be surprised to learn that Franklin Roosevelt began his tenure as president by selecting a Treasury Secretary who was an avid budget cutter and inflation hawk. Like President Hoover, Secretary Lewis Douglas believed that the best way to combat the Depression was to balance the government's books and restore investor confidence. During FDR's first 100 Days, Douglas launched a one-man crusade for economy in the federal budget, and one of his targets was federal funding for scientific research under the aegis of the Department of Agriculture. Secretary of Agriculture Henry Wallace vehemently opposed the cuts, and to sway the president, who repeatedly proclaimed his desire to trim fat from the budget, Wallace emphasized the electoral ramifications of these cuts. Wallace warned the president that if these cuts went through, "there will be such a large number of well-informed and disillusioned, highly trained, intelligent and influential people thrown in the ranks of the malcontents that the Democratic Party will probably never be able to carry the Middle West again."[6] Ultimately, Wallace's electoral appeal carried the day, and though some cuts were made, the larger project was spared.

Culling through the annals of presidential history, it is easy to find historical anecdotes to support both our theory of a particularistic president and its universalistic counterpart, which has become part of popular and academic presidential lore. But, when looking at the allocation of federal spending across the country writ large, which view best accords with reality? Do presidents routinely endeavor to target federal dollars to politically important constituencies? Or are federal dollars allocated seemingly without regard to presidential electoral and partisan pressures? To answer this question we must move beyond anecdote and the cases of single policies examined in previous chapters and instead systematically analyze all available grant spending from 1984 to 2008.

[5] Jerry Markon, "Obama showering Ohio with attention and money," *Washington Post*, September 25, 2012.
[6] Quoted in Adam Cohen. 2009. *Nothing to Fear: FDR's Inner Circle and the Hundred Days that Created Modern America*. New York: Penguin, p. 234. See also Wright (1974).

5.1   Why Budgetary Politics?

In three policy areas where presidents wield considerable unilateral authority – trade sanctions, base closings, and disaster declarations – we found considerable evidence of presidential particularism. Rather than pursuing economically optimal policies that serve the interests of the nation as a whole, presidents have used their authority to benefit disproportionately the most politically important constituencies: primarily constituencies in swing states and those dominated by their co-partisan base. Presidents are routinely particularistic in their policy outlook, rather than universalistic as many have argued. However, skeptics may counter that policy areas such as these, in which either Congress has delegated considerable authority to the president or presidents have claimed it as pursuant to their power as commander-in-chief, are exceptional. In other contexts where presidents must compete with Congress, interest groups, and other actors, presidents may be decidedly less successful in skewing outcomes to disproportionately advantage constituencies of the greatest political importance to the administration. We found evidence of particularism in the specific context of transportation grant spending. However, this is but one narrow type of spending program; does a particularistic president skew the allocation of federal dollars writ large?

Discretionary budgetary politics, such as the allocation of federal grants, is particularly well suited for examining the extent of presidential particularism for at least two reasons. First, prior scholarship has argued that in the realm of distributive politics Congress has jealously guarded its power, even as its influence in other areas, such as war powers, has waned. Thus, divide-the-dollar politics serves as a strong test case for our argument about the scope of presidential particularism. Second, in this policy venue the universalistic and particularistic frameworks offer clear and divergent expectations for the types of policies presidents should pursue. The universalistic framework posits a clear distinction between presidents and Congress in this policy realm. Congress should pursue pork, while presidents pursue the interests of the nation at large.

For reelection-seeking members of Congress, pork is a powerful electoral currency. Members engage in tacit log rolls to help one another bring home the bacon for their individual constituencies. Pundits routinely denounce congressional spending bills brimming with members' pet projects, ranging from badly needed road repairs or new bridges in their constituencies to the seemingly ridiculous, such as a $349,000 appropriation for swine waste management in North Carolina.[7] The annual *Citizens Against Government Waste Congressional Pig Book* identifies such projects by substantive policy area and by the member requesting them, showing the popularity of congressional earmarks on both sides of the aisle. Even in tough budgetary times when members of all stripes proclaim the need for restraint in government spending, scores of members aggressively seek funding for specific projects within their districts, even in cases where the larger benefits of such projects are tenuous at best.

Consider, for example, the 2012 battle over the Department of Defense appropriations bill. Facing inevitable cuts, the U.S. Army Chief of Staff Ray Ordiniero asked Congress to suspend production of the M1A1 Abrams tank and to postpone repairs. The tank was not in line with the military priorities of a post–Cold War age, and 2,000 tanks already sat idle in the California desert. In a climate of austerity, a rational observer might expect Congress to embrace the Army's proposed savings of almost $3 billion over three years. But instead, 173 members of Congress, Republicans and Democrats alike, petitioned the Secretary of Defense to overrule the Army and continue production of the tanks. Why? Production of M1A1 tanks involves more than 880 suppliers spread across the nation, and the main fabrication plant is located in the district of the ranking minority member of the House Armed Services Committee.[8]

Presidents, by contrast, are held to eschew pork barrel politics and instead to value universalism and efficiency. Tellingly, the aforementioned Citizens Against Government Waste gives the president a pass when it comes to pork barrel spending. One of the group's criteria for a project being designated as pork is that the request is *not* made by the president.[9] With a truly national constituency, the electoral payoff from benefits

---

[7] Paul Bedard, "Sen. John McCain's top 10 earmark tweets," *US News and World Report* Washington Whispers Blog, November 24, 2009. www.usnews.com/news/washington-whispers/articles/2009/11/24/sen-john-mccains-top-10-earmark-tweets.

[8] Drew Griffin and Kathleen Johnston, "Army to Congress: thanks, but no tanks," October 9, 2012. http://security.blogs.cnn.com/2012/10/09/army-to-congress-thanks-but-no-tanks/. Economists have long detailed the traditional holdup problem that plagues principal-agent relationships in which the agent can use its superior information to demand additional monies from the principal. This may be especially true of the military, which sees an unusual degree of deference from politicians. But in this case, paradoxically, the agent asked for less money from the principal who then rejected the savings. In sharp contrast to Congress's puzzling demand, President Obama's proposed budget heeded General Ordiniero's advice and eliminated funding for the superfluous tanks. "Tank glut shows congress is stuck in a pork barrel," *Sacramento Bee*, February 22, 2013, p. A8.

[9] http://cagw.org/sites/default/files/pdf/2012-pig-book.pdf.

received by one constituent is no more important than that from any other constituent. Thus, presidents, the universalistic framework argues, should favor a roughly equal – or perhaps more aptly, an apolitical – distribution of federal spending.

Our argument that presidents routinely respond to particularistic impulses directly challenges this perspective. Electoral incentives encourage presidents to target federal dollars toward swing states that have the most influence over the outcome of the next presidential election. As leaders of increasingly polarized political parties, presidents also have incentives to prioritize the needs of their core partisan base, even at the expense of nationally optimal policy outcomes. Furthermore, a long literature on distributive politics has argued that decisions over where federal dollars are allocated are essentially non-ideological.[10] Summarizing past research, Frances Lee argues, "Generally speaking, once a given level of federal funding for a program is established, liberalism and conservatism cannot guide members' decisions about how dollars should be divided."[11] As a result, if we see presidents channeling dollars to co-partisan constituencies, we argue it is partisan, not ideological, incentives about how best to achieve the national interest that are producing the observed inequities. Thus, as we examine the allocation of federal dollars across the country over time, we can test whether the data better fit the claims of the universalistic or particularistic presidency frameworks. Moreover, to the extent that we find evidence of presidential particularism, we can compare the magnitude of the presidentially induced inequities with those created by the parochial urges of members of Congress.

5.2 Presidential Capacity for Targeted Budgeting

Can presidents systematically influence the budgetary process to target federal grant dollars disproportionately to politically important constituencies? There are reasons to be skeptical. After all, the power of the purse is firmly lodged with Congress. Since the enactment of the Congressional Budget and Impoundment Control Act of 1974, Congress's budget committees have been charged with producing a budget resolution, which sets spending and revenue targets for the forthcoming fiscal year. Its substantive committees review all programs and determine the

---

[10] For example, Cox and McCubbins (2007, 46) contend that distributive politics, or how to divide the budgetary pie, cannot be placed on a traditional left-right dimension.
[11] Lee (2009, 59).

amount of federal spending they will authorize in each policy area. And each year the appropriations committees determine how much money to allocate to the myriad of government agencies and programs.

As a result, for decades political science scholarship on budgetary politics focused almost exclusively on the role of Congress in shaping the allocation of federal dollars across the country. Securing distributive benefits for which members could claim credit in their districts was viewed as an essential reelection-oriented activity, and a wealth of scholarship explored the moderating influence of committee assignments, majority party membership, and other institutional factors on a member's capacity to deliver pork to his or her constituency.[12]

While Article I of the Constitution plainly entrusts the power of the purse to the legislature, recent research has provided a corrective by emphasizing the critical role that presidents, through their multiple vantage points within the bureaucracy, play in the budgetary process.[13] Consider Lyndon Johnson's efforts to use NASA research grants to gain political leverage. Less than two months after ascending to the presidency following the assassination of John F. Kennedy, Johnson had firmly committed himself to enacting a civil rights bill as a tribute to his martyred predecessor. However, as had many similar initiatives before it, the bill remained where it was when President Kennedy died, caught in the iron grasp of the House Rules Committee. To force the committee's chair, Howard Smith, to hold hearings or risk losing his control over the bill, the administration and the bill's managers in the House had begun to collect signatures for a discharge petition that could force the bill to the floor for a vote without action from the Rules Committee. However, still forty votes short of the requisite majority and with few prospects for additional help from the Democratic side of the aisle, Johnson turned to the Republican leader, Charlie Halleck of Indiana. With Halleck before him in the Oval Office, wavering under the infamous Johnson treatment, the president picked up the phone and dialed NASA administrator James Webb, a political appointee selected by President Kennedy and asked to stay on the job by Johnson, to inquire what he and the agency could do for Halleck and his constituents.

Three days later, the NASA administrator, who had previously served as chief of the Bureau of the Budget under President Truman, met with Halleck and discussed a number of research grants that could be awarded

---

[12] As discussed in Chapter 2, this literature begins with Mayhew (1974a).
[13] Bertelli and Grose (2009); Larcinese et al. (2006).

to Purdue University, which happened to sit in the minority leader's district. The grants, Webb was quick to point out to Johnson, would be spread over three years and were renewable annually. Not mincing words, Webb concluded, "The net effect, Mr. President, is that if you tell him that you're willing to follow this policy as long as he cooperates with you, I can implement it on an installment basis. In other words the minute he kicks over the traces, we stop the installment."[14] To be sure, Johnson did not target these grants for electoral or partisan goals. In the concluding chapter, we discuss whether these goals are more pressing for contemporary presidents than for their predecessors. But the case does illustrate the capacity of the president to target federal grants to a specific constituency.

Archival records also show President Nixon using his influence over the budgetary process for political purposes. In one of his many memorable pre-Watergate exchanges recorded for posterity, Nixon demanded in writing that his chief domestic policy adviser, John Ehrlichman, intervene in the budgetary formulation process to punish the administration's political enemies by slashing federal funding for specific states. Nixon instructed Ehrlichman: "In your budget plans... I want Missouri, New York, Indiana, Nevada, Wisconsin, and Minnesota to get less than they have gotten in the past. New York is the only place where you must play a slightly different game because of Rockefeller [the governor of New York and an unsuccessful candidate for the Republican nomination in 1968 against Nixon]... the message can get across that states with Republican Senators are going to get a better audience at the White House than those with Democratic Senators who are constantly chopping at us."[15] President Nixon sought to exploit his influence over the budget to punish his enemies and reward his partisan base – precisely the type of core state targeting discussed in Chapter 2.

Of course, presidents and administration officials are often loath to publicly admit that they are using their leverage over the budget for political purposes. What in the early 1960s might have been viewed as simple horse-trading and even master bargaining today may be viewed as bribery: witness the public outcry at the 'Cornhusker Kickback' and the 'Louisiana Purchase,' which President Obama agreed to in exchange

---

[14] Caro (2012, 559–560); The "Presidential Recordings: Lyndon Johnson," January 21, 1964, conversation with James Webb, WH6401.18.
[15] Richard Reeves. 2001. *President Nixon: Alone in the White House.* New York: Simon and Schuster, p. 171.

for the initial support of Senators Nelson and Landrieu for health care reform. In a post-Watergate world, where administrations know that their every recorded utterance or written document can be subpoenaed or requested under the Freedom of Information Act, sincere first-hand accounts of the political motivations of presidential budgeting are nearly impossible to procure. This makes it difficult to assess how frequent or rare such direct presidential interventions in the budgetary arena are. But can presidents, through other mechanisms requiring less personal involvement, systematically influence the geographic allocation of federal grants in ways that serve their political needs?

Presidents have multiple opportunities to shape budgetary outcomes at the proposal and implementation stages. In some budgetary decisions, such as those regarding natural disaster relief discussed previously, presidents may have unilateral control over decisions about the allocation of funds. However, in most programs the primary mechanism through which presidents can shape budgetary outcomes is through the politicization of the federal bureaucracy.[16] Specifically, by appointing like-minded officials to the top levels of management at the departments and agencies charged with crafting budgetary requests and within the Office of Management and Budget, which coordinates and oversees the process, presidents empower officials who share their political outlook to pursue budgetary allocations that fit the administration's political needs.

Significant opportunities for executive branch influence emerge at the beginning of the budgetary process. The distributive politics literature has long emphasized that the power to offer the initial proposal gives an actor considerable influence over spending outcomes; indeed, this is the foundation of studies asserting the disproportionate influence that substantive committees wield over the allocation of federal largesse within their purview.[17] Yet, the power of proposal rests not with congressional committees, but with the White House. Since 1921, the Budget and Accounting Act has charged the president with preparing and submitting to Congress an annual budget proposal. This gives the president a significant advantage in defining the tenor and scope of the ensuing legislative debate. The administration begins formulating budgetary proposals on average nine months before the budget is even submitted to Congress. In practice, of course, presidents do not produce draft budgets; agency officials from across the federal bureaucracy do. The preferences

---

[16] Moe (1985a).
[17] McCarty (2000); Yildirim (2007).

of key officials in the agencies formulating budgetary requests may at times diverge from those of the president, and some agencies go to great lengths to gain and protect their autonomy.[18]

The bureaucracy is an interesting creature, lodged within the executive branch but potentially responsive to Congress, outside interests, and the preferences of career bureaucrats themselves. Nevertheless, contemporary presidents have increasingly sought to tighten their grip on the reins of bureaucratic power, in part by dramatically expanding the number of political appointees in virtually all reaches of the federal bureaucracy. Today the bureaucracy is populated with thousands of political appointees, including approximately 1,500 who are appointed by the president and confirmed by the Senate and another roughly 1,500 Schedule C appointees who are chosen by the president with no congressional input or review. These appointees logically tend to share the ideological orientation and programmatic vision of the president they serve.[19] As a result, by filling key posts with political loyalists, presidents can create an institutional structure that increases the probability that the budget recommendations that emerge from the bureaucracy will hew more closely to the White House's own preferences.

Moreover, presidents have centralized considerable budgetary power within the Office of Management and Budget (OMB), which is firmly lodged in the Executive Office of the President, to protect and advance the administration's priorities. Since the 1970s, many scholars have bemoaned the loss of "neutral competence" in OMB and the politicization of the office that has rendered it more attuned to the political needs of the president.[20] At the heart of this transformation lies the increased power of political appointees versus careerists within the office. Indeed, one of the key elements of the 1970 reorganization of the Bureau of the Budget into the OMB was the creation of a group of new program associate directors, appointed directly by the president, to oversee OMB's

---

[18] See, inter alia, Carpenter (2001). However, presidents enjoy a number of tools, foremost among them the capacity to populate the bureaucracy with political appointees who share the same basic political interests, through which presidents can exercise considerable bureaucratic and administrative control over policymaking (Dickinson 2005; Howell and Lewis 2002; Hudak and Stack 2013; Lewis 2003; Moe 1985b; Rudalevige 2002; Waterman 1989).

[19] Bonica et al. (2012) find that presidents appoint bureaucrats who match their ideologies, especially in contexts such as recess appointments, where the legislative oversight is limited.

[20] Heclo (1975); House (1995); Tomkin (1998).

examining divisions.[21] The examining divisions play a key role in shaping budgetary requests, and this reform created a second layer of political appointees to influence their actions. The number of political appointees and scope of their influence have only grown in intervening decades.

OMB plays an important role in shaping budgetary outcomes even before the departments and agencies begin to act. The process begins with OMB submitting planning guidance to executive agencies that shape their own requests. Moreover, after the agencies' initial proposals are complete, they are submitted to OMB for review to ensure that agency priorities accord with the program of the president. Taken together, the resulting process of formulating a presidential budget is stacked to create a document that reflects the president's priorities and needs.

Of course, congressional leaders may have different budgetary priorities and the final budget need not reflect the president's wishes. Nevertheless, the ability to set the agenda by providing the starting point for legislative debate is an important advantage. In Allen Schick's assessment, "Even when the president's budget is reputed to be dead on arrival, the president sets the agenda for the bargaining and legislative actions that follow."[22]

The power to propose the initial working document is far from the only institutional resource that presidents enjoy when trying to see their budgetary preferences enacted into law. For example, Schick calls the White House a "budget pulpit" from which "the president usually has the capacity to define the terms of the budget debate."[23] Brandice Canes-Wrone finds that when presidents go public on behalf of their budgetary initiatives, under certain conditions they can generate tangible influence in Congress.[24] During the legislative process itself, members of Congress frequently find themselves dependent on the expert testimony of other government officials, virtually all of whom are lodged within the executive branch. This informational asymmetry yields presidents important advantages in making the case for their budgetary priorities. Also, as Newt Gingrich and the Republican 104th Congress learned all too well, presidents retain a great institutional leverage point – the veto pen – to encourage members of Congress to return a bill that substantially matches

---

[21] Lewis (2008, 35–36).
[22] Schick (2000, 109).
[23] Schick (2000, 108).
[24] Canes-Wrone (2006).

the administration's budget priorities. It is important to remember that even when budget battles do not end in veto-laden showdowns and partial shutdowns of the federal government, the veto still may have a significant effect on policy.[25] Congressional leaders anticipating the possibility of a presidential veto often seek to craft a bill that the president will sign so as not to risk the potentially devastating political consequences of a high-profile budget stalemate.

Presidents also have a significant capacity to shape how federal dollars are ultimately allocated even after they are appropriated.[26] While Congress may determine the amount of money allocated to a specific department or agency, the bureaucracy itself often wields considerable influence over how such funds are ultimately distributed. Describing this reality, R. Douglas Arnold notes that "most decisions about geographic allocation are bureaucratic decisions."[27] While scholars continue to debate who controls the bureaucracy or whether bureaucrats typically enjoy considerable autonomy, a wealth of recent scholarship has emphasized the important levers through which presidents are able to exert influence over the workings of the executive branch writ large.[28] Here, again, presidential efforts to increase the number of political appointees and widen their reach down the organizational pyramids of many key federal bureaucracies loom large. Congressional statutes, even detailed ones, by necessity often delegate significant discretion over implementation to departments and agencies. By installing men and women who share the White House's priorities in positions of leadership throughout these arms of the executive branch, presidents stack the deck in their favor and raise the odds that policy as implemented will reflect their preferences and political imperatives to the greatest extent possible.[29]

Thus, through politicization of the departments and agencies, the empowerment of a responsive OMB, and occasional direct presidential involvement, presidents may wield considerable influence over budgetary

---

[25] Cameron (2000); Kiewiet and McCubbins (1988); McCarty (2000).

[26] Berry et al. (2010); Gordon (2011).

[27] Arnold (1979, 8).

[28] Dickinson (2005); Howell and Lewis (2002); Lewis (2003, 2008); Moe (1985b); Rudalevige (2002); Waterman (1989).

[29] Berry et al. (2010) argue that presidents desire to target federal dollars to constituencies represented by their co-partisans in Congress to build influence in the legislature. Berry and Gersen (2010, 12) show that politicized agencies – those that are heavily stacked with political appointees – are more likely to engage in such targeting than are less politicized agencies.

policymaking at the agenda-setting stage, during the course of the legislative debate, and during policy implementation. Presidents possess the institutional capacity to act on particularistic motives.

5.3 A Description of Federal Grants

To what extent do presidents influence the distribution of federal grants across the country? To answer this question, we compiled data from the Consolidated Federal Funds Report (CFFR) on every federal grant program from 1984 to 2008.[30] Each year, the federal government distributes hundreds of billions of dollars in grants to fund a myriad of projects across the country. From 1984 to 2008, grants accounted for between 10.3 percent and 14.6 percent of all federal spending reported in the CFFR. In 2008, the federal government awarded more than $575 billion of grants. Following a general increase in overall government spending, the total amount that the median county received gradually rose from just over $11 million in 1984 to nearly $40 million in 2008.

For each program, the CFFR reports the amount of money spent in each county in a given year. Some grants are narrowly targeted, such as those established by the abandoned mine land reclamation program or the Southern Nevada Land Management Act. For example, as part of the Omnibus Deficit Reconciliation Act of 1993, President Clinton secured the first appropriations to create empowerment zones in rural communities that were designed to stimulate investment and create new jobs, particularly among the chronically unemployed in economically depressed parts of the country. Through a series of legislative renewals, empowerment zones continued to receive funding throughout the 1990s and 2000s. The CFFR records that in 2008, the Department of Agriculture awarded almost $9.5 million of empowerment zone grants on a competitive basis to applicants spread over twenty-six counties from twenty-four different states. Yet others are broad. For instance, nearly every county in the United States receives money for highway planning and construction. In 2008 alone, under a single grant program the Department of Transportation allocated more than $37 billion to specific projects in more than 2,700 counties, making this one of the largest grant

---

[30] The CFFR distinguishes between several categories of federal spending, and we focus on grants, a decision that we describe in further detail shortly. In addition to grants, the CFFR includes spending on government salaries and wages, procurement, direct payments to individuals, other direct payments, direct loans, insured loans, and insurance.

programs in the entire federal budget. Other broad-based grant spending programs include community development block grants, airport improvement grants, and grants for disaster assistance.

In this chapter, we do not differentiate between individual programs but instead examine the distribution of all federal grant spending across the country. While at the most basic level, federal grants are government awards to some entity to carry out a public purpose authorized by statute, individual grant programs can differ greatly in terms of their objective, administration, and allocation of awards. For example, two major categories of federal grants are project grants and formula grants. To award project grants, a federal agency normally solicits competitive bids from aspiring applicants; then the agency evaluates the proposals to select which ones will receive federal funding. Examples of project grants range from agricultural research grants, to Air Pollution Control Program Support grants for states and localities, to distance education grants for learners in rural areas, to the urban and community forest program. By contrast, formula grants – such as the State Children's Insurance Program, Even-Start low-income educational programs, and many highway and transportation projects across the country – are allocated to all eligible recipients according to specific criteria as provided for by legislative statute.

This variation renders some grant programs more amenable to geographic targeting than others. However, even formula grants can be used to serve specific purposes by particularistic presidents. First, because the beneficiaries of formula grants are known, presidents can easily ascertain which constituencies would benefit most from a push to expand funding for a formula grant program. For example, by seeking additional funds in his budget for the Medical Assistance Program, a formula grant that provides federal assistance to low-income seniors for health care expenses, the president is not explicitly targeting funds to a certain locality, but rather pursuing a policy that will benefit all Americans who meet certain eligibility requirements. However, the president would surely know that a good portion of these additional federal dollars would find its way to Florida, a swing state with a large elderly population. Second, the formulas themselves are determined by the political process; thus, in some cases presidents may be able to alter the allocation of such funds by bargaining with Congress over how the formulas are computed.

Rather than making distinctions between programs, seeking to isolate only those over which presidents have the most levers of influence, in this chapter we cast a much broader net and look for evidence of presidential particularism in the allocation of all federal grant programs across the country. This allows us to examine whether presidential particularism systematically skews policy outcomes on a much larger scale.

5.4 Presidential Particularism and Grant Spending

Do presidents systematically target federal dollars to voters in swing states to bolster their prospects at the ballot box?[31] Do presidents behave as partisans-in-chief by seeking to channel federal grants disproportionately to core states dominated by their co-partisan base?

We use data from the CFFR to calculate the total amount of federal grants received by each county in each year from 1984 through 2008. To ensure comparability across years, we calculate all grant totals in inflation-adjusted 2008 constant dollars. Also, in order to ensure that outlying values do not drive our results, we analyze and present our finding on grant spending using the natural log of each county's annual grant total.[32]

We then construct a multiple regression model to assess the influence of a state's political characteristics on the share of federal grant spending that counties within that state receive. As described in the preceding chapter, we include two indicator variables identifying whether a county resides in a swing state or a core state. Swing states are those in which the losing candidate has averaged 45 percent or more of the two-party presidential vote over the preceding three elections.[33]

Our theory of presidential particularism also argues that partisan motivations, in addition to electoral incentives, may encourage presidents to target grants to a different type of constituency. Presidents as partisans-in-chief may pursue policies that reward members of their voting coalition.

---

[31] Two prior studies have looked for evidence of swing state targeting in federal spending writ large with conflicting results. Larcinese et al. (2006) find no evidence of swing state targeting in a state-level analysis of total federal expenditures from 1982 through 2000. Hudak (2014) finds modest evidence of swing state targeting in a state-level analysis of federal grant allocations from 1996 through 2008. Hudak (2014) also looks for evidence that the swing state effect varies with the electoral calendar or across presidential terms, but finds no significant evidence for either dynamic. The analyses that follow draw on Kriner and Reeves (2015).

[32] For additional discussion of the use of log transformations, as well as additional descriptions and details of the multivariate statistical analyses that follow, see Appendix C.

[33] Loser's share is a common measure of electoral competitiveness in both congressional and presidential election studies (Bartels, 1991; Jacobson, 2004; Mayhew, 1974b; Reeves, 2011; Shaw, 1999b). The 45 percent threshold is the one used in many congressional studies (e.g., Jacobson, 2004; Kriner and Reeves, 2012; Mayhew, 1974b).

As a result, our theory does not predict that all uncompetitive states will receive few federal grant dollars, but rather only states that are not competitive and that are firmly in the camp of the partisan opposition. If presidents target federal resources both to bolster their and their party's electoral prospects and to reward their core constituencies, then some communities at both ends of the competitiveness scale may receive disproportionate shares of federal grant dollars.

To test this core state hypothesis, our analysis includes an additional variable identifying whether or not a given state is a core state – that is, whether a significant majority of voters consistently back the party's candidate. We identify core states as those in which the incumbent presidential party's candidate has received an average of 55 percent or greater of the two-party vote share in the preceding three presidential elections.[34]

Last, by matching counties to congressional districts, we can look for evidence of another form of presidential particularism: whether presidents target resources toward counties represented by members of their party in Congress.[35] Targeting spending to help co-partisans in Congress may do little, at least directly, to bolster a president's own electoral prospects.[36] However, co-partisan targeting may serve both partisan and policy goals. First, contemporary presidents face strong pressures to be the leader of their political party. Rewarding co-partisan members of Congress with larger shares of the budgetary pie may help satisfy such demands for partisan leadership. Moreover, co-partisan targeting may be an important way in which the president can earn political capital with key members. By bolstering the electoral prospects of his party in Congress, such a strategy may prove quite useful at enabling the president to further his wider policy agenda in Washington. The strength of the president's party in Congress

---

[34] Reestimating the models that follow with alternative measures of a state's electoral competitiveness and the degree to which a state is a core state yields even stronger support for our hypotheses of swing state and core state targeting. For full results and additional discussion, see Appendix C.

[35] More than 80 percent of counties in our data matched uniquely into a single congressional district. For the counties that did not fall exclusively into a single district, we used geographic information systems (GIS) and census data to calculate the percentage of each county's population in each relevant district and assigned to that county the representative from the district that held the greatest share of the county's population. Replicating our analysis excluding counties that do not fall singly into a congressional district yields virtually identical results.

[36] However, to the extent that the president's and his congressional co-partisans' electoral fates are linked, improving the electoral performance and prospects of co-partisan members may well improve the situation for the president himself (e.g., Aldrich, 1995; Cox and McCubbins, 1993).

is perhaps the single most important predictor of his ability to accomplish his legislative agenda on Capitol Hill.[37] Even when acting as commander-in-chief, the president finds himself operating with a significantly freer hand when his party holds sway on Capitol Hill than when he faces a legislature controlled by the opposition.[38] As a result, presidents may have strong partisan and coalitional incentives to divert from the expectations of universalism in budgeting and instead to target federal grants to reward co-partisan members of Congress.

The multivariate analysis that we employ allows us not only to look for evidence of each of these three forms of presidential particularism but also to assess their relative magnitudes. In so doing, we can ascertain what types of incentives – electoral, partisan, or coalitional – most encourage presidents to depart from the norms and expectations of universalism.

However, presidents are not the only actors with the incentives and means to influence the allocation of federal grant dollars. Members of Congress also play a key role in such budgetary battles. Indeed, securing particularized benefits – such as post offices, roads, and bridges – for their districts is often seen as critically important electoral currency. We cannot fully assess the influence of presidential particularism on the distribution of federal dollars without comparing it to congressionally induced inequities. Are the inequalities induced by presidents pursuing electoral or other incentives insignificant compared to those produced by members of Congress using all resources at their disposal to secure federal benefits for their own constituencies? Or are presidents as, if not perhaps even more, effective at skewing the distribution of federal benefits across the country than are members of Congress?

Scholarship on federal spending has long emphasized the role played by the legislative branch, and with good reason. Since the dawn of the Republic, many members of Congress have channeled significant energy into bringing the proverbial bacon home to their districts. Perhaps among the most notorious was Bud Shuster, a Republican member of Congress from a district in south-central Pennsylvania that included Altoona. While chair of the House Transportation and Infrastructure Committee, Shuster was famous for his use of federal transportation funds within his district. Interviewed by the *New York Times* in his office adorned with 'Bud Shuster Highway' signs, he pointed out that "there's no such thing as a

---

[37] Bond and Fleisher (1990); Bond et al. (2003); Edwards (1989); Edwards et al. (1997).
[38] Howell and Pevehouse (2007); Kriner (2010).

Republican or a Democratic road or airport or bridge."[39] His constituents, he argued, cared little about the congressman's role in international affairs but instead focused on "what affects virtually every American. It's the ultimate quality-of-life issue." For Congressman Shuster, these quality-of-life issues included bringing the Bud Shuster Highway and Bud Shuster Bypass along with billions of dollars in other transportation projects home to his district.[40]

But which members of Congress are likely to be most successful in the race to secure federal grant dollars for their constituents? Existing scholarship offers two main hypotheses. First, scholars have argued that members of the majority party in Congress will seize a disproportionate share of federal dollars.[41] Legislative scholars have long noted the institutional advantages that members of the majority party enjoy, particularly in the House. Majority members enjoy greater powers of proposal; they largely determine what legislation the chamber will consider, and this power to set the legislative table affords considerable influence.[42] The majority party also wields considerable power to keep competing proposals that are less advantageous to its members off the agenda.[43] Recent game theoretic research shows how these powers can enable majority party members to reap a disproportionate share of the federal budgetary pie.[44]

---

[39] Richard L. Berke, "Lawmaker takes highway to power," *New York Times*, September 25, 1997. www.nytimes.com/1997/09/25/us/lawmaker-takes-highway-to-power.html.

[40] Eric Pianin and Charles R. Babcock, "Easy street: The Bud Shuster interchange," *Washington Post*, April 5, 1998. www.washingtonpost.com/wp-srv/politics/special/highway/stories/hwy040598c.htm.

[41] See, inter alia, Albouy (2013); Balla et al. (2002); Cox and McCubbins (2007); Levitt and Snyder (1995); Martin (2003).

[42] See, e.g., Cox and McCubbins (1993).

[43] Campbell et al. (2002); Den Hartog and Monroe (2011); Gailmard and Jenkins (2007); Lee (2009).

[44] Albouy (2013) finds empirical evidence consistent with this argument; states represented by more majority party members in the House and Senate reap a disproportionate share of federal spending. Others, however, have found weaker evidence for the majority party hypothesis. For instance, scholars have long noted that appropriations bills tend to pass by large margins (not the minimum winning coalitions we might expect if majority party members were simply trying to maximize their benefits at the expense of members of the opposition). Weingast (1979) argues that this is a result of members of both parties supporting rules and norms that produce a relatively even geographic distribution of federal dollars to protect themselves against significant losses should they switch from the majority to the minority. Similarly, early models of the appropriations process by Riker (1962) and Baron and Ferejohn (1989) also yield predictions of relative uniformity in the geographic allocation of federal dollars.

Thus, our analysis assesses the influence of whether a county's representative is a member of the majority party in the House on the share of federal grants that it receives. If the majority party is able to use its various levers of influence to skew federal dollars toward its members' districts, then we would expect counties represented by majority party members to receive, on average, more federal grants than counties represented by members of the opposition.

Other scholars of budgetary outcomes focus more on congressional committees than majority party status. Congress's committee system may enable some members to secure more federal resources for their constituencies than others can. Indeed, while scholars have posited a number of motives to explain the development of Congress's committees, one of the most important is the need to procure certain types of benefits for constituents. The heart of the distributive model of committees and committee assignments is the assumption that members with extreme preferences on an issue will seek a seat on the relevant committee (e.g., a farm state representative will pursue a seat on the agriculture committee) to help channel federal benefits to his or her constituency.[45] A number of researchers have examined the ability of members of specific committees to influence the distribution of federal spending within that specific sphere.[46] More generally, this scholarship points to the importance of institutional power structures in Congress in shaping the geographic allocation of federal benefits.

Two types of members may be particularly well positioned to seize a greater share of federal dollars for their districts. First, most committees can play an important role in the budget process. Most directly, committees are main actors in determining budgetary authorizations for programs under their substantive purview that will then serve as guides to congressional appropriators. Perhaps even more important, substantive committees forge relationships with the departments and agencies that administer policy in their portfolios. By cultivating and exploiting these relationships, committees can exert further influence over how and where federal dollars are spent. Much committee power resides with the chairs, who wield disproportionate influence over the happenings of congressional committees through their considerable powers of agenda control.

---

[45] See, e.g., Adler and Lapinski (1997); Deering and Smith (1997); Shepsle and Weingast (1981, 1987).

[46] Alvarez and Saving (1997); Ferejohn (1974); Lauderdale (2008); Lee (2000, 2003).

Through the power of the gavel, committee chairs may be able to use their institutional leverage to bring more federal benefits to their districts than do their peers who lack a similar position of institutional power within Congress. As a result, our models examine whether counties represented by committee chairs receive more federal grant dollars, on average, than other counties not represented by a committee chair.

Yet, all committees are not created equal when it comes to influencing the distribution of federal dollars. In the House, the two most influential committees are Ways and Means and Appropriations, which hold direct jurisdiction over all legislation involving revenue and over the appropriations process itself. All members of these committees hold important vantage points from which they might pursue federal resources for their districts. To account for this possibility, our models also assess whether a county that is represented by a member of either Ways and Means or Appropriations receives a greater share of federal grants, on average, than does a county not represented by a member of these control committees.

Last, our statistical analysis includes a number of important controls. Most important, we control for each county's population in each year.[47] We also include two controls for a county's socioeconomics: per capita income in constant 2008 dollars and the poverty rate.[48] Both variables may be positively correlated with federal spending. Counties with high per capita incomes may have greater demand for federal grant programs. Counties with high poverty rates have a greater need for federal assistance. Our models also include a series of fixed effects for counties and years. The former allow us to establish a county-specific baseline level of grant funding for each of the more than 3,000 counties across the country. The latter allow us to account for temporal factors that affect funding levels from year to year. By including these fixed effects, we can identify the influence of presidential and congressional particularism after controlling for a host of often unobservable factors that might affect the baseline level of grant funding received in a county.

---

[47] Because of the skewed nature of this variable, we include its logged values in our models. An alternative operationalization for the dependent variable is logged per capita grants. We note that by controlling for logged population, this model is algebraically equivalent to that presented in the text.

[48] Annual county-level personal income data was obtained from the Bureau of Economic Analysis. County-level poverty data was available from U.S. Census county and city data books for 1980, 1989, 1997, and 2000.

5.5 Evidence of Presidential Particularism

Our results are presented in Column 1 of Table 5.1. Strongly consistent with our particularistic presidency framework, we find evidence of all three forms of particularism: electoral, partisan, and coalitional. Counties in swing and core states received significantly more federal grant spending – almost 5 percent and 7 percent more, respectively – on average than did counties not located in swing or core states. Counties represented by presidential co-partisans in the House also received a considerably smaller, though still significant, 2.2 percent increase in grant spending versus counties represented by members of the opposition party.

What do these percent increases mean for average Americans? In 2008, Dutchess County, New York, home to Franklin Roosevelt's Hyde Park estate, received roughly $428 million in federal grants. In 2008, it was what we call the population-weighted median county – half of Americans lived in counties that received more grant dollars than Dutchess County did, and half of Americans lived in counties that received fewer grant dollars than did residents of Dutchess County. In 2008, New York was solidly in the Democratic column; as a result, it was neither a swing state nor a core state. As shown in Figure 5.1, our model suggests that if Dutchess County were in neighboring Pennsylvania, a swing state, its residents would have enjoyed an influx of $17 million simply by virtue of being in a battleground state.[49] Such swing state bonuses in grant spending can be a significant windfall for a county; the additional funds could hire dozens of police officers or teachers, improve key stretches of road in bad repair, or expand a government-subsidized daycare program that helps many transition from welfare to work. This is strong evidence that presidents engage in particularism to bolster their and their party's prospects at the next election. Rather than treating all voters equally, presidents treat some voters as more important to electoral calculations. Presidents systematically target disproportionately large shares of federal dollars to voters living in swing states that could tip the scales in the next electoral contest.

The data also yield strong evidence that presidents engage in another form of particularism: they pursue budgetary policies that disproportionately advantage counties located in core states that solidly backed the president's party in recent elections. If John Kerry had won the 2004

---

[49] We found no evidence that counties represented by committee chairs or by members of the Appropriations or Ways and Means Committees received a greater-than-expected share of federal grant funding; hence, these factors are not included in Figure 5.1.

TABLE 5.1. *Presidential Particularism and the Allocation of Federal Grants, U.S. Counties, 1984 to 2008. Least squares model with fixed effects for counties and years. Dependent variable is the natural log of federal grant spending in each county in a given year. Robust standard errors clustered on county are in parentheses.*

	Base (1)	Election Year (2)	Reelection (3)	Within State (4)
Swing state	0.039	0.031	0.030	0.017
	(0.005)	(0.006)	(0.006)	(0.006)
Core state	0.064	0.065	0.064	0.036
	(0.006)	(0.006)	(0.006)	(0.007)
Swing state × Election year		0.032 (0.006)		
Core state × Election year		−0.001 (0.008)		
Swing state × Reelection year			0.050 (0.007)	0.050 (0.007)
Swing state × Successor election			0.018 (0.007)	0.018 (0.007)
Core county				−0.011 (0.008)
Core county × Swing state				0.040 (0.009)
Core county × Core state				0.054 (0.011)
Member of Congress from presidential party	0.020 (0.004)	0.020 (0.004)	0.020 (0.004)	0.015 (0.004)
Member of Congress from majority party	0.025 (0.004)	0.025 (0.004)	0.025 (0.004)	0.025 (0.004)
Member of Congress chair	−0.021 (0.010)	−0.022 (0.010)	−0.021 (0.010)	−0.030 (0.009)
Member of Appropriations or Ways and Means	−0.010 (0.005)	−0.010 (0.005)	−0.010 (0.005)	−0.010 (0.005)
County population (logged)	0.234 (0.031)	0.233 (0.031)	0.234 (0.031)	0.231 (0.031)
Poverty rate	0.005 (0.001)	0.005 (0.001)	0.005 (0.001)	0.005 (0.001)
Per capita income	0.004 (0.002)	0.004 (0.002)	0.004 (0.002)	0.005 (0.002)
Constant	14.926 (0.302)	14.246 (0.301)	14.919 (0.302)	14.822 (0.304)
Observations	76,937	76,937	76,937	76,296
R^2	0.619	0.619	0.619	0.621

FIGURE 5.1. Presidential Particularism and Federal Grant Spending (County-Level Effects). Each bar presents the additional estimated amount of money that the population-weighted median county receives if it is in a swing state (electoral particularism) or core state (partisan particularism), is represented in the House of Representatives by a member of the president's party (coalitional particularism), or is represented by the majority party in Congress. The effects are estimated from the model in Column 1 of Table 5.1. Amounts are relative to those received by a comparable county in a non-core, non-swing state represented by a member of Congress not of the president's party. *For example, the model estimates that a county in a swing state sees $17 million more in federal grant spending than a comparable county in a non-swing and non-core state.* The I-bars around the top of each bar represent the uncertainty (95% confidence interval) around each estimate.

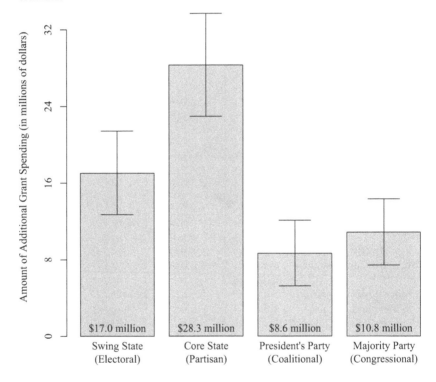

presidential election, in 2008 New York would have been a core state rather than a state that solidly backed the opposition party. If New York were a core state, our model estimates that Dutchess County would have received more than $28 million more in grant spending.

Of course, we do not have direct evidence that presidents are manipulating the allocation of federal dollars to disproportionately reward swing states. Nevertheless, the most plausible interpretation of the spending data is that presidents are responsible for many of the significant inequalities in grant spending. Who else benefits from federal grant dollars being targeted to swing states especially, as we shall see shortly, in the immediate lead-up to a presidential election? Neither the Speaker of the House nor the chairman of the Ways and Means Committee nor the median member of the majority party in Congress has clear incentives to pursue such an allocation of federal dollars. Only the president does. In a similar vein, members of Congress have no incentives to channel federal dollars disproportionately to parts of the country that voted heavily for the president's party in recent elections. Rather, such core constituency targeting makes sense only if presidents are using the institutional vantage points at their disposal to shape the geographic distribution of federal spending. Thus, while it is always difficult to speak with certainty about causal relationships in politics, we are confident that the only compelling explanation for the consistent, systematic patterns we find in the allocation of federal grant dollars across the country is presidential targeting.

We also find evidence consistent with the argument that presidents might geographically target funds to counties represented by co-partisans in Congress to bolster their influence in the legislature. Echoing findings presented by Christopher Berry, Barry Burden, and William Howell, we find that counties represented by a member of the president's party received approximately 2 percent more in grant spending, on average, than counties represented by the partisan opposition.[50] For example, our model estimates that if Dutchess County had been represented instead by one of President Bush's fellow Republicans in 2008, it would have received an infusion of $8.6 million in additional grant spending.[51] This is a substantial sum; however, compared to swing state and core state targeting, the average effect of this form of particularism is fairly modest. Indeed, the increase in grant spending such counties receive is roughly half the boost received by counties in swing states.

Taken altogether, this initial cut of the data offers striking evidence of presidential particularism. Rather than pursuing policies that do not discriminate between beneficiaries on the basis of their political characteristics, the data suggest that presidents pursue budgetary policies

[50] Berry et al. (2010).
[51] Because the GOP was also in the House majority in 2008, our model estimates that Dutchess County would have received both an $8.6 million boost from being represented by a presidential co-partisan and an increase of $10.8 million from being represented by a member of the majority party.

that channel federal grant dollars systematically toward constituencies in swing states and core states, as well as toward constituencies that have elected co-partisans to Congress.

Our analysis does reveal some evidence of congressional particularism. After all, for decades political scientists have documented the needs for members to bring home targeted benefits for their constituents to bolster their hopes of reelection. Indeed, the image of the pork-barreling legislator is burned into our national consciousness; we expect congressional budgeting to be characterized by rampant parochialism. Yet, the evidence for it is surprisingly modest. Counties represented by the majority party in the House receive only about 3 percent more in grant spending, on average, than counties represented by the minority party. Moreover, we found no evidence that counties represented by committee chairs or members of the Appropriations or Ways and Means Committee enjoyed any more benefits, on average, than those represented by rank-and-file members.

Surprisingly, our data suggest that presidential particularistic impulses are an even greater source of inequality in the distribution of federal grants across the country than is congressional particularism. That is not to say that budgetary politics would necessarily be more efficient if Congress alone made decisions concerning how federal dollars are spent across the country. Indeed, there are good reasons to think it would not be so. However, our findings suggest that presidents, not legislators, are the most important actors causing systematic inequalities in federal spending across constituencies based on their political characteristics.

5.5.1 *Particularism and the Electoral Cycle*
Presidents appear to possess powerful incentives to target federal grants to both swing states and core states. However, these incentives may vary with the electoral calendar.

The motivations driving swing state targeting are unambiguous: presidents endeavor to target federal dollars to constituencies in swing states specifically to bolster their or their partisan successor's chances of winning the White House in the next election. To meet this objective, presidents may always try to steer additional federal dollars to swing states. However, this incentive should increase as the next presidential election nears. Political scientists have shown that voters enter the voting booth with remarkably short memories. For example, in a comprehensive analysis of decades of data on voting behavior, Larry Bartels paints a portrait of the "myopic voter" who fails to consider economic performance over the course of an entire presidential term and instead responds to only the most recent changes in the state of the economy.[52] Voters tend to prioritize actions and developments that happened recently and to discount developments that happened in the more distant past. Bartels goes so far as to suggest that presidents may be able to manipulate elections by pursuing policies that produce short-term economic benefits in the run-up to an election that will distract voters from poor economic stewardship in prior years. As a result, the particularistic incentive to target federal grant dollars to swing states should be strongest in election years. Therefore, if our theory is correct, we should see swing states reaping even larger shares of federal grant dollars in election years than they do in non-election years.

By contrast, several different motivations may encourage presidents to pursue policies that target federal dollars disproportionately to constituencies dominated by their fellow partisans. First, presidents may target core partisan constituencies in an effort to keep them solidly in the partisan win column. While core states are seemingly safe, history is full of surprising reversals of fortune. For example, in Indiana the Republican presidential candidate won, on average, more than 60 percent of the two-party presidential vote over the 1996, 2000 and 2004 elections. However, in one of the most shocking results of the 2008 election, Indiana narrowly awarded its eleven electoral votes to the Democrat Barack Obama. Targeting federal dollars to core states may not be as electorally efficient as targeting swing states is; however, it may nonetheless serve electoral purposes by solidifying the partisan base. If electoral incentives are primarily responsible for core state targeting, then we should find greater evidence of this targeting in election years. Indeed, we see some evidence supporting this possibility in the politics of disaster declarations in the preceding chapter.

However, presidents may pursue policies that channel federal benefits to co-partisan constituencies for reasons besides electoral concerns. Presidential candidates first secure the nomination and then ultimately win the presidency by espousing programmatic agendas that appeal to coalitions of constituencies. Most often, presidents advocate budgetary policies and priorities that reward key blocs of voters within their co-partisan constituency. Thus, presidents need not explicitly endeavor to target funds geographically to their core constituencies; rather, simply by pursuing their stated policy agenda and catering to the desires of their

---

[52] Bartels (2008). See also Bartels and Zaller (2001); Erikson (1989); Erikson et al. (2001); Lewis-Beck and Stegmaier (2000).

co-partisans, as opposed to the national median voter, they may push policy in a direction that channels more resources toward key constituent blocks. The end result is that core constituencies receive more federal grant aid than they would under an opposition party president. Under this alternative mechanism, core state targeting does not serve an electoral need, and therefore core state targeting should not be more prominent in election than in non-election years.

By examining whether core state targeting is stronger in election years, we can gain greater insight into the forces driving this type of presidential particularism. If core state targeting increases in election years, then electoral incentives may well be driving this behavior. By contrast, if core state targeting is a constant and does not increase in election years, then a programmatic story is a more compelling explanation for this form of presidential particularism.

To test these additional hypotheses about the forces underlying presidential particularism, we slightly modify the analysis from the preceding sections to examine whether the degree of swing and core state targeting varies across election years and non-election years. The results are presented in Column 2 of Table 5.1. Figure 5.2 illustrates the main effects.

The data show that counties in swing states always receive a disproportionately large share of federal grants. In non-election years, the median county in a swing state receives approximately $13.5 million more than does the median county in an electorally uncompetitive state, all else being equal. However, strongly consistent with our theory, we find that this swing state advantage increases significantly during election years. Because voters reward presidents for only the most recent policy developments, the electoral incentive to target federal dollars to swing states is strongest in the immediate run-up to the election. As a result, during election years counties in swing states receive twice as much additional federal grant funding as they do in non-election years. In election years, the median county in a swing state receives $27.8 million, or fully 6.5 percent more federal grant dollars than a similar county in a non-swing state.

The true magnitude of swing state targeting is perhaps easier to capture when we aggregate up from the county to the state level. Even after controlling for the influence of Congress on the allocation of federal grant dollars, we find strong evidence that swing states receive considerably more grant funding, all else being equal, than do noncompetitive, non-core states. Figure 5.3 presents the swing state boost in grant spending received by each electorally competitive state in 2008. To calculate this, we use our model first to estimate how much money each county in each

FIGURE 5.2. Presidential Particularism and the Political Business Cycle (County-Level Effects). The bars present the estimated additional amount of federal grant dollars that a population-weighted median county receives in a swing state or core state in election versus non-election years. The effects are estimated from the model in Column 2 of Table 5.1. *For example, the model estimates that in an election year a median county in a swing state sees $27.8 million more in federal spending than does a comparable county in a non-swing and non-core state. Counties in swing states see a significant increase in federal spending during election years when compared to non-election years. Counties in core states see no such election-year increase.* The I-bars around the top of each bar represent the uncertainty (95% confidence interval) around each estimate.

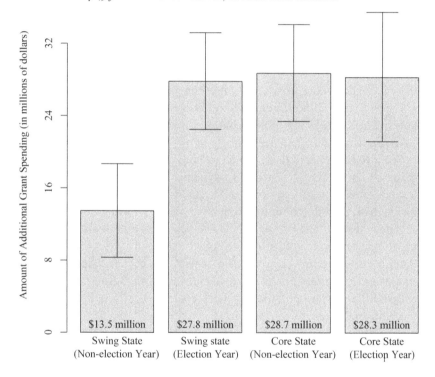

swing state would have received if it had been located in a non-swing, non-core state.[53] The swing state boost then is the difference between this figure and the amount of grant spending the county actually received. According to our model, in the election year of 2008 four hotly contested swing states – Florida, Ohio, Pennsylvania, and Michigan – received more

[53] Algebraically, we do this by dividing each county's actual grants total by the exponentiated swing state coefficient because our dependent variable is logged grants, and all other state characteristics remain unchanged.

FIGURE 5.3. Estimated Increases in Grant Spending Secured by Swing States in 2008.

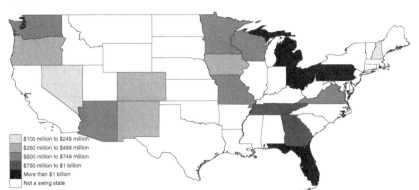

than $1 billion more in grant funding than they would have if they had not been battleground states. Eight additional competitive states received upward of half a billion dollars more in federal grants than they would have received if they had been solidly in the Democratic column.

We also continue to find strong evidence that presidents target federal grants to core states; however, this dynamic does not vary with the electoral calendar. Counties in core states always receive more grant dollars, on average, than do counties in non-core states, regardless of whether it is a presidential election year. This suggests that presidents do not primarily target grant dollars to core constituencies for electoral purposes. If simply shoring up the partisan base was the primary aim, then core state targeting should also increase in election years. Rather, the constant nature of core state targeting is more consistent with a programmatic mechanism. Democratic presidents tend to pursue budgetary policies that disproportionately reward Democratic constituencies and vice versa for Republicans. This creates sharp geographic inequalities in the allocation of federal resources that fall along partisan lines.

As shown in Figure 5.4, core states in 2008 also reaped significant increases in grant spending versus states that reliably backed the opposition party. Texas was the big winner, securing in excess of $2 billion more in federal grants than it would have if a Democrat had resided in the Oval Office. Indiana and North Carolina both reaped in excess of half a billion dollars more in grant spending by virtue of being core states, and other states solidly in the GOP column – including South Carolina, Alabama, Mississippi, and Kentucky – also secured core state boosts of more than $375 million each.

FIGURE 5.4. Estimated Increases in Grant Spending Secured by Core States in 2008.

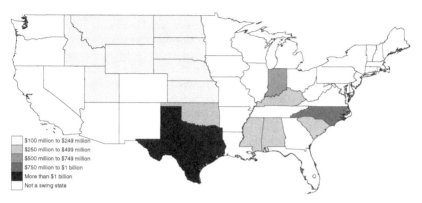

Last, we consider one further observable implication of our theory of electoral particularism. Presidents may well face incentives to target federal dollars to swing states even in their second terms (when they are barred from seeking reelection) in an effort to help boost the prospects of their co-partisan successor. Ensuring a successor president of the same party is perhaps the best way for presidents to defend their policy legacies from incursions and reversals by a new president of the opposition party. However, it stands to reason that the electoral incentive for swing state targeting should be strongest when the president himself is set to face the voters in a reelection battle. Of the seven elections in our data set, four (1984, 1992, 1996, and 2004) were reelection contests; three (1988, 2000, and 2008) were open-seat races. If the swing state advantage is the result of presidential targeting for electoral gain, then swing states should reap the greatest rewards in presidential reelection years. Presidents face strong incentives to elect co-partisan successors, but the drive for reelection is likely even stronger.[54]

To test this final hypothesis, we reestimated our statistical model with an additional set of variables to explore whether counties in swing states receive an even greater infusion of grant dollars when the incumbent president is seeking reelection than in other election years, in which a partisan successor is vying to follow the incumbent. The results are

[54] In a similar vein, research by Jacobson et al. (2004) suggests that President Clinton's fundraising efforts during his second term seem inefficient in terms of helping congressional Democrats' chances of retaking the House.

FIGURE 5.5. Presidential Particularism, and Presidential Incumbency (County-Level Effects). Each bar presents the estimated additional amount of federal grant dollars that the population-weighted median county receives in an election year if the county is in a swing state. The effects are estimated from the model in Column 3 of Table 5.1. The first bar is the effect if the incumbent president is not running for reelection, and the second bar is the effect when he is. The amounts are relative to those received by a comparable county in a non-core, non-swing state. *For example, the model estimates that, in an election year when the incumbent president is running for reelection, the median county in a swing state sees $35.6 million more in federal spending than does a comparable county in a non-swing and non-core state. Counties in swing states see significantly more federal money in years when a president is running for reelection than when the president is a lame duck and his partisan successor is running for reelection.* The I-bars around the top of each bar represent the uncertainty (95% confidence interval) around each estimate.

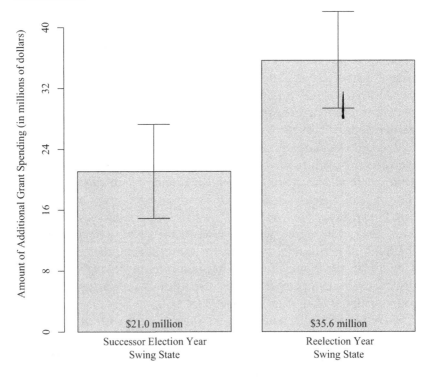

presented in Column 3 of Table 5.1, and the main effects are summarized in Figure 5.5.

Consistent with our electoral logic, we find that swing state targeting is most intense in years during which the incumbent president is seeking reelection. Indeed, in these years counties in swing states receive an estimated 8.3 percent more in grant spending than an otherwise similar county in a state that reliably backed the opposition party, all else being equal. For the median county, this would translate into a $35.6 million infusion of federal largesse. Counties in swing states also receive more money than counties in non-battleground states in other election years when the incumbent president is not on the ballot, all else being equal; however, the swing state bonus is significantly smaller than that observed in reelection years.

When aggregating to the state level, we see that this swing state boost can translate into massive increases in grant spending in a reelection year. For example, our model estimates that in 2004, Florida and Pennsylvania each received more than $1.5 billion in grant spending than they would have received if they were not swing states. Ohio, Michigan, and North Carolina are each also estimated to have received swing state boosts of more than $1 billion in the immediate run-up to President Bush's reelection bid.

5.5.2 *Within-State Targeting*

Last, we can push our theory of electoral particularism further and derive one additional implication that can be tested by analyzing grant spending at the county level. Thus far, we have argued only that the combination of the Electoral College and winner-take-all apportionment encourages presidents to target federal dollars to swing states that may decide the next presidential election. But states are large, heterogeneous constituencies that offer a myriad of diverse electoral landscapes. James Carville famously described the political disposition of the swing state of Pennsylvania as "Philadelphia and Pittsburgh, with Alabama in between."[55] If a president wants to maximize his chances of securing Pennsylvania's electoral votes by using all available levers to influence budgetary policy, how should he proceed? Does an additional dollar of federal grants have the same influence on the likelihood of winning the election regardless of where in the state it is spent? Or can presidents gain more votes by targeting dollars to certain constituencies within a swing state rather than others?

Political operatives and scholars alike have long debated this question. Since resources are finite, where should they be concentrated? Some argue

---

[55] Quoted by Terry Madonna and Michael Young, "It's Pennsylvania stupid," February 13, 2002. www.fandm.edu/politics/politically-uncorrected-column/2002-politically-uncorrected/it-s-pennsylvania-stupid.

that the best way forward is to target undecided voters. According to this logic, presidents may possess incentives to target federal dollars to marginal constituencies within swing states, where the electorate does not lean heavily one way or the other. By contrast, others argue that presidents should instead focus on turning out their base, because the margin of return is much higher on such voters than it is when trying to persuade marginal voters to come to the polls. These competing strategies were on vivid display in the 2004 battle for Ohio between George W. Bush and John Kerry. The Kerry campaign, led by Mary Beth Cahill, fought hard for undecided voters, convinced that the uncommitted were ripe for the picking and poised to vote against the incumbent. By contrast, the Bush campaign, led by Karl Rove and chief strategist Matthew Dowd, opted to focus primarily on turning out base Republican voters within the state.[56] Ultimately, Bush's strategy proved more successful, and the president won reelection thanks to Ohio's twenty electoral votes.

Within political science, scholars have also long debated the theoretical underpinnings and relative explanatory power of the core voter[57] and swing voter[58] models. The former posits that the most efficient way to maximize votes is for a political actor to target resources to constituencies in which they previously enjoyed considerable electoral support. For risk-averse politicians, the optimal strategy is to target spending to shore up support among loyal voters and solidify the political base of their reelection coalition. By contrast, the latter model outlines, like Kerry's campaign, the logic for targeting swing voters. Recent research by Gary Cox argues that expanding the scope of the formal models to focus on the capacity of resource targeting not only to persuade voters but also to improve coordination and mobilization only tilts the balance toward the core voter model.[59] If this perspective is correct, then we should see evidence of presidents targeting federal grants disproportionately to core constituencies within swing states. That is, presidents should gain the proverbial biggest bang for the buck by targeting grant dollars to strongly co-partisan counties with a track record of voting for the president's party that are within swing states that are in play in the upcoming presidential election.

A within-state analysis may also shed insight into the forces driving core constituency targeting. As discussed previously, a programmatic

---

[56] www.pbs.org/wgbh/pages/frontline/shows/architect/interviews/dowd.html.
[57] Cox and McCubbins (1986).
[58] Lindbeck and Weibull (1987).
[59] Cox (2010).

rationale, rather than electoral incentives, better fits the pattern observed in the last section. Counties in core states consistently receive more grant dollars than do counties in other states; this gap does not vary with the electoral calendar. As a further test of the programmatic story underlying such core constituency targeting, we can also examine whether counties that are heavily composed of presidential co-partisans receive a dispropor-tionate share of federal grant dollars. If core constituency targeting is truly the result of presidents championing policies that most benefit their core voters, then we should see counties that voted heavily for the president and his party in recent elections also receiving a disproportionate share of federal dollars. In this way, by pursuing a specific programmatic agenda, presidential budgetary influence may result in core counties receiving sig-nificantly more federal grants than counties that are not heavily populated with presidential partisans.

To examine where presidents target grants within swing states, we estimate a model with three new variables: an indicator for core counties, defined as those in which the president's party averaged 55 percent or more of the two-party vote in the preceding three elections, and the interactions of this variable with both swing and core state indicator variables. Column 4 of Table 5.1 presents the results. Figure 5.6 provides a substantive interpretation of the main results for the median county.

Strongly consistent with our theory of electorally motivated presiden-tial particularism, we find robust evidence that presidents target fed-eral dollars for electoral gain even at the county level. Presidents do not simply target federal dollars to swing states that have the greatest probability of influencing the outcome of the next election; rather, the results in Table 5.1 show that there is a strong association between pres-idential electoral incentives and the distribution of federal grant dollars *within* a swing state. Specifically, consistent with a line of game theoretic arguments concerning how politicians should allocate scarce resources to maximize vote totals, we find that presidents do not target money blindly within swing states. Rather, presidents send money disproportionately to core constituencies within swing states. As shown in Figure 5.6, our model estimates that the average core county in a swing state receives about 3 percent more in federal grants than does the average non-core county within the same state.[60] For the median county in 2008, this trans-lates into a boost of $12.6 million in grant spending above and beyond the increase received by virtue of residing in a swing state.

---

[60] Both counties (core and non-core) receive an additional infusion of grant dollars by virtue of being located in a swing state versus similar counties in non-battleground states.

FIGURE 5.6. Presidential Particularism within States (County-Level Effects). The first bar presents the estimated additional amount of federal grant dollars that a core county in a swing state receives and the second bar estimates the amount for a core county in a core state. The effects are estimated from the model in Column 4 of Table 5.1. For the first bar, the amount is relative to a non-core county in the same swing state. For the second bar, the amount is relative to a non-core county in the same core state. *The model estimates that the median core county in a swing state receives $12.6 million more in federal spending than does a comparable non-core county in the same swing state. The model estimates that a core county in a core state receives $18.8 million more in federal spending than does a comparable non-core county in the same core state.* The I-bars around the top of each bar represent the uncertainty (95% confidence interval) around each estimate.

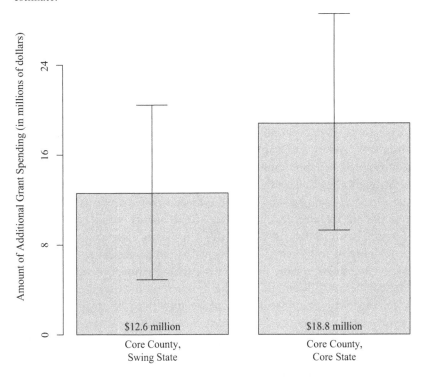

We also find that core counties in core states receive more federal grants on average than do other counties within the same state. For the median county in 2008, this translated into an additional $18.8 million in grants, above and beyond the increase received by that county because it was located in a core state. However, core counties in states that reliably backed the opposition party do not receive a boost in spending.

We are wary of inferring too much from this finding; however, it is inconsistent with a purely programmatic mechanism suggesting that the advantages reaped by core constituencies is the offshoot of presidents pursuing policies that disproportionately benefit blocs of Americans that tend to vote for their party. If that were the case, all core counties should benefit, not just those in swing or core states. Yet, the data suggest that counties with many presidential co-partisan voters in states that support the other party do not receive the same infusions of grant spending that similar counties in core states do. This pattern is at least consistent with the idea that core state targeting is the result of presidents intentionally channeling federal benefits to the most important components of their partisan base – core counties in core states – rather than simply pursuing policies that benefit groups of voters that tend to support their party, regardless of where they are located.

5.6 Summary

By examining the share of federal grant dollars each U.S. county received in each year from 1984 to 2008, we find strong evidence for our theory of a particularistic presidency. Presidents are not purely universalistic actors who pursue policies that maximize the national good. Rather, such impulses in presidents are tempered by both electoral and partisan motivations.

First-term presidents desire, perhaps above all else, a second term, and second-term presidents prefer a co-partisan successor who will protect and defend their legacies. Consistent with this logic, we find that swing state targeting increases significantly in election years, and is at its peak when the president himself is seeking reelection. Furthermore, presidents do not target grants blindly within swing states. Rather, they systematically target dollars to core counties within swing states where federal spending should have the largest electoral impact by helping turn out the partisan base. Taken together, the collective weight of the evidence strongly supports our theory of electoral particularism.

Presidents also consistently reward their core co-partisan constituencies. Parts of the country that reliably back the president's party at the polls routinely receive billions of dollars more in federal grant spending than do constituencies that back the opposition party. Far from portraying presidents as impartial defenders of the national interest, the data show presidents systematically skewing budgetary policies to the advantage of their core partisan constituencies. Last, we found evidence of presidents targeting federal grants to constituencies represented by their co-partisans in Congress in an apparent attempt to build political capital with legislators. However, this form of particularism paled in comparison to the magnitude of swing state and core state targeting.

While the evidence of presidential particularism in its various forms is considerable, we find surprisingly modest evidence for traditional sources of congressional parochialism. Undoubtedly, members of Congress play a tremendously important role in shaping the allocation of federal dollars, and some individual members of Congress – as a quick perusal of any newspaper come ribbon-cutting time will readily reveal – routinely succeed in securing seemingly disproportionate shares of federal resources for their districts. However, we find only modest evidence that members of the majority party, committee chairs, or members of key budgetary committees have any systematic influence on the geographic distribution of federal dollars.[61] Indeed, whatever geographic inequalities in federal spending that we can attribute to Congress are dwarfed by those that result from presidential particularistic impulses.

Our results turn the conventional wisdom on its head to some extent. Rather than presidents being the voice of reason and providing the universalistic counterbalance to the parochial drives of members of Congress, we find that presidents routinely inject considerable geographic inequalities into the allocation of federal grants across the country, inequalities that fall along patently political lines.

---

[61] Of course, substantive committees may be particularly well situated to secure disproportionate shares of funding for committee members in the narrow policy areas within their purview. This is a dynamic we do not test when looking at grant spending as a whole.

6

The Electoral Rewards of Presidential Particularism

> The fault, dear Brutus, is not in our stars, But in ourselves . . .
> – William Shakespeare's *Julius Caesar* (I, ii, 140–141)

Throughout this book, we find compelling evidence that presidents target federal dollars to electorally valuable constituencies, inducing economic inequality among the communities that find themselves as political winners or losers. Thus far, we have speculated that presidents are motivated to pursue this behavior because voters, perhaps shortsightedly, reward them for it. While considering the state of the national economy and the competency with which the president runs the executive branch, voters are also rewarding presidents at the ballot box for increased levels of spending in their communities. This is not the usual lens through which scholars, pundits, or journalists view presidential accountability. Additionally, our contemporary era is one in which government spending in the face of massive deficits is a highly politicized issue. National, not local, factors are supposed to dominate presidential electoral politics. Moreover, public opinion polls repeatedly tell us that most Americans believe that government is too big, that Washington wastes too many tax dollars, and that federal spending should be reduced. In a December 2013 Pew poll, a near-majority of Americans (49 percent) replied that it was more important to cut spending and reduce the deficit than to increase spending to spur economic recovery.[1] In a Fox News poll conducted in

---

[1] Pew Research Center for the People and the Press Political Survey, December 3–8, 2013, USPSRA.121913.R33.F2. Only 44% favored "more spending to help the economy recover."

October, 86 percent of Americans believed that the federal "government could spend less and save more without hurting people."[2] In a May 2013 poll, 54 percent of Americans, when asked whether the 2014 budget should feature increased or decreased levels of spending compared with the preceding year, favored spending cuts, versus only 16 percent who preferred more federal spending.[3] This raises the specter that voters may view local federal spending as waste and be more likely to punish than reward politicians for it.

Even though they may oppose spending in the abstract and in the aggregate, how will Americans respond to federal spending within their local communities? Will opposition remain high? And will they credit the commander-in-chief for new airport runways, remodeled hospital wings, and repaired highway spans? We first seek insight into these questions through an original survey experiment. Then, after establishing in a controlled setting that Americans like government spending so long as it is within their local communities, we turn to an analysis of electoral returns to see if presidents reap electoral gains in places where federal grant spending is increasing.

6.1 Targeted Spending and Public Opinion: An Experimental Approach

Do Americans respond differently to targeted federal spending programs when the dollars are allocated to their local communities? There are strong reasons to think they will. One man's pork may be another man's vital governmental investment. Why would politicians go to such great lengths to secure federal funding for localized projects – from $250,000 for a wireless network for Hartselle, Alabama, to $225,000 for exhibit restoration at the St. Louis Art Museum, to $693,000 to support "beef improvement research" in Missouri and Texas – if they did not believe such projects would bolster their support back home?[4] Yet, there is surprisingly little empirical evidence to substantiate such claims, in large part because identifying the influence of pork barrel spending on public opinion is difficult from observational data alone.

Here, we employ an experimental approach. In an experimental setting, we can inform participants about the level of federal spending in their

---

[2] Fox News Poll, October 20–22, 2013, USASFOX.102413.R16.

[3] Reason-Rupe Poll, May 9–13, 2013, USREASON.13MAY.R05.

[4] These three examples are taken from the NASDAQ OMX Group's list of the ten most bizarre pork items from the 2010 budget. www.nasdaq.com/article/the-10-most-absurd-pork-barrel-spending-items-of-2010-cm32756.

communities and then examine the impact of this information on their political preferences and judgments. Therefore, we embedded an experiment within an online survey to explore the influence of information about geographically targeted federal transportation grants on Americans' support for transportation spending and attitudes toward President Barack Obama. The sample that we recruited online is not nationally representative. However, it is demographically and geographically diverse, including respondents from every state except North Dakota. Moreover, recent research across disciplines has shown that the treatment effects observed on samples recruited in this way mirror those observed using nationally representative samples.[5] Thus, while we cannot infer that the characteristics and attitudes of our respondents mirror those of the country, we are confident that the experimental results are reflective of the way many Americans would respond to the experimental stimuli.

At the beginning of the survey, participants were asked several basic demographic questions including their current state of residence. After answering several questions that were completely unrelated to our focus of interest, participants were randomly assigned (without their knowledge) to one of three groups. The first group, the control, received no information about geographically targeted spending programs. The second group, by contrast, was asked to read a short statement by President Obama patterned after numerous real-world examples announcing a $50 million grant by the Department of Transportation to fund infrastructure projects within the subject's home state. We used the self-reported home state information from the beginning of the survey to customize this treatment so that each subject read about a grant award directed at his or her home state. The full text of the brief statement read:

> President Obama announced today that the Department of Transportation has awarded $50 million in new transportation grants to [the home state of the respondent]. "Investments in transportation projects like these," President Obama emphasized, "create jobs right away in communities across [the home state of the respondent], and lay a foundation for future economic growth." President Obama argued, "these projects in [the home state of the respondent] reflect my Administration's commitment to making smart investments in our nation's transit infrastructure."

Participants in the second treatment received the same statement, with one small twist: the state identified as receiving the $50 million

---

[5] See Berinsky et al. (2012). For additional discussion of how we recruited our sample as well as its demographic characteristics, see Appendix D.

TABLE 6.1. *Support for Increased Transportation Spending across Experimental Groups. The average in the home state treatment is statistically larger than the average in the control or non-home state treatment, p < .05.*

	Control	Home State	Non-Home State
Support	72%	78%	70%

transportation grant was not the respondent's home state, but one of the other forty-nine states, chosen at random. Participants in this treatment thus received information about a new federal spending program in another state.

All participants were then asked the same two questions. First, they were asked whether they approved or disapproved of increasing federal spending for transportation infrastructure projects. Later in the survey, participants were also asked to rate how they felt about President Obama on a feeling thermometer. Participants were shown a slider bar that ranged from 0 to 100 and were asked to indicate how they felt toward President Obama, with 0 being cold, 100 being warm, and 50 indicating neither warm nor cold.[6]

Because participants were randomly assigned to one of the three treatment groups, to estimate the effect of our grant spending treatments, we can compare the mean levels of support for increased transportation funding and attitudes toward Obama across the three groups. The only factor that distinguishes respondents, on average, across the three groups is the nature of the treatment they received concerning grant spending backed by the Obama administration.

Table 6.1 illustrates the effects of our treatments concerning geographically targeted federal spending on support for transportation spending. As shown in the control group, a substantial majority of our sample – 72 percent – supported increased federal investments in infrastructure. However, support for infrastructure spending was even higher among the subset of our sample told that the administration had announced a $50 million grant earmarked for transportation projects within their home state. In the home state treatment group, 78 percent of respondents supported increased transportation spending. This suggests that a significant infusion of grant spending within a state should increase support for transportation spending among voters in that state by approximately

---

[6] At the end of the survey, participants were debriefed concerning the hypothetical nature of our experimental manipulation and the purpose of the study.

TABLE 6.2. *Obama Feeling Thermometer Ratings across Experimental Groups. The average feeling thermometer rating in the home state treatment is statistically larger than the average in the control or non-home state treatment, $p < .05$.*

	Control	Home State	Non-Home State
Temperature	60°	68°	63°

6 percent. In a closely divided public, a shift of this size could be of considerable political importance. By contrast, among those respondents informed of a new grant award in another state apart from where they lived, support for increased spending on transportation infrastructure stood at only 70 percent, a full 8 percentage points lower than that observed among those told of grant spending in their home state. Thus, our experiment provides strong evidence that voters respond to localized federal spending when forming their preferences within that policy area. Those who see the tangible benefits of federal transportation spending in their home state are more supportive of increased spending in this area than those who do not.

Yet, just because learning of administration-backed grant spending in one's home state increases support for transportation spending in general does not mean that it will also affect attitudes toward the president. A long line of public opinion scholarship has shown that Americans' issue-specific opinions and policy preferences are considerably more malleable than are their assessments of political leaders and voting behavior. While most voters lack sophisticated policy-specific knowledge on which to base their policy preferences, when evaluating political leaders, partisanship provides most voters a clear heuristic. All else being equal, we like politicians who share our partisan affiliation and dislike those who do not. Indeed, our assessments of presidents are based on a myriad of factors that have unfolded and developed over the course of a presidential term in office. Therefore, the deck may be stacked against finding any evidence that such a modest cue about the administration's spending priorities and impact on voters' geographic constituencies will influence evaluations of the president.

Table 6.2 presents the average feeling thermometer ratings for President Obama in the control group and two treatment groups.[7] In the

---

[7] To disguise our purpose, we asked respondents to rate several additional political figures, both from the United States and foreign countries, using feeling thermometers. These additional feeling thermometers afford a strong placebo test. Because none of these political

control group, the average feeling thermometer rating for President Obama was 60 points on a 100-point scale, indicating a slightly more positive than neutral feeling toward the president.[8] However, among those who earlier in the survey read the statement by the president announcing transportation grant projects in their home state, the average feeling thermometer for the president was significantly higher at 68. This suggests that learning of the home state grants increased respondents' feelings toward Obama by almost 15 percent on average.[9] Finally, among those participants who learned of an influx of transportation grant spending in another state, the average feeling thermometer was 63. This figure is significantly lower than that observed in the home state spending treatment and statistically indistinguishable from the average observed in the control group.

Thus, geographically targeted spending can do more than merely raise support for the specific spending program among those who disproportionately benefit from it. Rather, geographically targeted spending can also increase support for the president among those who receive the increased benefits. After his five years in office and the accumulation of innumerable bases and issues on which to judge the president, voters who learned of increased spending in their home states were significantly more likely to view President Obama favorably than those who were not told of an infusion of federal grant spending in their home state.

6.2 The Electoral Politics of Federal Spending

Targeted federal grants may boost public support for a federal program – and even support for the president – among grant recipients. But does this increased support generated from targeted spending actually translate into more votes at the ballot box?

Virtually every academic inquiry into the electoral consequences of federal spending has focused on Congress. A lengthy literature has examined

---

figures were linked to our experimental treatments, we should not observe any significant differences in thermometer ratings for them across the three experimental treatments, and, indeed, we found none. Four respondents gave zeros to all five feeling thermometers on the survey. This is almost certainly indicative of inattentive respondents trying to skip through the survey. Therefore, we dropped these four respondents from the analysis. The results, however, are virtually identical if they are included in the final sample.

[8] For comparison, the average feeling thermometer rating for President Obama in the 2012 National Election Study pre-election wave was 58.3.

[9] Put slightly differently, the average feeling thermometer rating for President Obama in the home state spending group was .27 standard deviations higher than the mean rating in the control group.

the variable capacity of members of Congress to channel distributive benefits to their districts.[10] A wealth of scholarship has focused on the flip side of the equation, whether such pork barrel spending actually nets members of Congress more votes in the next election.[11] The image of pork-barreling legislators battling to channel federal dollars to their districts to secure reelection is firmly entrenched in both the popular and the academic consciousness.[12] Yet, in stark contrast to this conventional wisdom, most studies have found scant evidence that increased federal spending translates into extra votes for congressional incumbents.[13] We argue that one reason scholars have encountered so much difficulty in finding evidence for the electoral consequences of federal spending is that they have looked in the wrong place.

We live in an increasingly president-centered political world. For decades, scholars have examined the central role of presidents in American politics and noted the increasingly heavy weight of expectations heaped on them by an anxious public.[14] Against the backdrop of these lofty expectations, presidential power has grown dramatically in the modern era.[15] While the president's powers may still be far exceeded by popular demands for action, compared to a seemingly feckless Congress with historically low approval ratings, presidents may be the logical focus for voter accolades or animus. Voters living in a community with crumbling infrastructure may blame the president, not members of Congress or state or local officials, for governmental failings. If voters perceive that their community is not getting a fair share of federal dollars, they may blame the White House for the lack of federal assistance – if only the president

---

[10] See, inter alia, Anzia and Berry (2011); Atlas et al. (1995); Balla et al. (2002); Bickers and Stein (2000); Ferejohn (1974); Lee (2000, 2004); Lee and Oppenheimer (1999); Levitt and Poterba (1999); Stein and Bickers (1994).

[11] See, inter alia, Alvarez and Saving (1997); Alvarez and Schousen (1993); Bickers and Stein (1996); Lazarus and Reilly (2010); Levitt and Sndyer (1997); Sellers (1997).

[12] Inter alia Mayhew (1974a).

[13] Summarizing the literature, Lazarus and Reilly (2010, 344) describe the results of these primarily House-centered studies as exhibiting a general "pattern of non-findings." Some studies buck this general trend. For instance, Bickers and Stein (1996, 1319) find that a two-standard-deviation increase in district-level awards modestly decreases the likelihood of a quality challenger by "only two percentage points" in the primary election and by "slightly less than four percentage points" in the general election. Levitt and Snyder (1995, 51), who address the endogeneity of electoral vulnerability and increased grant dollars through an instrumental variables approach, do find a significant effect. This analysis yields an effect of "an extra 5 percent" with a one-standard-deviation increase in high variation federal spending.

[14] Neustadt (1990 [1960], 7). See also Rossiter (1960).

[15] See, inter alia, Dickinson (1999); Howell (2003); Rudalevige (2002).

would curb government waste and channel the savings into improving roads and bridges in the community! By contrast, if a federal grant funds the opening of a new clinic that significantly improves the quality and convenience of medical services in the region, voters in that community may reward the president rather than members of Congress for the federal largesse.

Thus, we predict that voters reward or punish presidents at the ballot box for the share of federal spending that their communities receive. Voters who see firsthand the benefits brought to their communities by an infusion of federal dollars may logically conclude that the president's priorities are responsive to the needs of their local community and reward him accordingly. By contrast, voters who see their share of federal dollars shrink may punish the chief executive for heading a government that seemingly fails to prioritize the needs of their communities.

6.3 The Electoral Benefits of Federal Grant Spending

Our experimental evidence suggests that when we directly expose an individual to information that the president has increased federal spending in his or her community, the response is to reward the president. But do we observe this relationship in actual election outcomes? To answer this question, we investigate whether incumbent presidents and their partisan successors fare better in counties that received an election-year infusion of federal grant dollars.

Toward this end, we first must construct a measure of presidential electoral performance in a county that accounts for the baseline partisan orientation of voters in that constituency. For example, President Clinton received 79 percent of the two-party vote in Suffolk County, Massachusetts, in 1996. That year, Suffolk County also received almost $5 billion in federal grants, one of the largest hauls in the nation. It might be tempting to treat this as superficial evidence that presidents do indeed reap electoral rewards in counties that receive large amounts of federal dollars. However, Suffolk County, which is dominated by liberal-leaning Boston and its surrounding suburbs, has long favored the Democratic Party in presidential contests. Indeed, Clinton won 72 percent of the two-party vote in 1992 when he challenged the incumbent President George H. W. Bush. Similarly, Al Gore carried Suffolk County in 2000 with 78 percent of the two-party vote. To account for this Democratic lean, we examine *the change in two-party vote share* in a county from the preceding to the current election. To continue our prior example, Bill Clinton exceeded his prior performance in Suffolk County by 7 percent in 1996, and Al

Gore fell 1 percent off Bill Clinton's prior pace in the county when he ran for president in 2000. Using this metric allows us to control for a myriad of often unobservable county characteristics – for example, a county's socioeconomic characteristics, racial composition, and mix of urban and rural regions – that may make the county lean toward one party or the other. It allows us to focus on the more politically relevant factor: the influence of localized grant spending on the change in vote share above or below its "baseline" level in a constituency.

In a similar vein, for our main explanatory variable we use the percentage change in grant spending that a county receives in an election year from its preceding year baseline.[16] This measure also maximizes controls by accounting for the widely varying levels of grant funding that counties across the country receive. For example, because Suffolk County contains a major city, several leading research universities, and world-class medical centers, its grant totals are routinely among the highest in the nation. By looking at the change in grant dollars that Suffolk County receives, we can account for its high baseline and focus on the electoral consequences of changes in federal support above or below this baseline.

Moreover, our focus on election-year changes in spending accords with a vast literature arguing that voters respond only to the most recent economic conditions. For example, in the fall of 1983, President Ronald Reagan appeared eminently beatable to many. The country had experienced a sharp and painful recession in 1982. Unemployment sat above 9 percent, and Reagan's approval rating languished in the low to mid-40s. However, a year later, the economy had begun to pick up, consumer optimism was rising, and voters had largely forgotten the pain of the preceding two years. Reagan rode an electoral landslide to a second term, trouncing his Democratic opponent Walter Mondale. An additional practical advantage of using the percentage change is that it allows us to provide a standard measure of change in spending across counties, one that is consistent across counties with widely varying base levels of grant funding.[17]

Figure 6.1 illustrates the distribution of changes in federal grant spending at the county level for presidential elections years from 1988 to 2008.

---

[16] In other words, this variable is calculated as the amount of federal grants a county received in an election year minus the amount it received in the preceding year, divided by this prior year baseline.

[17] For example, in 2008 the average county received $1,940 per person in grant spending. However, 10% of counties received less than $1,020 per person in grant spending, whereas 10% received in excess of $3,466 per person in grant spending. Thus, a $175 per person increase in grant spending (the median change in per capita grant spending from 2007 to 2008) represents a much bigger increase for residents of some counties than for others.

FIGURE 6.1. Distribution of Election-Year Change in Grant Spending at the County Level, 1988 to 2008.

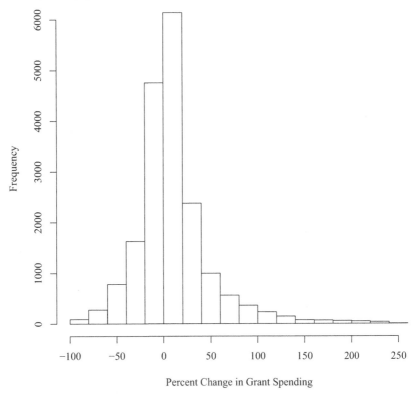

Percent Change in Grant Spending

In an election year, the median county sees a 10 percent increase in grant spending, but the figure shows substantial variation across the country. Changes range from a decline of nearly 100 percent to an increase of more than 240 percent. This range reflects the sometimes dramatic changes in year-to-year spending levels observed in prior research on federal budgeting.[18] Do these sometimes significant swings in grant spending drive changes in presidential electoral fortunes at the county level?

---

[18] For example, this changing distribution of grant spending is aptly characterized as "hyperincrementalism" by Jones and Baumgartner (2005, 112), who also point out that "sometimes programs received huge boosts, propelling them to double or triple their original sizes or more. Sometimes, but less often, programs lost half or more of their funding." A small number of counties (approximately 1%) experienced election-year increases of more than 240%. To ensure that these extreme outlying values are not driving our results, we omitted them from the figure as well as from the statistical analyses that follow. All analyses, however, are robust to their inclusion. See Appendix D for additional robustness checks and discussion.

FIGURE 6.2. Changes in Grant Spending, Florida in 2008.

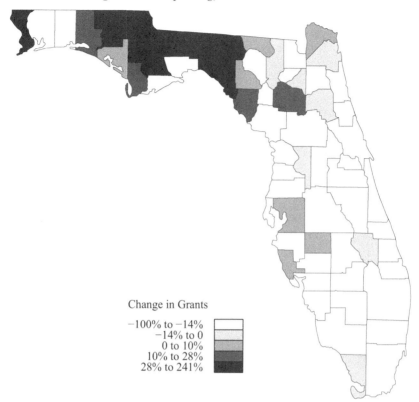

Change in Grants

−100% to −14%
−14% to 0
0 to 10%
10% to 28%
28% to 241%

6.3.1 *Grant Spending and John McCain's Fortunes in 2008*

As an initial inquiry into the electoral consequences of shifts in local grant spending, consider the case of Florida in 2008. The average Florida county saw its grant totals decrease by roughly 8 percent from 2007 to 2008; however, as shown in Figure 6.2, there was considerable variation about that mean. Counties in light shades on the map saw larger decreases, and those in darker shades experienced increases in grant spending. For example, while many of the more Democratic-leaning areas in southeast Florida experienced decreases in grant spending in the lead-up to the 2008 vote, many counties in the more traditionally Republican panhandle saw significant increases in grant spending. Indeed, ten of Florida's sixty-seven counties experienced election-year increases in grant spending of more than 50 percent over their 2007 total.

FIGURE 6.3. Changes in Grant Spending and Change in GOP Vote Share, Florida in 2008.

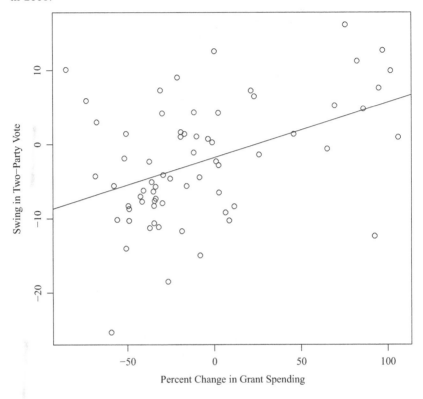

Can these changes in grant spending help explain shifts in the Republican Party's electoral fortunes in Florida from 2004 to 2008? The scatter plot in Figure 6.3 suggests that they may. The horizontal axis shows the change in federal grant spending that a county received from 2007 to 2008, and the vertical axis shows the change between the share of the two-party vote received by George W. Bush in a county in 2004 and that secured by John McCain in 2008. While there is considerable variation, Figure 6.3 does show a clear positive correlation between changes in grant funding in a county and changes in Republican vote share. As we might expect, John McCain, facing a stiff headwind against Republicans in 2008, underperformed President Bush's 2004 vote tally in forty of Florida's sixty-seven counties. Yet, in the twelve counties that received significant election-year increases of grant spending of 25 percent or more, McCain fared substantially better at the polls. Indeed, in nine of these twelve counties, McCain actually surpassed President Bush's 2004 performance. In the key battleground state, McCain appears to have reaped significant electoral advantages in counties that received an influx of grant spending in the immediate lead-up to the election.

Stepping back and examining data from counties nationwide in 2008 tells a similar story. For example, in the 1,182 counties that experienced decreases in grant spending, McCain underperformed President Bush by an average of 4 percent. McCain also lost ground, on average, in the 1,930 counties that experienced increases in grant spending. However, in these counties, the loss was significantly smaller, only 2.5 percent on average.[19] Thus, superficially at least, we find considerable evidence suggesting that voters from counties that were showered with additional grant dollars rewarded George W. Bush's partisan successor at the polls, while voters who saw their community's share of federal largesse shrink punished the Republican candidate at the ballot box.

6.3.2 A Comprehensive Approach

While the 2008 results from Florida and elsewhere support our contention that voters reward and punish presidential candidates for the share of federal grants they receive, the results offer only circumstantial support for our argument. First, we examine data from only a single election. Second, the scatter plots and comparisons make no effort to control for other factors that might also drive changes in partisan vote share across two elections. Accordingly, to provide a more convincing test of our hypothesis, we estimate a series of more comprehensive statistical models using data on all presidential elections from 1988 through 2008.[20]

We model the change in the share of the two-party vote that the incumbent presidential party receives in a county as a function of how much grant spending has increased or decreased in that county during the year immediately preceding the election. We also control for a number of factors that prior scholarship suggests drive variation in presidential

---

[19] Put slightly differently, McCain actually outperformed Bush in 26% of counties that experienced an election-year increase in grant spending. By contrast, in counties that experienced a decrease in grant spending, McCain outperformed Bush in only 16% of counties.

[20] The Consolidated Federal Funds Report (CFFR) data on county-level grant spending begins in 1983, and data is available for the 1984 election. However, beginning in 1984, CFFR began reporting county-level distributions for seven grant programs accounting for 40% of all grant spending that in the 1983 report had been assigned to the state capital's county. As a result, we are unable to construct the change in county-level grant spending measure for the 1984 election, and our models therefore begin with the 1988 election.

election returns at the county level. First, given the importance of economic conditions in almost all studies of electoral behavior, and particularly of retrospective calculations, we control for the percentage change in per capita personal income in a county during the year preceding the election.[21] Logically, the incumbent presidential party might perform better in counties where incomes are rising than in counties where incomes are stagnating or even decreasing. Second, our statistical model allows us to control for the dynamics of the campaigns. Specifically, we include two variables measuring the differential in both TV advertising and campaign appearances between the incumbent party candidate and the challenger within each state.[22] This allows us to account for the probability that the incumbent party will receive a boost in states where it out-campaigns the opposition and perhaps will suffer setbacks in states where the challenger runs a stronger campaign.

Other scholarship has also argued that war can affect electoral outcomes. Moreover, because all parts of the country do not experience a war and its costs equally, counties that have witnessed high casualty tallies may punish the incumbent party more than counties that have been comparatively insulated from battle deaths.[23] To account for this possibility, we control for the number of Iraq War casualties that each county had suffered as of the 2004 and 2008 elections.

The model includes two additional variables to account for possible changing political dynamics within a county: the change in vote share secured by the House candidate of the incumbent president's party from the midterm to the current election and the percentage change in county population during the year preceding the election.[24] The change in the House vote affords a strong control for recent changing political dynamics within a county. The other measure allows us to be sure that population flows into and out of a county are not driving any correlation between spending and presidential vote share. Last, as in previous chapters, our

[21] Inter alia, see Erikson (1989); Fiorina (1981); Hibbs (1987).
[22] These measures are drawn from Huang and Shaw (2009); Shaw (1999a, 2006).
[23] Gartner et al. (2004); Grose and Oppenheimer (2007); Karol and Miguel (2007); Kriner and Shen (2007).
[24] As discussed previously, while more than 80% of counties match uniquely into a single district, some counties straddle multiple districts. In such cases, we use the data from the congressional district that contains a plurality of the county's population. Our results are robust to excluding this variable, or to limiting our analysis to only those counties that match uniquely into a single congressional district. See Appendix D for additional discussion and robustness checks. Furthermore, because our data is time series, cross-sectional, all of our models also include both county and year fixed effects.

TABLE 6.3. *Effect of Federal Spending on Incumbent Presidential Vote Share, U.S. Counties, 1988 to 2008. Least squares model with fixed effects for counties and years. Dependent variable is the percent change in county-level vote for the incumbent president (or the incumbent party) since the previous presidential election. Increased grant spending leads to increased incumbent presidential vote share. This relationship is particularly strong in swing states. Robust standard errors clustered on county are in parentheses.*

	(1)	(2)
% change in grants	0.707	
	(0.119)	
% change in grants × Uncompetitive state		0.493
		(0.146)
% change in grants × Competitive state		1.134
		(0.187)
Change in per capita income (in thousands)	0.170	0.169
	(0.029)	(0.029)
Television ad difference	0.070	0.071
	(0.012)	(0.012)
Campaign appearance difference	0.210	0.208
	(0.018)	(0.019)
Change in presidential party House vote	0.012	0.013
	(0.003)	(0.003)
Iraq War casualties in county, 2004	−0.487	−0.485
	(0.125)	(0.125)
Iraq War casualties in county, 2008	−0.269	−0.266
	(0.075)	(0.075)
% change in county population	−0.366	−0.440
	(1.209)	(1.209)
Competitive state (within 5%)		−0.000
		(0.108)
Constant	−2.716	−2.725
	(0.144)	(0.151)
Observations	17,959	17,959
R^2	0.499	0.500

models include both county and year fixed effects. Results are presented in the first column of Table 6.3, and a full series of robustness checks is presented in Appendix D.

After expanding the scope of analysis to include all counties and all elections from 1988 to 2008, we continue to find strong evidence supporting our contention that voters reward presidents for increased grant spending in their communities and punish presidents for decreases in

FIGURE 6.4. Effect of Federal Spending on Incumbent Presidential Vote Share, U.S. Counties, 1988 to 2008. Effects are generated by increasing the variable from one standard deviation below the mean to one standard deviation above the mean. Point estimates are presented with 95% confidence intervals indicated by line segments through the points.

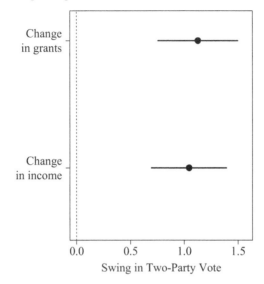

spending. Perhaps the easiest way to visualize the electoral consequences of federal spending is to consider the swing in the two-party vote generated by a given increase (or decrease) in grant spending in a county. For example, if a given change in grant spending increases the incumbent's share of the two-party vote by 1 percent from 51 percent to 52 percent, it also by definition decreases the challenger's share of the two-party vote by 1 percent, from 49 percent to 48 percent. The resulting swing in the two-party vote share is thus 2 percent.

Figure 6.4 presents the effect of a two-standard-deviation increase in grant spending on the change in the two-party vote swing. As a basis of comparison, we also present the effect of a two-standard-deviation increase in per capita income – a factor long held to be a primary driver of presidential electoral fortunes – on the swing in the two-party vote. Clearly, voters do significantly reward or punish presidents for the share of federal spending their communities receive. An 80 percent increase in federal grant spending, which represents an increase from one standard deviation below to one standard deviation above the mean value, generates a more than 1.1 percent swing in the two-party vote share in that county. This suggests that, in eight of the darkly shaded counties in

Florida's panhandle shown in Figure 6.2, John McCain enjoyed a more than 1 percent swing at the polls because of election-year infusions of federal grant dollars into these communities.

Moreover, as Figure 6.4 illustrates, this change in electoral fortunes is comparable to that generated by an identically sized shift in per capita income, a factor long held to influence voting behavior significantly in presidential elections. A two-standard-deviation increase in per capita income yields a 1 percent swing in the two-party vote.

At first blush, a 1.1 percent swing in the two-party vote may appear relatively modest, even if it is as large as the swings generated by other important variables, such as changing income levels, that are emphasized in the literature on presidential elections. However, it is important to remember that a 1.1 percent swing in the two-party vote is potentially decisive in an era of razor-thin presidential electoral margins. One need only remember 2000, a year in which several hundred ballots in Florida decided the election and the winner of the popular vote failed to secure the presidency, to appreciate the potential importance of a swing of this size.

6.3.3 Effects in Swing States

As the 2000 election made patently clear, voters do not directly decide who will become the next president of the United States: electors in the Electoral College do. These electors are apportioned state by state. Therefore, the electoral importance of a 1.1 percent swing in vote share at the county level depends on the competitiveness of the state in which it is located. If presidents receive electoral rewards for increased spending only in states where the final outcome is not in doubt, then the electoral consequences of spending would be minimal. Moreover, this would call into question our theory emphasizing the electoral incentives that drive electoral particularism. If presidents reap benefits at the polls from geographically targeted spending, but only in parts of the country that are not electorally in play, then presidents would have few incentives to try to target funds to specific constituencies for electoral gain. However, if we find evidence that patterns in grant spending also affect electoral outcomes in swing states, then the foundations for our theory of electoral particularism would be strong indeed.

There are strong reasons to expect that the effects of increased federal spending may be even larger in competitive battleground states where campaigns explicitly prime voters to consider the achievements of the incumbent administration, including its ability to direct federal grants to voters. Presidential candidates spend most of their time and target their financial resources overwhelmingly in battleground states.[25] As Chapter 1's descriptions of President Obama's whirlwind efforts to claim credit for the stream of federal benefits that poured into Ohio (from manufacturing innovation centers to small business loans for cheese producers) make clear, campaigns can and do tout increased levels of federal spending and the associated economic benefits they have delivered to local constituencies. President Obama is far from the only incumbent to highlight the discrete benefits that his administration has secured for a politically valuable constituency. For instance, in February 1996, the Clinton administration announced a plan to spend billions of dollars restoring the Florida Everglades. The *New York Times* noted that the proposal enjoyed broad support in Florida, an important swing state coveted by the administration that no Democrat had captured since Jimmy Carter in 1976. Less than a month before the election, Clinton triumphantly signed the measure into law.[26] Eight years later, another president seeking reelection, George W. Bush, followed in his predecessor's footsteps and announced just before the 2004 election a new $1.5 billion in funding to continue the almost decade-old cleanup of the Everglades. The announcement, covered extensively in local media outlets, was made at Boynton Beach in Palm Beach County, a major epicenter of the recount battle that narrowly awarded Bush the presidency in 2000. The potential electoral impact of the infusion of federal dollars did not go unnoticed by Bush's opponents, who attempted to counteract that announcement with local appearances by Ted Danson and other celebrities.[27] Given the disproportionate elite mobilization in battleground states, voters in these areas may be primed to consider the role of presidents in providing federal dollars and therefore more likely to reward them for those grants.[28]

Accordingly, to examine the real-world importance of the spending effect, we examine whether increases in grant spending have different effects in battleground versus non-battleground states. We again

[25] Goldstein and Freedman (2002); Shaw (2006).

[26] Todd Purdum, "President signs a bill to restore the Everglades," *New York Times*, October 13, 1996. http://www.nytimes.com/1996/10/13/us/president-signs-a-bill-to-restore-the-everglades.html.

[27] Craig Pittman, "Everglades plan leads to campaign battle in swamp," *St. Petersburg Times*, October 15, 2004.

[28] When voters are primed to link increased federal spending to the president's actions, presidents should be more likely to receive credit (Arceneaux, 2006; Malhotra and Kuo, 2008). Alternatively, battleground states may have more voters who are undecided between the two candidates and who are more likely to switch their vote choice if given a nudge by increased federal spending in their community.

FIGURE 6.5. The Effect of Federal Spending and Electoral Competitiveness on Incumbent Presidential Vote Share, U.S. Counties, 1988 to 2008. For grant spending and income, the effect on vote swing is generated by increasing the variable from one standard deviation below the mean to one standard deviation above the mean. Competitiveness is a binary indicator and its independent effect is indistinguishable from zero. Effects are estimates based on the model presented in Column 2 of Table 6.3. Point estimates are presented with 95% confidence intervals indicated by the line segments through the points.

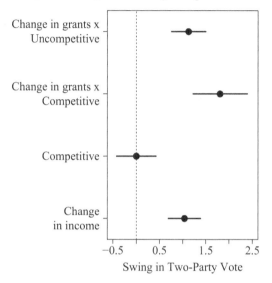

define competitive states as those in which the losing candidate averaged 45 percent or more of the two-party vote share in the preceding three electoral contests.

The results of the revised model that allows us to test for the relative electoral consequences of federal spending in swing states versus non-battleground states are presented in the second column of Table 6.3. Figure 6.5 illustrates the main results. Our revised analysis shows convincingly that the change in grant spending that a county receives affects presidential vote swings in both battleground and unbattleground states.[29] For example, in uncompetitive states, a two-standard-deviation increase in grant spending yields a .79 percent swing in the two-party vote. Even more important for our argument, in the most electorally important

---

[29] The competitive variable in the figure shows that the incumbent did not perform any better, on average, in swing states than in non-battleground states. Thus, the increased electoral success illustrated in the "Change in grants × Competitive" variable is exclusively the result of grant spending.

battleground states, the effects are significantly larger. In competitive
states, a similar increase in grant spending within a county produces an
estimated 1.8 percent shift in the two-party vote – an electoral boost
that is more than twice the magnitude of that observed in uncompetitive
states. This effect is substantively much greater than an equivalent shift
in the county's personal per capita income.

Politically, swings of this magnitude are substantively significant. In
2004, a 1.8 percent swing in the two-party vote could have flipped nine
states, including delegate-rich Michigan, Ohio, and Pennsylvania, from
one partisan side to the other. Moreover, even within individual counties, a shift of this size could be consequential. For example, a 1.8 percent
swing for President Bush in Milwaukee and Dane Counties in Wisconsin
in 2004 would have netted him more than 13,500 additional votes. Senator Kerry won the state by less than 12,000 votes that year. A similar
shift in almost any Florida county in 2000 would also have changed the
outcome of the election.

Thus, across a range of models we find strong evidence consistent with
our argument that voters reward or punish presidents for the share of federal grant spending that their communities receive. This is the lynchpin of
our larger argument that voters incentivize electoral particularism. Voters
reward presidents for the share of government benefits their communities
receive. Because the Electoral College ensures that some voters have more
electoral value then do others, a rational president has incentives to target
federal dollars toward some constituents, particularly toward those who
live in swing states, and away from others.[30]

6.4 Presidential Swing State Targeting Revisited

The analysis in Chapter 5 modeled the overall level of federal grant
spending that a county receives. On average, counties in swing states
receive tens of millions dollars more than do other counties in non-swing
states, all else being equal. But does a state's electoral importance to the
president influence the probability of counties within that state receiving one of the very large increases in grant spending – 80 percent or

---

[30] In previous research, Kriner and Reeves (2012) demonstrate that the electoral effects
of federal spending are even greater in certain types of counties (i.e., in counties represented by presidential co-partisans, and in counties with smaller shares of conservative
voters) and among some voters (i.e., among liberal and moderate voters) than others.
See our prior research for theoretical and empirical extensions to our core argument here
emphasizing the foundations of electoral particularism.

more – that are shown to have such significant electoral consequences in the preceding analysis?

First, it bears emphasizing that such massive infusions of grant spending into a county are not rare occurrences. For example, just over 15 percent of counties in 2008 received an increase in grant spending of 80 percent or more over the previous year's total. Are counties located in swing states more likely to receive such significant increases in grant spending?

To test this final implication of electorally induced presidential particularism, we construct another statistical model to understand the factors influencing the probability of a given county receiving such a large infusion of grant spending. Our dependent variable is an indicator variable identifying whether or not each county in each year from 1985 to 2008 received an infusion of grant spending of 80 percent or more over the preceding year.[31] Our main independent variable is the interaction between the swing state variable and an indicator variable identifying election years. Because only election-year infusions of grant spending translate into more votes at the ballot box, being located in a swing state should increase a county's probability of receiving a massive increase in grant spending in an election year. Our logistic regression model controls for all of the other explanatory variables used in the models reported in Chapter 5 and includes county and year fixed effects.[32] Table 6.4 presents the results.

In a final piece of evidence for presidential swing state targeting, we find that counties in swing states are much more likely to receive such large infusions of grant spending, particularly in election years. In an election year, our model suggests that the probability of the average county receiving a major infusion of grant spending increases from .16 in a county located in a non-swing state to .23 in a county located in a swing state, all else being equal. This represents a 44 percent increase from the baseline.[33]

---

[31] As discussed previously, because the CFFR changed its reporting for many grant programs in 1984, our analysis must begin here with 1985.

[32] The inclusion of county fixed effects causes the model to drop counties that never received a major infusion of grant spending of this magnitude. Alternatively, we estimated the same model specification with state fixed effects, instead of county fixed effects. This yielded virtually identical results: counties in swing states are much more likely to receive large infusions of grant spending, particularly in election years. For full results, see Appendix D.

[33] Counties in core states are no more or less likely than counties in non-core, non-swing states to receive a major increase in election-year grant spending.

TABLE 6.4. *Swing State Counties Secure Large Increases in Grant Spending. The dependent variable identifies counties that received an 80% or greater increase in grant spending over the preceding year. Large, electorally significant increases in grant spending occur disproportionately in swing states during presidential election years. Model is a logistic regression with fixed effects for county and year. Standard errors are in parentheses.*

Swing state	0.096
	(0.063)
Swing state × Election year	0.284
	(0.085)
Core state	0.010
	(0.060)
Member of Congress from presidential party	−0.021
	(0.045)
Member of Congress from majority party	0.027
	(0.045)
Member of Congress chair	0.334
	(0.094)
Member of Appropriations or Ways and Means	−0.115
	(0.053)
Per capita income	−0.009
	(0.006)
Poverty rate	−0.027
	(0.007)
Population (natural log)	−0.655
	(0.139)
Observations	46,237

Thus, a substantial number of counties do routinely receive the large increases in grant spending that have significant electoral consequences. Counties in swing states are much more likely to receive such election-year infusions of cash than are counties in non-battleground states. Despite their protestations to the contrary, when allocating federal dollars across the country, presidents appear more like reelection-driven politicians than unbiased stewards of the national interest.

6.5 Summary

The combination of survey experimental evidence and analysis of the correlations between electoral returns and patterns of federal spending yields strong support for the motivating assumption behind core state targeting: voters reward presidents at the polls for federal dollars channeled to their communities.

To be sure, each component of the analysis has limitations. For example, experiments often sacrifice external validity for internal validity. That is, experiments conducted in highly controlled settings allow us to be sure that our treatment is causing any observed differences across treatment and control groups, but through the very process of creating this level of control our study becomes removed from the real world. In our experiment the president announced the grant program, and then shortly thereafter respondents were asked for their opinions on transportation spending and their attitudes toward the president. In the real world, when presidents announce new grant programs, they are not the only ones who claim credit for them. Members of the House and Senate, governors, and even local politicians who may have petitioned Washington for assistance can all seek to claim credit for the benefits brought home to a constituency. Moreover, in the lead-up to an election, voters are bombarded with a wide array of competing information designed to influence their final decisions at the ballot box. However, our experiment does show conclusively that Americans incorporate information about the localized consequences of federal spending into their policy preferences and political judgments. All else equal, voters who see an influx of federal spending in their communities are more likely to support that type of spending and to approve of the president who helped bring it to their constituency. This direct experimental evidence at the individual level complements the results of our statistical models of real-world election data in the aggregate.

By contrast, the analysis of observational data in which we show strong correlations between increases in localized federal spending and increased electoral support for the president has high external validity; all of the data is taken from actual elections. Yet, from such aggregate data alone we cannot be positive that voters are observing the increases in spending, updating their political assessments and calculations, and increasing their probability of voting for the incumbent president accordingly. It is the most logical explanation underlying the patterns we see, but not the only plausible one.

Nevertheless, when taken together, the observational and experimental evidence for the causal logic underlying our theory of presidential electoral particularism is compelling. Voters respond to spending within their more narrow geographic constituencies, and they reward presidents at the ballot box for increases in grant spending and punish them for decreases. This, in turn, combined with the structure of our electoral system, gives presidents strong incentives to target federal resources disproportionately to voters in swing states, something they do every four years.

7

Conclusion

We have searched for and found evidence of presidential particularism in a diverse range of policy realms, from the implementation of U.S. trade law to decisions concerning military base closures to natural disaster declarations to the allocation of hundreds of billions of grant dollars across the country. Even in the realm of the federal government's response to natural disasters – a policy venue where presidents have unilateral authority and where all would hope that economic need alone drives policy choices – we found unambiguous evidence of presidents catering to swing states and privileging the interests of core political constituencies at the expense of a politically neutral distribution of federal resources. The sheer breadth of evidence for presidential particularism shows that it is far from the exception in presidential policymaking.

Given our findings of particularism across a range of policy areas, we suspect the influence of presidential particularism extends beyond the policies examined in this book. For example, election watchers have long noted that presidential candidates are reluctant to criticize federal ethanol subsidies, despite voluminous evidence of their inefficiencies and perverse unintended consequences.[1] The rush to expand ethanol production has been linked to the destruction of pristine habitats and conservation lands, contamination of water supplies with fertilizers, and rising food prices, all while failing to reduce significantly the carbon footprint of energy

---

[1] The economic literature on this question is vast. Among others, see David Pimental. 2003. "Ethanol fuels: Energy balance, economics, and environmental impacts are negative." *Natural Resources Research* 12: 127–134; Jason Hill, et al. 2006. "Environmental, economic, and energetic costs and benefits of biodiesel and ethanol biofuels." *Proceedings of the National Academy of Sciences* 103: 11206–11210.

generation.[2] Why would presidents champion a position that, according to many, is detrimental to the best interest of the nation? One answer is particularism. Although Iowa is not always considered a swing state in general election contests, it enjoys privileged status as the nation's first caucus state in the presidential nomination calendar.[3] Time and again Iowa's electoral importance has blunted any executive initiative to change the nation's energy policies. Indeed, executive branch policies under Presidents Bush and Obama have further bolstered ethanol, despite its widespread environmental and social costs.[4]

Consider another policy venue – immigration – where President Obama's executive actions in 2013 directed the Department of Justice to, in effect, implement key provisions of the Development, Relief, and Education for Alien Minors Act, more commonly known as the DREAM Act. The administration was unable to push the act through the

---

[2] Dina Cappiello and Matt Apuzzo, "The secret environmental cost of US ethanol policy," *Associated Press*, November 12, 2013. http://bigstory.ap.org/article/secret-dirty-cost-obamas-green-power-push-1.

[3] We do not explicitly consider the influence of primary elections on presidential behavior. On one hand, this makes sense because incumbent presidents rarely have cause for worry in a primary contest. On the other hand, there is at least anecdotal evidence that presidential candidates pander to important primary states. In 2012, during a GOP primary debate, Governor Romney chastised his fellow candidate Newt Gingrich for promising particularistic spending to each of the new primary states to which he traveled. Romney noted, "[W]e've seen politicians ... go from state to state and promise exactly what that state wants to hear. The Speaker comes here to Florida, wants to spend untold amounts of money having a colony on the moon. ... In South Carolina, it was a new interstate highway, and dredging the port in Charleston. In New Hampshire it was buying a power line coming in from Canada and building a new VHA hospital in New Hampshire so that people don't have to go to Boston." Transcript of CNN Florida Republican presidential debate, January 26, 2012. http://archives.cnn.com/TRANSCRIPTS/1201/26/se.05.html.

[4] Writing on agricultural policy more generally, Graham Wilson explicitly challenges the notion that universalistic presidents protect consumers, who are the vast majority of the population, while Congress, dominated by extreme preference outliers on the Agriculture Committee, defends farmers. "The traditional argument is that the President is the custodian of general interests. Elected by the people, he is held ransom by none. In particular, it would be argued that farmers, though now a small proportion of the population (5 per cent), can maintain their influence with Congress because of the unequal distribution of power within Congress typified by the committee system. Consumers and taxpayers who are, of course, more numerous, find their interests better protected by the President. No matter how plausible such an argument, it is incorrect. Presidents have shown an eagerness to court the farm vote which fully matches and probably exceeds competition for the farm vote in Britain" (Wilson, 1977). This accords with the example in Chapter 5 of Franklin Roosevelt in 1933 sparing cuts in agricultural research at the behest of Secretary of Agriculture Henry Wallace, who warned that doing so would forever lose the farm vote for Democrats. See Rosenstone et al. (1996) for a discussion of the agriculture sector as a swing constituency.

Republican-controlled House. Almost certainly, President Obama believed that not deporting young illegal immigrants who meet certain criteria was the right thing to do and in the national interest. However, the timing of the decision, announced in the summer of 2012, suggests that electoral calculations also factored into the decision. The Latino vote was widely anticipated to be pivotal in a number of swing states, and his actions were also interpreted by many as a means of rewarding Latino Americans who voted almost two-to-one for the president in 2008. The administration's unilateral actions regarding immigration speak to the difficulty of disentangling presidential motive; but they remind us of the many pathways through which particularistic forces can influence both the content and the timing of presidential behaviors.

Even the wartime president and his allies across the administration may be influenced by particularistic impulses. Before the first ordinance of the "shock and awe" campaign against Baghdad rained down, the Bush administration awarded Kellogg, Brown and Root, a subsidiary of Vice President Dick Cheney's former employer Halliburton, a multibillion-dollar no-bid contract to rebuild Iraq's oil production capacity. A leaked Department of Defense e-mail noted that Undersecretary of Defense for Policy and head of the Office of Special Plans Douglas Feith signed off on the deal and anticipated "no issues since action has been coordinated w VP's office."[5] The contract was awarded over the strenuous objections of the Army Corps of Engineer's Principal Assistant Responsible for Contracting and Competition Advocate.[6] Haliburton was far from the only company with political ties to the Bush administration to benefit greatly from government contracts to rebuild postwar Iraq. After conducting a six-month review of more than seven million contracting actions related to the war, the nonprofit Center for Public Integrity alleged multiple instances of cronyism in contracts and charged that the Bush administration systematically rewarded companies who gave more to President Bush's campaign coffers than to any other politician over the preceding twelve years.[7] In two more empirical studies of Iraq War contracting,

[5] Timothy Burger and Adam Zagorin, "The paper trail," *Time*, May 30, 2004.
[6] For full details of Ms. Greenhouse's allegations, see the memorandum from Michael Kohn, Stephen Kohn, and David Colapinto to Les Brownlee, Office of the Acting Secretary of the Army, October 21, 2014. www.documentcloud.org/documents/239357-attorney-letter.html.
[7] Bryan Bender, "Study finds cronyism in Iraq, Afghanistan contracts," *Boston Globe*, October 31, 2003. See also Center for Public Integrity, "Winning contractors," October 30, 2003. www.publicintegrity.org/2003/10/30/5628/winning-contractors.

Michael Long and colleagues have shown that past campaign contributions are significant predictors of a potential company securing a postwar contract. Moreover, companies that secured a contract in Iraq or Afghanistan were then significantly more likely to donate substantially to the GOP in the next electoral cycle than those who did not receive a contract.[8] Political and ideological imperatives, not the pursuit of maximum efficiency, appear to best explain patterns and abuses in Iraq War contracting.

Thus, across the gamut of issue areas, policy outcomes are routinely skewed by presidential particularistic forces. But have presidents always faced such strong incentives to prioritize the needs and wants of some Americans over others? Or is presidential particularism a more recent phenomenon?

7.1 The Past and Future of Presidential Particularism

Most of the data sources we used to demonstrate the influence of particularistic forces reach back only to the 1980s. As a result, in many instances we lack directly comparable data to assess the relative weight of particularistic factors today versus in earlier eras of American history. However, returning to the mechanisms generating electoral, partisan, and coalitional particularism, there are reasons to think that each incentive may be stronger for contemporary presidents than for their predecessors.

7.1.1 *Reforming the Electoral College*
The institutional foundations of presidential particularism – the Electoral College and widespread adoption of unit rule apportionment of electors – did not emerge from the Constitution fully formed like Athena from the head of Zeus. Rather, they emerged and were shaped slowly by political and social forces of the times. By 1832 all but one state allowed the popular election of presidential electors. Most dramatic for our study was the development of the all-or-nothing allocation of electoral votes, which was not part of the "warp and woof" of the U.S. Constitution,

---

[8] Michael Long, Michael Hogan, Paul Stretesky, and Michael Lynch. 2007. "The relationship between postwar reconstruction contracts and political donations: The case in Afghanistan and Iraq." *Sociological Spectrum* 27: 453–472. Michael Hogan, Michael Long, Paul Stretesky, and Michael Lynch. 2006. "Campaign contributions, post-war reconstruction contracts, and state crime." *Deviant Behavior*, 27: 269–297.

but rather the result of a series of decisions by states that evolved over decades.[9]

However, there are strong reasons to believe that the pressures presidents face to engage in particularism in pursuit of electoral rewards have increased significantly in recent decades. Consider presidential elections from Truman through Obama. Before Bill Clinton's election in 1992, the winner of post-World War II presidential elections averaged a margin of more than 300 votes in the Electoral College. For example, Ronald Reagan won 91 percent of the electoral votes in 1980 and increased that margin to 98 percent in 1984. Political pundits and analysts still divided states into battleground and non-battleground states, but the winners of presidential contests routinely emerged victorious in wide swaths of the country. Between 1992 and 2012, however, the average Electoral College margin of victory shrunk significantly to 130 votes, with two elections in that span decided by fewer than 40 electoral votes.[10]

This development reflects the larger growth of polarization in the country writ large. Much has been written on the emergence of red and blue America. However, what is often overlooked is that in such an environment, the importance of swing state voters – and catering to their interests – has been magnified significantly. In 1960, John Kennedy became, in the assessment of many analysts, the first candidate to focus intently on swing states. Vice President Nixon, by contrast, employed a more traditional fifty-state strategy.[11] Modern presidential candidates focus on courting swing state voters. Technological advances in diverse fields from polling to social media have allowed candidates to identify pockets of potentially pivotal voters and microtarget their messaging more than ever before. As a result, contemporary presidents may have even greater incentives to pursue particularistic policies for electoral gain than did their predecessors.[12]

---

[9] Dougherty (1906, 11). Dougherty further details the extent to which constitutional scholars mostly ignored the method of allocation of electors throughout the nineteenth century.

[10] The average margin of victory in the popular vote has also decreased significantly, from more than 10 percent in elections from 1948 through 1988 to less than 5 percent in elections from 1992 through 2012.

[11] Robert Dallek. 2003. *An Unfinished Life: John F. Kennedy, 1917–1963*. Boston: Little, Brown and Company, p. 295.

[12] We note that there were previous eras in American politics that saw competitive presidential elections where swing states determined which party would hold the presidency. Several works document the policy effects as a result of presidential behavior in this competitive Electoral College environment (James, 2000; James and Lawson, 1999).

While scholars debate the extent to which there really is a "red" and "blue" America, there is little prospect that the number of swing states will increase in the near future. As a result, the incentives for swing state targeting should remain strong. The only way to change such incentives would be to reform the Electoral College system. Of course, not even the fiasco of the 2000 election resulted in any serious action to amend the Constitution or reform the Electoral College. The barriers to ratification of a constitutional amendment are simply too high. Instead, perhaps the most viable option is the National Popular Vote bill, which endeavors to change the system not through the constitutional amendment process but through direct action in state legislatures. The Constitution grants states complete freedom in deciding how to allocate their electoral votes. All but two states currently embrace the unit rule, in which all of the state's electors are awarded to the winner of the state's popular vote tally. The National Popular Vote bill, if enacted by enough states, would bind states that adopt the bill to award their electors not to the candidate that won a plurality of votes within the state but to the victor in the national popular vote tally. As of early 2015, ten states and the District of Columbia, representing 165 electoral votes, have adopted the reform, and the bill has passed at least one chamber of the state legislatures in another eleven states.[13]

Proponents of the National Popular Vote system emphasize the Electoral College's affront to the principle of one person, one vote articulated by the Supreme Court in *Baker v. Carr* (1962). In his preface to *Every Vote Equal*, a plan put forth by a nonprofit group arguing for a national popular vote, former Indiana Senator Birch Bayh argues: "In the United States every vote must count equally. One person, one vote is more than a clever phrase, it's the cornerstone of justice and equality. We can and must see that our electoral system awards victory to the candidates chosen by the most voters."[14] In this altered electoral environment, candidates would no longer concentrate their energies solely on a handful of swing states while largely ignoring voters in other states, including some of our most populous states such as California, Texas, and New York. Rather, candidates would be forced to battle for every vote, regardless of where in the country the person lives.

Yet, the consequences of such a reform could extend far beyond changing the way that candidates campaign for the presidency. Our theory and

[13] http://www.nationalpopularvote.com/map.php, accessed January 8, 2015.
[14] Koza et al. (2013, xxxi).

evidence suggest that it could also fundamentally influence presidential policymaking. Ironically, the Electoral College, an institution created by the Founders in large part to promote geographic equality, has became a major source of geographic *inequality* as presidents have systematically pursued a range of policies designed to disproportionately benefit voters in swing states, particularly in election years. Under the National Popular Vote system, this incentive would disappear.

But would another form of electoral targeting rise up to take its place? Under a popular vote system, presidents could possess incentives to target more federal resources to urban constituencies where there are the greatest concentrations of voters. This might lead to a significant shift in how federal resources are allocated. However, rather than leading to skewed outcomes, such a shift may simply rebalance a system that currently favors rural constituencies. For example, analyses of data from 1981 through 2005 conducted by the Tax Foundation show rural states consistently receiving significantly more in federal benefits than they contribute in federal taxation and more heavily urbanized states receiving less than they pay in taxes.[15] Like almost all reforms, a move to the National Popular Vote would generate some unintended consequences with important implications for public policymaking. However, absent some overhaul of the Electoral College system, the imperative to target federal resources to swing states is likely to remain an important source of politically induced inequality for years to come.

7.1.2 *Polarization and Presidential Particularism*

When most scholars talk about partisan polarization in contemporary Washington, they focus first and foremost on Congress. Perhaps the most ubiquitous illustration of partisan polarization is a graph compiled by Nolan McCarty, Keith Poole, and Howard Rosenthal showing the steadily widening ideological gap between the average Democrat and average Republican in Congress over the past three decades.[16] What has received less attention, however, is how partisan polarization has also given rise to a polarized presidency.[17]

For some Americans, President Barack Obama appears to be a hyperpartisan, whereas for others he is not partisan enough. For his idealistic

---

[15] Tax Foundation Special Report No. 158. "Federal tax burdens and spending by state." http://taxfoundation.org/article/federal-taxes-paid-vs-federal-spending-received-state-1981-2005.

[16] McCarty et al. (2006, 36).

[17] Cameron (2002).

early followers, Obama has failed to follow through on his promise to provide "post-partisan" leadership and to rise above traditional partisan cleavages. To other Democrats, the president has often appeared weak and indecisive, incapable of marshaling the strength and resolve needed to overcome Republican intransigence. Sidney Milkis and colleagues have argued that Obama's failings are not entirely or even primarily personal. Rather, they can better be understood as an inevitable by-product of trying to balance two competing approaches to presidential leadership. The first, which dominated the era of Franklin Roosevelt, Dwight Eisenhower, and Lyndon Johnson, emphasizes almost "nonpartisan administration of the welfare and national security states." The second, and more contemporary paradigm all but demands that presidents be partisan leaders willing to battle tirelessly to enact the party's program.[18] Nicely capturing the partisan pressures presidents face, Marty Cohen and colleagues have argued that "the American people may want a president who will rise above party and govern as the president of the whole nation. Parties, however do not."[19]

In an era of intensifying partisan polarization, the ties between presidents and their political parties have strengthened to the extent that parties have become almost executive-centered in orientation. Presidents sit at the top of a national partisan apparatus and are almost universally expected to be strong party leaders. In such an environment, the incentives to pursue partisan goals and policy objectives have become paramount.[20]

As a result, the same partisan polarization that has bifurcated Congress into warring partisan camps, bringing business in the legislature to a veritable halt in the process, has encouraged presidents to embrace overtly partisan policy postures. As presidents have increasingly assumed responsibility for building and leading a national partisan organization, the incentives to target the benefits of federal policies to their core partisan base have grown exponentially. This is not to say that past presidents never sought to reward core constituencies. Indeed, in the era of patronage (also a period of intense partisan polarization), participating in the spoils system and showering core supporters with material rewards was part and parcel of politics. And even in the more recent past, presidents

---

[18] Milkis and Rhodes (2007); Milkis et al. (2012).

[19] Cohen et al. (2008, 87).

[20] Galvin (2009) shows that presidents, particularly Republican presidents, played important roles as party leaders in earlier eras. However, Galvin (2013) notes that the overt partisanship of George W. Bush was enabled by the increasingly partisan era in which he acted.

have pursued policies that reward base supporters at the expense of groups that reliably back the opposition. However, in the contemporary era when partisan leadership is all but demanded of our nation's chief executives, such incentives are as strong as they have been since the late nineteenth and early twentieth centuries.

The rising tide of polarization may also have intensified the incentives for co-partisan targeting – what we have labeled coalitional particularism – by forcing presidents to rely increasingly on the ranks of their co-partisans to enact their legislative agendas. In his landmark study of legislative productivity from 1946 through 1990, David Mayhew found little evidence that Congress passed more significant legislation in periods where the same party controlled both chambers of Congress and the presidency than during divided government.[21] However, for much of this period, presidents found a substantial number of potential coalition partners on both sides of the partisan aisle. Lyndon Johnson worked with Everett Dirksen to pass the Civil Rights Act of 1964. In the early 1980s, Ronald Reagan successfully courted conservative Boll Weevil Democrats to support major tax cuts and increases in defense spending. For much of the post–World War II era, there were a significant number of what Richard Fleisher and Jon Bond labeled "cross-pressured" members of Congress: members of one party who were ideologically closer to the center of the other party than to their own. However, beginning in the 1980s and accelerating in the 1990s, the number of centrist, cross-pressured members began to decline dramatically.[22] In tandem, party unity votes – those on which a majority of voting Republicans oppose a majority of voting Democrats (and vice versa) – have soared in recent decades.[23]

As a result, presidents are forced to rely on their fellow partisans more than ever before to advance their legislative agendas on the Hill. Indeed, according to research by Frances Lee, public presidential involvement in an issue in and of itself leads to higher levels of partisan polarization, minimizing the president's prospects of successfully reaching across the aisle.[24] Absent major changes, this reliance will persist for the foreseeable future. In such a setting, pursuing policies that concentrate benefits among constituencies that elect co-partisans and withhold benefits among those that vote for the opposition in House races will remain a sound presidential strategy.

---

[21] Mayhew (2005).
[22] Fleisher and Bond (2004).
[23] Davidson et al. (2013, 256–257).
[24] Lee (2009).

7.2 The Dangers of Delegation

In Chapter 1, we identify numerous commentators who have called for increased delegation of policymaking power to the executive branch as a means to cut through our dysfunctional political process. This growing chorus makes many cogent arguments. However, after surveying the copious evidence for dramatic presidentially induced inequalities in policy outcomes, we offer a strong cautionary note. The contemporary Congress often seems wrought with paralysis, stymied by arcane legislative procedures, intransigent minorities, and partisan and parochial bickering. Contrasted with institutional failure on Capitol Hill, the energy and dispatch of a unitary executive who responds to the needs of a national constituency holds obvious appeal. If only it were so. Too often, presidents pursue policy outcomes that are in their individual political interests, not those of the nation as a whole.

In the cases of trade policy and disaster declarations, Congress delegated unilateral authority to the president to grant or refuse requests for protectionist measures or to issue natural disaster declarations precisely in the hopes of removing parochial political impulses from the equation. However, rather than acting solely on objective economic criteria, in both realms presidents have used their unilateral power to pursue their interests, as opposed to those of powerful members of Congress. Congressional parochialism has been replaced with presidential particularism.

For decades, students of Congress have noted the institution's negligence of bureaucratic oversight. James Pearson sums up this perspective: "Oversight is a vital yet neglected congressional function."[25] A now-textbook response to this concern is that congressional oversight is effective in that Congress does nothing until a "fire alarm" is sounded. In their study of congressional oversight, Mathew D. McCubbins and Thomas Schwartz argue, "[i]nstead of sniffing for fires, Congress places fire-alarm boxes on street corners, builds neighborhood fire houses, and sometimes dispatches its own hook-and-ladder in response to an alarm."[26] In some respects, the fire alarm method is an effective protection in the cases we examine. For instance, when the executive branch pursued base closings with such partisan vengeance in 1990, the fire alarm eventually sounded, and the process was altered. Yet, in the overall picture of federal spending, there is no fire alarm. The presidential influence is on the marginal

---

[25] Pearson (1975, 288) quoted in McCubbins and Schwartz (1984).
[26] McCubbins and Schwartz (1984, 166).

dollar. As we described in Chapter 2, presidents place their thumb on the scale, which has the effect of diverting billions of federal taxpayer dollars. As Congress delegates power to the executive branch, members of Congress are slowly giving weight to presidential prerogatives in the division of resources across the nation.

One of the most uncomfortable virtues of the U.S. Constitution is that it encourages gridlock. Power is dispersed through nearly ninety thousand units of government at different levels and within the different branches of government.[27] Such are the checks and balances of the U.S. political system. When Congress eschews this feature by delegating authority to the president, it acts at its own peril. Members of Congress have to fight among themselves for resources in a context where their voting power influences the amount they can procure.[28] Yet, if the president acts, he exercises his prerogatives without competing against hundreds of other agents vying to implement the preferences of their respective principals. While some would urge Congress to delegate powers to the executive allowing for equitable outcomes without political rancor, we argue that this perspective misconstrues the incentives of presidents.

Few would argue that contemporary Washington is not broken. Real leadership is needed, both in the White House and on Capitol Hill, to make our government function to address the vexing new challenges of the twenty-first century. Simply delegating power to the executive and hoping for the best is not a viable solution.

7.3 The President's Opposition

The evidence of rampant American particularism that we have amassed across policy areas also has important implications for how citizens and scholars think about presidential systems writ large. Throughout the book, we focus on the windfalls produced by particularism enjoyed by voters lucky enough to find themselves living in communities in battleground or core states. But we can recast this finding by considering the millions of Americans who receive fewer federal tax dollars for schools, highways, hospitals, or other infrastructure simply because of the electoral characteristics of the states in which they live. Americans in these communities suffer the collateral damage of presidential particularism,

[27] www.census.gov/compendia/statab/2012/tables/12s0428.pdf.
[28] On the relationship between legislative voting and distributive outcomes, see, for example, Ansolabehere et al. (2002, 2003).

ranging from grants for airport improvements that are awarded instead to a different jurisdiction to the closure of a military base while similar installations across state lines remain open. Across policy areas, voters living in counties and states that consistently vote against the incumbent president's party are the biggest losers. They receive fewer dollars, their industries are less likely to receive protection from foreign competition, they are less likely to receive federal assistance when disasters strike, and they are more likely to see bases closures than are other constituencies.

Our findings echo Juan Linz's criticisms of presidential systems. Linz argues that the electorate's perception of the presidency is ultimately the underpinning of the institutional weakness of presidential systems:

> Perhaps the most important consequences of the direct relationship that exists between a president and the electorate are the sense the president may have of being the only elected representative of the whole people and the accompanying risk that he will tend to conflate his supporters with "the people" as a whole. The plebiscitarian component implicit in the president's authority is likely to make the obstacles and opposition he encounters seem particularly annoying. In his frustration he may be tempted to define his policies as reflections of the popular will and those of his opponents as the selfish designs of narrow interests. This identification of leader with people fosters a certain populism that may be a source of strength. It may also, however, bring on a refusal to acknowledge the limits of the mandate that even a majority – to say nothing of a mere plurality – can claim as democratic justification for the enactment of its agenda. The doleful potential for displays of cold indifference, disrespect, or even downright hostility toward the opposition is not to be scanted.[29]

In an ironic twist, this passage suggests that presidential systems – precisely because presidents see themselves as national representatives and their agendas as blessed by a national mandate – may be particularly apt to lead to policies that disadvantage groups in the political minority. The prospects of a tyranny of the majority is precisely what our Madisonian system of checks and balances was designed to guard against.

In a similar vein, writing almost thirty years ago, Theodore Lowi warned that the plebiscitary presidency and the myths about presidential governance it perpetuates encourage the erosion of our separation of powers system and the dangerous concentration of power in the executive.[30] The universalistic paradigm encourages Americans to think of

---

[29] Linz (1990, 61).

[30] This proceeds under liberal and conservative administrations alike. For example, in his critique of Reagan, Lowi argues that even as Reagan paid lip service to shrinking

presidents as representatives of the whole nation and to support the concentration of greater policymaking authority in their hands. In Lowi's assessment, this view has fueled the increasing delegation of power from Congress to the president with the result being an exponential growth in executive power. "A system dependent for its restraints on the persons who occupy the White House," Lowi admonished, "is a system without effective restraints at all."[31]

It is little wonder, then, that recent observers have decried the rise of a "new imperial presidency."[32] Lulled into a false sense of complacency and succored by a belief that expanded presidential authority will most often result in more nationally optimal, less parochial policy outcomes, Americans have largely stood by and watched with approval the transferral of power from one end of Pennsylvania Avenue to the other. Perhaps such shifts in the equilibrium of our governing system are inevitable. However, we should be aware of their potential costs. Presidents, like members of Congress, will frequently pursue policies that benefit politically important constituencies. Americans in core co-partisan constituencies and in those pivotal to the president's electoral prospects are systematically rewarded at the expense of others.

The paradigm of presidential universalism is pervasive. It persists throughout American history and, as observed by Juan Linz, it looms over other presidential political systems as well. In *The American Commonwealth*, his famous treatise on American politics, James Bryce wrote in 1888 that the president "has the weight of the people behind him. The people regard him as an indispensable check, not only upon the haste and heedlessness of their representatives, the faults which the framers of the constitution chiefly feared, but upon their tendency ... to yield either to pressure from any section of their constituents, or to temptations of a private nature."[33] Bryce also acknowledged the dangerous "one man power" of the presidency but quickly dispensed with this concern

government, his policies failed to do so, and if anything they expanded presidential power and influence. "But from the start, President Reagan's expressed desire to get the government off our backs was complete phony. All his domestic budget cuts were neutralized by the great increase in the defense budget; and since a large share of the defense budget is spent for ordinary old patronage politics – the pork barrel – this conservative president had plenty of discretionary resources with which to placate the wealthier oligarchs of his party" (Lowi, 1985, 158–159).

[31] Lowi (1985, 159).
[32] Rudalevige (2006); Savage (2007).
[33] Bryce (1924 [1888], 60).

because Congress could easily "checkmate him by stopping supplies."[34] The view of the presidency that Bryce describes persist today, but presidential power has grown immensely since the first administration of Grover Cleveland when Bryce wrote. Scholars, jurists, and legislators should be careful to examine critically the extent to which a president is equipped and incentivized to act in accordance with the preferences of the general public.

[34] Bryce (1924 [1888], 68).

Appendix A

Technical Appendix to Chapter 3

A.1 Swing States and the 1990 Cheney List

The statistical analysis in Chapter 3 focuses almost exclusively on when the first Bush administration used its control over the military base closure process in 1990 to try to concentrate the economic pain of closings in Democratic districts. Yet, presidents may also have strong incentives to try to protect swing states from base closures. To test this additional hypothesis, Table A.1 estimates the models presented in Table 3.1 with one additional variable: an indicator identifying whether a congressional district is located in a swing state. As we discuss in greater detail in Chapter 4, we define a swing state as one in which the losing candidate averaged 45 percent or more of the two-party vote over the preceding three presidential elections.

The coefficient for the swing state variable in the first column of Table A.1 is negative and statistically significant. All else being equal, a district in a swing state was significantly less likely to have a base identified for closure by Cheney and the Bush administration than was a district in a non-battleground state.[1] The coefficient for the swing state variable in the jobs-lost regression model is negative, as expected, though it is not statistically significant. Taken together, however, there is

---

[1] One concern is that California, which contained the greatest number of closures and was not a swing state in 1990, might be driving the results. To test this, we estimated the logistic regression in Table A.1 excluding California. Even after excluding California, the Democratic member coefficient is positive and significant, and the coefficient for being in a swing state is still negative and statistically significant. An outlier, California, is not skewing our results.

186

Appendix A

TABLE A.1. *Protecting Districts in Swing States – the 1990 Cheney List.*
Logistic and least squares regression models. Democratic districts were
disproportionately targeted for base closures and military and civilian job
losses, even after controlling for the number of bases in a district. However,
districts in swing states were protected from closures. Robust standard
errors are in parentheses.

	Closure	Jobs Lost
Democratic member	1.272	382.211
	(0.473)	(143.021)
Swing state	−1.240	−100.409
	(.562)	(196.755)
Military installations in district	0.247	139.342
	(0.084)	(75.498)
Constant	−3.485	−65.100
	(0.430)	(76.48)
Observations	435	435
R^2		0.029

considerable evidence that the Bush administration used its control over
base closures in 1990 to craft a list that would serve its electoral and
partisan goals.

A.2 Member Ideology and the 1990 Cheney List

In February 1990, Secretary of Defense Dick Cheney publicly defended
his list of proposed base closings from charges that he was playing politics
with the nation's defense apparatus. Cheney denied allegations that he
had sought to concentrate cuts in Democratic districts, particularly in
the districts of liberal Democrats.[2] In Chapter 3, we present a statistical
analysis showing that, even after controlling for the number of bases
in a district, Democratic districts were disproportionately targeted for
base closures. But were liberal Democrats in particular also targeted?
To explore this we estimated the logistic and linear regression models in
Table A.1 only for Democrats and with each member's first dimension
NOMINATE score as the independent variable of interest. NOMINATE
is a measure of member liberalism obtained from roll-call vote analysis. It

[2] Mike Mills, "Cheney's plan for shutdowns a new salvo in a long fight," *CQ Weekly*,
February 3, 1990, p. 340.

TABLE A.2. *Targeting Liberal Democrats – the 1990 Cheney List. Logistic and least squares regression models. Models limited to Democratic members with member ideology being the new independent variable of interest. Member ideology is defined such that positive values are conservative and negative values are liberal. Thus, districts represented by liberal Democrats had a higher probability of closure and sustained more job losses than districts represented by conservative Democrats. Robust standard errors are in parentheses.*

	Closure	Jobs Lost
Member ideology	−2.448	−2198.782
	(1.357)	(1224.661)
Swing state	−1.578	−308.316
	(.624)	(311.736)
Military installations in district	0.264	281.477
	(0.108)	(166.223)
Constant	−2.947	−437.029
	(0.547)	(402.897)
Observations	259	259
R^2		0.053

is coded between −1 and 1, with negative numbers on the first dimension indicating more liberal representatives. In 1990, the median Democrat had a NOMINATE score of −.318, and the most liberal Democrat had a NOMINATE score of −.751. Table A.2 presents the results.

In both models, the coefficient for member ideology is negative and statistically significant ($p < .10$, two-tailed test). Because first-dimension NOMINATE scores are coded such that negative numbers indicate greater liberalism, this means that districts represented by liberal Democrats were more likely to experience both a closure and to sustain greater job losses than were districts represented by conservative Democrats. This ideological component – something specifically denied by the Secretary of Defense – adds a further dimension to partisan particularism in base closings.

Appendix B

Technical Appendix to Chapter 4

B.1 Disasters: An Alternative Statistical Model

In Chapter 4, we consider the influence of presidential particularism on the dynamics of presidential disaster declarations. To this end, we analyze county-level disaster declarations from 1984 through 2008.[1] To test our hypotheses that presidents will disproportionately reward counties in swing and core states, we identified swing states as those in which the losing candidate averaged 45 percent or more of the two-party vote over the preceding three elections and core states as those in which the president's party averaged 55 percent or more of the two-party vote over the preceding three contests. We then constructed a logistic regression model analyzing the factors driving whether a county received one or more disaster declarations in a given year. In addition to considering whether a county was in a swing or core state, our model controlled for actual storm damage within the county in a given year based on data from Hazards and Vulnerability Research Institute (2009); the number of severe weather events in a county that year; and its per capita income, a measure of the county's capacity to address storm damage on its own.

While most counties received one or zero disaster declarations in a given year, some did receive more than one. As a robustness check, we therefore estimate a poisson regression model, which models the number of disaster declarations in each county in each year. Table B.1 presents the results, which are similar to those of the logistic regression models

[1] For election years, we include only disaster declarations made from January 1 to October 31.

TABLE B.I. *A Model of County-Level Presidential Disaster Declarations, 1984 to 2008, Poisson Regression Model. Robust standard errors are in parentheses.*

	(1)	(2)
Swing state	0.079	−0.017
	(0.024)	(0.025)
Core state	0.196	0.148
	(0.024)	(0.026)
Member of Congress from presidential party	0.140	0.139
	(0.015)	(0.015)
Swing state × Election year		0.427
		(0.042)
Core state × Election year		0.219
		(0.048)
Election year		−0.051
		(0.050)
Severe disaster events	0.058	0.059
	(0.005)	(0.005)
Disaster damage (logged 2005 dollars)	0.120	0.119
	(0.004)	(0.004)
Personal income (logged 2005 dollars)	−0.479	−0.455
	(0.125)	(0.126)
County population (logged, in millions)	−0.186	−0.223
	(0.149)	(0.149)
Observations	63,175	63,175
Number of counties	2,999	2,999

presented in Chapter 4. In the base model in Column 1, we find evidence of all three forms of presidential particularism: electoral, partisan, and coalitional. The coefficients for the swing state, core state, and co-partisan House member variables are all positive and statistically significant. The model in Column 2 again uses a series of interactions to explore whether swing and core state targeting varies with the electoral cycle. As in the logit models presented in Chapter 4, both swing and core state target-ing intensifies in election years. Indeed, swing state targeting occurs only in election years, when the electoral bang for the buck is greatest. The results suggest that presidents always disproportionately respond to dis-asters occurring in counties within core states with disaster declarations; the coefficient for the main effect is positive and statistically significant. However, counties in core states are even more likely to receive disas-ter declarations, controlling for objective need, in election years. The coefficient on this interactions variable is also positive and statistically significant.

B.2 Transportation Grants

Chapter 4 continues by shifting focus from disaster declarations, a policy venue where presidents have unilateral authority over distributive politics, to a policy area where presidents must compete for influence with members of Congress: transportation grants. In the chapter, we find strong evidence of electoral and coalitional particularism: The coefficients for the swing state and co-partisan House member variables were positive and statistically significant. We also find modest evidence of partisan particularism in the allocation of transportation grants: the coefficient for the core state variable was positive, although it failed to meet conventional levels of statistical significance.

B.2.1 *Alternative Measures of Competitiveness and Presidential Party Strength*

As an initial robustness check on our results, we first estimate our models using an alternative operationalization of whether a state is a swing state or core state. In Chapter 4, we employ a binary measure of whether or not a state is a swing state. States in which the losing candidate averaged 45 percent or more of the two-party vote over the preceding three elections are competitive swing states; states in which the losing candidate averaged less than this threshold are not competitive. We argue that such a metric best reflects how campaigns view states: either as battleground or not. Alternatively, we can employ a continuous measure of how competitive a state is: the simple average of the losing candidate's share of the two-party vote over the last three contests. As this variable increases, so does a state's competitiveness. Similarly, rather than employing a binary indicator for whether a state is a core state, we can use the continuous measure (theoretically ranging from 0 to 100) of the average share of the two-party vote won in a state by the president's party over the past three contests. Table B.2 estimates our statistical model using these continuous measures of a state's electoral competitiveness and how strongly aligned it is with the president's party (i.e., how "core" it is). The model specification is otherwise identical to that presented in the chapter.

The results are similar to those presented in the chapter. The biggest difference is that the coefficient for the continuous measure of core state

TABLE B.2. *Targeting of Transportation Grants to Counties – Continuous Measures of Swing and Core States. Dependent variable is logged Department of Transportation grants awarded to each county in a given year. Models also include both county and year fixed effects. Robust standard errors clustered on county are in parentheses.*

State electoral competitiveness	2.471
	(0.787)
Presidential party strength in state	1.283
	(0.307)
Member of Congress from presidential party	0.127
	(0.035)
Member of Congress from majority party	0.032
	(0.037)
Member of Transportation Committee	0.003
	(0.051)
Lane mileage (in 1000s)	0.007
	(0.002)
County population (logged)	−0.159
	(0.186)
Per capita income	0.000
	(0.008)
Unemployment rate	−0.018
	(0.011)
Constant	13.253
	(1.926)
Observations	76,930
R^2	0.040

targeting – presidential party strength in the state – is now positive and highly statistically significant. In this model we find strong empirical evidence of all three forms of presidential particularism.

As a final robustness check, we also employ another set of operationalizations for whether a state is a swing state or core state using data only from the most recent election, instead of an average of electoral performance over the preceding three contests. While these measures are more volatile to sudden swings and idiosyncratic forces, they provide an additional opportunity to assess the robustness of our results. Column 1 of Table B.3 estimates the model from Chapter 4 but includes swing and core state indicator variables based solely on election results in the last election. Column 2 of Table B.3 replicates the model from Table B.2 but with continuous measures of swing and core derived only from the most recent election. In both models, we continue to find strong and

TABLE B.3. *Targeting of Transportation Grants to Counties, Swing and Core Measures Using Only Last Election. Dependent variable is logged Department of Transportation grants awarded to each county in a given year. Binary (swing state; core state) and continuous (state electoral competitiveness; presidential party strength in state) measures of a state's electoral competitiveness and support for the president's party are based only on the most recent presidential election, rather than on the three preceding races. Models also include both county and year fixed effects. Robust standard errors clustered on county are in parentheses.*

	(1)	(2)
Swing state	0.228	
	(0.070)	
Core state	0.280	
	(0.066)	
State electoral competitiveness		2.292
		(0.665)
Presidential party strength in state		1.546
		(0.364)
Member of Congress from presidential party	0.132	0.133
	(0.035)	(0.035)
Member of Congress from majority party	0.037	0.036
	(0.037)	(0.037)
Member of Transportation Committee	−0.002	0.004
	(0.051)	(0.051)
Lane mileage (in 1000s)	0.008	0.008
	(0.002)	(0.002)
County population (logged)	−0.083	−0.118
	(0.183)	(0.183)
Per capita income	−0.001	−0.000
	(0.008)	(0.008)
Unemployment rate	−0.017	−0.016
	(0.011)	(0.011)
Constant	13.872	12.700
	(1.930)	(1.958)
Observations	76,930	76,930
R^2	0.040	0.040

statistically significant evidence of swing state, core state, and co-partisan House-member targeting.

B.2.2 *A Further Search for Congressional Influence*
In the model presented in Chapter 4, we find strikingly little evidence of congressional influence over the geographic allocation of transportation

TABLE B.4. *Targeting of Transportation Grants to Counties – Chair and Ranking Member Measures. Dependent variable is logged Department of Transportation grants awarded to each county in a given year. Models also include both county and year fixed effects. Counties represented by the chair or ranking member of the Transportation and Infrastructure Committee secure more transportation grants than other counties. Robust standard errors clustered on county are in parentheses.*

Swing state	0.152
	(0.054)
Core state	0.063
	(0.052)
Member of Congress from presidential party	0.146
	(0.036)
Member of Congress from majority party	0.013
	(0.039)
Member of Transportation Committee	0.025
	(0.053)
Chair of Transportation Committee	1.084
	(0.484)
Ranking minority member of Transportation Committee	0.426
	(0.224)
Lane mileage (in 1000s)	0.008
	(0.002)
County population (logged)	−0.038
	(0.193)
Per capita income	−0.004
	(0.009)
Unemployment rate	−0.016
	(0.011)
Constant	13.674
	(2.032)
Observations	73,768
R^2	0.041

dollars. Neither majority party members nor members of the Transportation and Infrastructure Committee appear to have secured disproportionate shares of federal transportation dollars, all else being equal. However, two members who might be particularly well positioned to secure transportation projects for their districts are the chair and ranking member of the committee. After all, it was Congressman Don Young's position as chair of the Transportation and Infrastructure Committee that enabled him to secure the millions needed for the infamous "Bridge to Nowhere." To probe further for signs of congressional influence, we estimate the model from the chapter with two new indicator variables identifying counties represented by either the chair of the Transportation and Infrastructure Committee or its ranking member. Table B.4 presents the results. We continue to find evidence of all three forms of presidential particularism; the coefficients are virtually unchanged from those observed in Chapter 4. However, in this revised model specification we do find evidence of focused congressional influence. While majority party members and members of the Transportation and Infrastructure Committee writ large appear unable to systematically secure larger shares of federal transportation dollars, the chair and ranking member of the committee have succeeded in channeling a disproportionate share of transportation grants to their districts.

Appendix C

Technical Appendix to Chapter 5

C.1 Measuring Federal Grants

We take the natural log of federal grants to construct our dependent variable to ensure that our results are not skewed by outlying values. At the county level, the variation in federal grant spending is extreme. For example, whereas the median county received roughly $40 million in federal grant spending in 2008, more than 160 counties received in excess of $500 million in grant spending that year. After taking the logarithmic transformation, our dependent variable is roughly normally distributed, as shown in Figure C.1.

C.2 Robustness Check: Counties and Congressional Districts

To account for Congress's influence over the budgetary process, we control for several characteristics of each county's representative in the House in our statistical models. Roughly 85 percent of counties in our data uniquely match into a single congressional district. When a county spanned multiple congressional districts, the models in Table 5.1 assign the county to the congressional district in which the greatest share of county residents live. However, to ensure that this approximation has not skewed our results, Table C.1 estimates the models from Table 5.1 for only those counties that matched uniquely into a single congressional district. Across all four specifications, the results are virtually identical to those presented in Table 5.1 when using all counties.

FIGURE C.1. Histogram of Logged County Federal Grant Totals, 1984–2008.

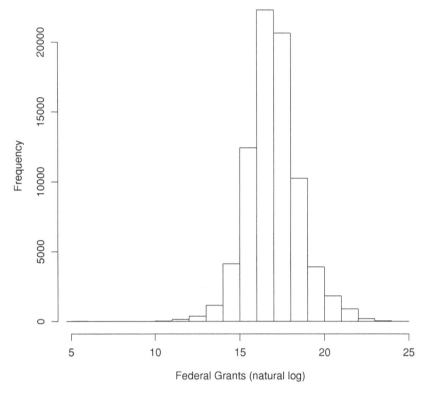

Federal Grants (natural log)

C.3 Robustness Check: Additional Controls

The models presented in Chapter 5 consider three main congressional variables highlighted in the existing literature as having the greatest potential impact on the geographic allocation of federal dollars across the country. However, other congressional variables could also affect the distribution of federal grant dollars. Accordingly, Table C.2 estimates the base model from Table 5.1 but with all of the control variables from the models in Berry et al. (2010).

First, in addition to accounting for whether a county was represented by a committee chair, we add a variable to capture whether a county's representative was a ranking minority member on any House committee. Members of the leadership structures of both parties may also possess an array of resources on which to draw to influence legislative outcomes, including the distribution of federal spending. To examine whether leaders are better able to channel federal dollars to their constituencies, we

TABLE C.1. *Federal Grant Spending and Presidential Particularism. A robustness check where we exclude counties that are not 100% matched to a single Congressional district. As in the main results, counties in swing states, core states, those represented in Congress by the president's party and the majority party see more federal grant spending than do other counties (Column 1). Swing states receive an additional increase in grant spending in presidential election years (Column 2) particularly when the incumbent president is seeking reelection (Column 3). Core counties in swing states and core states see larger increases in federal grant spending than do other counties in the same state (Column 4). Model is a least squares regression with fixed effects for county and year. Robust standard errors clustered on county are in parentheses.*

	(1)	(2)	(3)	(4)
Swing state	0.037	0.026	0.027	0.013
	(0.006)	(0.006)	(0.006)	(0.006)
Core state	0.067	0.066	0.067	0.034
	(0.006)	(0.007)	(0.006)	(0.008)
Swing state × Election year		0.042		
		(0.007)		
Core state × Election year		0.005		
		(0.008)		
Swing state × Reelection year			0.051	0.051
			(0.008)	(0.008)
Swing state × Successor election			0.028	0.028
			(0.008)	(0.008)
Core county				−0.013
				(0.008)
Core county × Swing state				0.039
				(0.010)
Core county × Core state				0.063
				(0.012)
Member of Congress from presidential party	0.018	0.017	0.017	0.012
	(0.004)	(0.004)	(0.004)	(0.004)
Member of Congress from majority party	0.023	0.023	0.023	0.023
	(0.004)	(0.004)	(0.004)	(0.004)
Member of Congress chair	−0.018	−0.019	−0.018	−0.029
	(0.011)	(0.011)	(0.011)	(0.010)
Member of Appropriations or Ways and Means	−0.011	−0.011	−0.011	−0.012
	(0.006)	(0.006)	(0.006)	(0.006)
County population (logged)	0.207	0.206	0.207	0.202
	(0.035)	(0.035)	(0.035)	(0.035)
Poverty rate	0.006	0.006	0.006	0.006
	(0.001)	(0.001)	(0.001)	(0.001)
Per capita income	0.006	0.006	0.006	0.006
	(0.002)	(0.002)	(0.002)	(0.002)
Constant	14.975	14.292	14.967	15.001
	(0.336)	(0.334)	(0.336)	(0.338)
Observations	67,713	67,713	67,713	67,072
R^2	0.601	0.601	0.601	0.603
Number of counties	2,920	2,920	2,920	2,891

TABLE C.2. *Federal Grant Spending and Presidential Particularism. A robustness check where additional congressional controls are included. These are the same controls used by Berry, Burden, and Howell (2010). As in the main results, counties in swing states, core states, those represented in Congress by the president's party and the majority party all see more federal grant spending than other counties. Model is a least squares regression with fixed effects for county and year. Robust standard errors clustered on county are in parentheses.*

	(1)
Swing state	0.037
	(0.005)
Core state	0.064
	(0.006)
Member of Congress from presidential party	0.014
	(0.004)
Member of Congress from majority party	0.025
	(0.004)
Member of Congress chair	−0.018
	(0.010)
Member of Appropriations or Ways and Means	−0.012
	(0.006)
Member of Congress ranking member	0.002
	(0.009)
Member of Congress leader	0.019
	(0.020)
Member of Congress Republican	0.031
	(0.005)
Member of Congress first term	0.017
	(0.003)
Member of Congress close race	0.014
	(0.006)
County population (logged)	0.229
	(0.031)
Poverty rate	0.005
	(0.001)
Per capita income	0.005
	(0.002)
Constant	14.947
	(0.301)
Observations	76,653
Number of counties	3,082
R^2	0.619

also include a variable indicating whether or not a county is represented by a member of either party's leadership.

Last, the model includes three additional controls. Because other scholars have argued that Democratic members are more likely to bring home federal benefits to their districts than are Republicans, we include an indicator variable identifying whether a county is represented by a Republican in the House.[1] Other scholarship suggests that new members, who lack the institutional clout of their more senior peers, may be at a disadvantage in the appropriations process. Accordingly, we include a variable indicating whether or not a county is represented by a first-term member of the House to examine whether such counties receive disproportionately less federal funding than others do. Third, prior research has argued that parties may seek to target funds toward their most electorally vulnerable members.[2] To account for this dynamic, our models include a variable identifying counties represented by members who narrowly won their last electoral contest (by 5 percent or less).

The results from the model in Table C.2, which includes the full range of control variables, are virtually identical to those in Table 5.1. We continue to find strong evidence of both swing and core state targeting. Consistent with prior scholarship, we find evidence that presidents also target federal grants to counties represented by congressional co-partisans; however, the effect is considerably smaller than swing or core state targeting.[3] Lastly, some of the coefficients for the congressional variables are statistically significant; for example, as in Table 5.1, we continue to find evidence that majority party members secure a larger share of federal grant dollars, on average, than do minority party members. However, the other coefficients cut against theoretical expectations drawn from existing literatures.

C.4 Robustness Check: Alternative Measures of Swing and Core

As a further robustness check, we estimate our base model from Table 5.1 using the continuous measures of state electoral competitiveness or the strength of the president's party in the state as described in Appendix B. Column 1 of Table C.3 includes just the state electoral competitiveness measure. Strongly consistent with our theory of electoral particularism,

[1] Alvarez and Saving (1997).
[2] Stein and Bickers (1995).
[3] Berry et al. (2010).

TABLE C.3. *Federal Grant Spending and Presidential Particularism – Continuous Measures of Swing and Core. A robustness check where continuous measures are used for competitiveness and core. State electoral competitiveness is measured as the average statewide vote share of the losing candidate averaged over the previous three presidential elections. Core is measured as incumbent party vote share averaged over the previous three elections. As in the main results, counties in swing states, core states, those represented in Congress by the president's party and the majority party all see more federal grant spending than other counties. Model is a least squares regression with fixed effects for county and year. Robust standard errors clustered on county are in parentheses.*

	(1)	(2)
State electoral competitiveness	0.776	1.020
	(0.103)	(0.103)
Incumbent party vote share in state		0.495
		(0.036)
Member of Congress from presidential party	0.025	0.017
	(0.004)	(0.004)
Member of Congress from majority party	0.023	0.023
	(0.004)	(0.004)
Member of Congress chair	−0.022	−0.021
	(0.010)	(0.010)
Member of Appropriations or Ways and Means	−0.005	−0.008
	(0.005)	(0.005)
County population (logged)	0.210	0.206
	(0.031)	(0.031)
Poverty rate	0.005	0.005
	(0.001)	(0.001)
Per capita income	0.005	0.005
	(0.002)	(0.002)
Constant	14.860	14.529
	(0.297)	(0.295)
Observations	76,937	76,937
R^2	0.618	0.620
Number of counties	3,082	3,082

the coefficient is positive and statistically significant. Column 2 adds the continuous measure of how "core" a state is: the strength of the president's party in the state over the past three elections. Even with these different operationalizations, we continue to find strong evidence of electoral and partisan targeting; both coefficients are positive and statistically significant.

TABLE C.4. *Federal Grant Spending and Presidential Particularism – Swing and Core Measures Using Only Last Election. A robustness check where binary and continuous measures of state competitiveness and partisanship are based solely on the results of the last election. As in the main results, counties in swing states, core states, those represented in Congress by the president's party and the majority party all see more federal grant spending than other counties. Model is a least squares regression with fixed effects for county and year. Robust standard errors clustered on county are in parentheses.*

	(1)	(2)
Swing state	0.064	
	(0.008)	
Core state	0.082	
	(0.008)	
State electoral competitiveness		0.340
		(0.080)
Presidential party strength in state		0.496
		(0.046)
Member of Congress from presidential party	0.021	0.019
	(0.004)	(0.004)
Member of Congress from majority party	0.025	0.025
	(0.004)	(0.004)
Member of Congress chair	−0.020	−0.021
	(0.010)	(0.010)
Member of Appropriations or Ways and Means	−0.010	−0.010
	(0.006)	(0.006)
County population (logged)	0.238	0.237
	(0.031)	(0.031)
Poverty rate	0.005	0.005
	(0.001)	(0.001)
Per capita income	0.004	0.004
	(0.002)	(0.002)
Constant	14.866	14.525
	(0.300)	(0.306)
Observations	76,937	76,937
Number of counties	3,082	3,082
R^2	0.619	0.619

As in Appendix B, we replicate our base targeting models for all grants using both binary and continuous measures of swing and core states based only on the results of the last election, rather than the average performance across the three preceding contests. Table C.4 presents the results. Across both specifications, we find strong evidence of swing state and core state targeting. The coefficients for the binary swing state and core state variables, as well as for the continuous state competitiveness and presidential party strength variables, are all positive and statistically significant. Thus, our results are robust to multiple operationalizations of whether a state is swing or core.

Appendix D

Technical Appendix to Chapter 6

D.1 Experimental Sample and Demographics

In March 2013, we recruited an online sample of 933 participants via Amazon's Mechanical Turk service. Summary statistics for the demographic characteristics of the experimental sample are presented in Table D.1. As documented in previous research on the external validity of conclusions made from MTurk samples, Democrats are somewhat overrepresented in the sample, and the sample is both younger and more educated than the general population as a whole. However, the sample did have considerable geographic diversity. Participants in our sample hailed from forty-nine of fifty states. Moreover, given the importance of geographical representation to our study emphasizing the importance of home state spending, we compare the percentages of our sample hailing from each state with that state's share of the U.S. population as a whole. The two series are almost perfectly correlated, $r > .90$. Recent research has demonstrated that experiments implemented on samples recruited in this way yield treatment effects very similar to those observed in experiments run with nationally representative samples (Berinsky et al., 2012).[1]

D.2 Robustness Checks on Experimental Results

Because participants were randomly assigned to either the control or one of the two experimental treatments, the simple differences in means

---

[1] For additional research validating the use of Mechanical Turk in the social sciences, see also Buhrmester et al. (2011); Kittur (2008); Mason and Suri (2012); Paolacci et al. (2010); Ross et al. (2010).

TABLE D.I. *Demographic Characteristics of Experimental Sample.*

	Mean	Standard Deviation
% Democrats (including leaners)	60	(49)
% Republicans (including leaners)	18	(39)
% Male	59	(49)
% College graduates	44	(50)
Median age	29	
Number of states represented	49	

are unbiased. However, as a robustness check, we also estimate multivariate models assessing the effects of our home state and non-home state spending treatments controlling for participants' demographic characteristics.

Table D.2 presents results from two logit models assessing the effects of the experimental treatments on participants' probability of supporting increased federal spending on transportation infrastructure. The model in Column 1 includes only two indicator variables identifying assignment

TABLE D.2. *Logit Models Assessing Effect of Spending Treatments on Support for More Federal Transportation Funding. Standard errors are in parentheses.*

	(1)	(2)
Home state spending	0.325	0.256
	(0.186)	(0.197)
Non-home state spending	−0.055	−0.197
	(0.175)	(0.188)
Democrat		1.114
		(0.193)
Republican		−0.569
		(0.219)
Female		−0.424
		(0.167)
Education		0.189
		(0.090)
Age		0.012
		(0.007)
Constant	0.925	−0.109
	(0.125)	(0.349)
Observations	933	926

TABLE D.3. *Least Squares Regression Models Assessing Effect of Spending Treatments on Feeling Thermometer Rating of President Obama. Standard errors are in parentheses.*

	(1)	(2)
Home state spending	8.022	4.878
	(2.403)	(1.815)
Non-home state spending	3.157	0.732
	(2.366)	(1.793)
Democrat		28.473
		(1.944)
Republican		−18.588
		(2.404)
Female		0.691
		(1.560)
Education		−0.565
		(0.855)
Age		−0.137
		(0.068)
Constant	60.270	51.691
	(1.670)	(3.440)
Observations	911	904
R^2	0.012	0.447

to either the home state or the non-home state spending treatments. The control group is the omitted baseline category. Consistent with expectations, the coefficient for the home state spending treatment is positive and statistically significant; learning of a federal transportation grant to a participant's home state increases his or her support for more federal transportation spending. By contrast, the coefficient for the non-home state spending treatment is negative and statistically insignificant. The model in Column 2 controls for each participant's partisanship, age, gender, and educational attainment. The coefficient in the home state spending treatment is again positive; the coefficient for the non-home state spending treatment is negative; a Wald test shows that the two are statistically different from one another, $p < .05$.

Table D.3 presents results from a pair of multiple regression models of the effects of the experimental treatments on participants' feeling thermometer ratings of President Obama. The model in Column 1 includes only two dummy variables identifying assignment to either the home state or non-home state spending treatments. The control group is the omitted baseline category. Consistent with expectations, the coefficient for the home state spending treatment is positive and statistically significant; learning of a federal transportation grant to a participant's home state significantly increases his or her rating of President Obama on the feeling thermometer. The coefficient for the non-home state spending treatment is also positive but smaller and statistically insignificant. The model in Column 2 controls for participants' partisanship, age, gender, and educational attainment. The coefficient in the home state spending treatment is again positive and statistically significant. The coefficient for the non-home state spending coefficient is also positive but statistically insignificant and substantively trivial. A Wald test shows that the coefficients for the home state and non-home state spending variables are statistically different from one another, $p < .05$.

One final potential concern is that the underrepresentation of Republicans in our sample may be leading us to overestimate the effect of the home state spending cue. If Republicans are not responsive to home state spending (either because they are ideologically opposed to it or because they simply refuse to reward President Obama for it), then our experiment may significantly overstate the effect of home state spending on public opinion. To address this concern, we estimated our analysis (both the simple difference in means and the regression models) for only Republican respondents. Importantly, learning of a grant to a Republican participant's home state significantly increased his or her feeling thermometer rating of President Obama ($p = .05$). Additionally, the coefficients for the home state and non-home state spending treatments in the support transportation spending model are significantly different from one another, ($p = .10$).

D.3 Localized Grant Spending and Electoral Outcomes

To assess the effect of federal grant spending on presidential electoral fortunes, we estimate a series of least squares models. As an initial inquiry, we begin by modeling the change in the incumbent party's vote share within a county solely as a function of the percentage change in federal grant spending within that county over the preceding year.[2] Because the

---

[2] As discussed previously, our use of change in grant spending in the last year is consistent with many studies that emphasize the influence of short-term economic changes on electoral outcomes. For example, the Abramowitz (2008) forecast model uses annualized

data are time series, cross-sectional, all models also include both county and year fixed effects and report standard errors clustered on the county.

The first column in Table D.4 presents the bivariate results for our base model of all counties in all presidential elections from 1988 to 2008. Consistent with our theory that voters will reward presidents for increases in federal largesse in their local communities, the coefficient for the change in federal grant spending in the county is positive and highly statistically significant.[3]

Given the long-documented retrospective tendencies of many American voters (inter alia Erikson, 1989; Fiorina, 1981; Hibbs, 1987), the model in Column 2 of Table D.4 also includes the percentage change in per capita personal income (in constant 2008 dollars), obtained from the Bureau of Economic Analysis, in each county during the year immediately preceding each election contest. The coefficient for increasing income levels is positive and statistically significant as expected, while the coefficient for federal spending also remains substantively large and statistically significant.

Column 3 of Table D.4 presents the expanded specification we report in Chapter 6. It includes a number of additional control variables to account for other factors, including campaign activity, that might also drive electoral outcomes. In this expanded model specification, we continue to find a strong and statistically significant positive relationship between federal spending and incumbent vote share. Moreover, the control variables all largely accord with theoretical expectations derived from past research. The greater the incumbent party candidate's campaign efforts in a state relative to the challenger, the stronger his electoral performance. President Bush and John McCain performed worse, *ceteris paribus*, in counties that had suffered greater numbers of casualties in the Iraq War in 2004 and 2008, respectively. Presidents also enjoyed greater electoral success in counties where their party's House candidate also enjoyed increasing electoral fortunes.

GDP growth rate in the second quarter of the election year, and the Lewis-Beck and Tien (2008) forecast model considers gross national product growth from the fourth quarter of the year before the election to the second quarter of the election year.

[3] To examine whether voters reward or punish presidents for increases or decreases in grant spending to different degrees, we also replicated all three model specifications in Table D.4 and disaggregated the change in grant spending measure into two variables capturing increases and decreases in grant spending in the county. In each specification, both coefficients were in the expected direction, of similar magnitudes, and statistically significant.

TABLE D.4. *The Effect of Federal Spending on Incumbent Presidential Vote Share, U.S. Counties, 1988 to 2008. Least squares model with fixed effects for counties and years. Dependent variable is the percent change in county-level vote for the incumbent president (or the incumbent party) since the previous presidential election. Increased grant spending leads to increased incumbent presidential vote share. Robust standard errors clustered on county are in parentheses.*

	(1)	(2)	(3)
% change in grants	0.860	0.773	0.707
	(0.117)	(0.119)	(0.119)
Change in per capita income (in 1,000s)		0.198	0.170
		(0.028)	(0.029)
Television ad difference			0.070
			(0.012)
Campaign appearance difference			0.210
			(0.018)
Change in presidential party house vote			0.012
			(0.003)
Iraq casualties in county, 2004			−0.487
			(0.125)
Iraq casualties in county, 2008			−0.269
			(0.075)
% change in county population			−0.366
			(1.209)
Constant	−6.426	−0.291	−2.716
	(0.077)	(0.077)	(0.144)
Observations	18,464	18,137	17,959
R^2	0.477	0.481	0.499

Last, we find no evidence that incumbent-party candidates are simply enjoying greater electoral success in counties that had experienced significant changes in population. A potential concern is that our finding of the relationship between federal grant spending and change in incumbent-party vote share may be driven exclusively by one of the six elections investigated. To alleviate such concerns, we follow a procedure similar to that employed by Berry et al. (2010, 795) and replicate our models, sequentially dropping one election at a time. In each case, the coefficient for change in grant spending is positive and statistically significant.

D.3.1 Robustness Check: Change in Logged Grant Spending

In Chapter 5, we model the forces driving the logged amount of federal grant spending received by a county in a given year. As a robustness

TABLE D.5. *The Effect of the Change in Logged Federal Spending and Electoral Competitiveness on Incumbent Presidential Vote Share, U.S. Counties, 1988 to 2008. Least squares model with fixed effects for counties and years. These models replicate the results from the chapter using the change in logged grants received by a county as the independent variable of interest, instead of the percentage change in grant spending in the county. The results are substantively identical to those presented in Chapter 6. Competitive states are those in which the losing candidate has averaged 45% or more of the two-party vote in the preceding three presidential elections. Counties in competitive states reward presidents for federal spending at higher levels than do counties in uncompetitive states. Robust standard errors clustered on county are in parentheses.*

	(1)	(2)
Change in Ln(grants)	0.572	
	(0.107)	
Change in Ln(grants) × Uncompetitive state		0.394
		(0.124)
Change in Ln(grants) × Competitive state		0.983
		(0.187)
Competitive state – within 5%		0.029
		(0.098)
Change in per capita income (in 1,000s)	0.175	0.173
	(0.027)	(0.027)
Television ad difference	0.069	0.068
	(0.011)	(0.011)
Campaign appearance difference	0.212	0.211
	(0.017)	(0.017)
Change in presidential party House vote	0.013	0.013
	(0.002)	(0.002)
Iraq casualties in county, 2004	−0.485	−0.483
	(0.114)	(0.113)
Iraq casualties in county, 2008	−0.274	−0.272
	(0.070)	(0.070)
% change in county population	−0.249	−0.413
	(1.083)	(1.085)
Constant	−2.605	−2.622
	(0.129)	(0.135)
Observations	18,135	18,135

check, we estimate the analyses presented in Chapter 6 using the change in the logged amount of federal grants a county receives over the year preceding the election as the independent variable of interest. Results are presented in Table D.5. As seen in Column 1, the coefficient for the

TABLE D.6. *The Electoral Consequences of the Change in Federal Grant Spending per Capita. These models replicate the results from Chapter 6 using the change in per capita grant spending in a county as the independent variable of interest, instead of the percentage change in grant spending in the county. The results are substantively identical to those presented in Chapter 6. Increased per capita grant spending in a county boosts the incumbent party's prospects in the next presidential election, particularly in counties from competitive states. Robust standard errors clustered on county are in parentheses.*

	(1)	(2)
Change in per capita grants	0.552	0.493
(in 1,000s)	(0.111)	(0.112)
Change in per capita grants ×		0.341
Uncompetitive state		(0.140)
Change in per capita grants ×		0.792
Competitive state		(0.168)
Change in per capita income	0.225	0.196
(in 1,000s)	(0.031)	(0.032)
Television ad difference	0.066	0.067
	(0.012)	(0.012)
Campaign appearance difference	0.214	0.212
	(0.019)	(0.019)
Change in presidential party House vote	0.013	0.013
	(0.003)	(0.003)
Iraq casualties in county, 2004	−0.485	−0.483
	(0.125)	(0.125)
Iraq casualties in county, 2008	−0.264	−0.263
	(0.074)	(0.074)
% change in county population	−0.291	−0.320
	(1.231)	(1.232)
Competitive state − within 5%		0.057
		(0.108)
Constant	−0.112	−0.305
Observations	17,976	17,976
R^2	0.479	0.481

change in logged grants in a county is positive and statistically significant. In Column 2, this variable is interacted with indicator variables to assess the effect of the change in logged grants on the president's vote share in both swing and non-battleground states. Both coefficients are positive and statistically significant; however, a Wald test shows that spending has a significantly greater effect on electoral outcomes in swing states than in non-swing states.

TABLE D.7. *Swing State Counties Secure Large Increases in Grant Spending, State Fixed Effects Model. The dependent variable identifies counties that received an 80% or greater increase in grant spending over the preceding year. Large, electorally significant increases in grant spending occur disproportionately in swing states during presidential election years. Model is a logistic regression with fixed effects for state and year.*

Swing state	0.078
	(0.059)
Swing state × Election year	0.288
	(0.089)
Core state	−0.023
	(0.058)
Member of Congress from presidential party	0.027
	(0.039)
Member of Congress from majority party	−0.006
	(0.042)
Member of Congress chair	0.353
	(0.081)
Member of Appropriations or Ways and Means	−0.123
	(0.047)
Per capita income	0.015
	(0.005)
Poverty rate	−0.044
	(0.004)
Ln Population	−0.527
	(0.024)
Observations	73,744

D.3.2 Robustness Check: Change in Per Capita Grant Spending

As an additional robustness check, Table D.6 replicates the models presented in the chapter using the change in per capita grants that a county receives as the independent variable of interest. Results are virtually identical to those presented in the chapter. Counties that experience an increase in per capita grant spending reward the president and his party at the ballot box; this is particularly true in counties located in swing states.[4]

D.3.3 Robustness Check: Major Increases in Grant Spending

Chapter 6 concludes with an analysis of which counties receive the large-scale infusions of grant spending (increases of 80 percent or more) that

[4] For a host of additional robustness checks, see Kriner and Reeves (2012) and its accompanying online appendix.

might have a significant impact on voting within the county. The model reported in Table 6.4 includes county fixed effects. This allows us to estimate a unique baseline for each county and therefore affords an important measure of control. However, including county fixed effects also requires us to drop all counties that never received an annual increase in grant spending of this magnitude from the analysis. An alternative strategy is to estimate the same model specification with state fixed effects instead of county fixed effects. The results, presented in Table D.7, are similar to those reported in the chapter. Most important, the coefficient for the Swing State × Election Year interaction is positive (virtually the same magnitude) and statistically significant. Counties in swing states in election years are the most likely to receive significant infusions of grant spending. This is strongly consistent with our theory of electoral particularism.

References

Abramowitz, Alan I. 2008. Forecasting the 2008 Presidential Election with the Time-for-Change Model. *PS: Political Science & Politics*, 41(4), 691–695.

Abrams, Burton A., and Butkiewicz, James L. 1995. The Influence of State-Level Economic Conditions on the 1992 U.S. Presidential Election. *Public Choice*, 85(1–2), 1–10.

Acemoglu, Daron, and Robinson, James A. 2006. *Economic Origins of Dictatorship and Democracy*. Cambridge, MA: MIT Press.

Achen, Christopher H., and Bartels, Larry M. 2004. Blind Retrospection: Electoral Responses to Drought, Flu, and Shark Attacks. Typescript.

Adler, E. Scott, and Lapinski, John S. 1997. Demand-Side Theory and Congressional Committee Composition: A Constituency Characteristics Approach. *American Journal of Political Science*, 41(3), 895–918.

Albouy, David. 2013. Partisan Representation in Congress and the Geographic Distribution of Federal Funds. *The Review of Economics and Statistics*, 95(1), 127–141.

Aldrich, John H. 1995. *Why Parties? The Origin and Transformation of Political Parties in America*. Chicago: University of Chicago Press.

Alesina, Alberto, Londregan, John, and Rosenthal, Howard. 1993. A Model of the Political Economy of the United States. *American Political Science Review*, 87(1), 12–33.

Alvarez, R. Michael, and Nagler, Jonathan. 1995. Economics, Issues and the Perot Candidacy: Voter Choice in the 1992 Presidential Election. *American Journal of Political Science*, 39(3), 714–744.

Alvarez, R. Michael, and Saving, Jason. 1997. Congressional Committees and the Political Economy of Federal Outlays. *Public Choice*, 92(1–2), 55–73.

Alvarez, R. Michael, and Schousen, Matthew M. 1993. Policy Moderation or Conflicting Expectations: Testing the International Models of Split-Ticket Voting. *American Politics Quarterly*, 21(4), 410–438.

Ansolabehere, Stephen, Gerber, Alan, and Snyder, James. 2002. Equal Votes, Equal Money: Court-Ordered Redistricting and Public Expenditures in the American States. *American Political Science Review*, 96(4), 767–778.

Ansolabehere, Stephen D., Snyder, Jr. James M., and Ting, Michael. 2003. Bargaining in Bicameral Legislatures: When and Why Does Malapportionment Matter? *American Political Science Review*, 97(3), 471–481.

Anzia, Sarah F., and Berry, Christopher R. 2011. The Jackie (and Jill) Robinson Effect: Why Do Congresswomen Outperform Congressmen? *American Journal of Political Science*, 55(3), 478–493.

Arceneaux, Kevin. 2006. The Federal Face of Voting: Are Elected Officials Held Accountable for the Functions Relevant to Their Office? *Political Psychology*, 27(5), 731–754.

Armey, Richard. 1988. Base Maneuvers. *Policy Review*, 43, 70–75.

Arnold, R. Douglas. 1979. *Congress and the Bureaucracy: A Theory of Influence*. New Haven, CT: Yale University Press.

Atlas, Cary M., Gilligan, Thomas W., Hendershott, Robert J., and Zupan, Mark A. 1995. Slicing the Federal Government Net Spending Pie: Who Wins, Who Loses, and Why. *American Economic Review*, 85(3), 624–629.

Balla, Steven J., Lawrence, Eric D., Maltzman, Forrest, and Sigelman, Lee. 2002. Partisanship, Blame Avoidance, and the Distribution of Legislative Pork. *American Journal of Political Science*, 46(3), 515–525.

Banzhaff, III, John F. 1968. One Man, 3.312 Votes: A Mathematical Analysis of the Electoral College. *Villanova Law Review*, 13(Winter), 303–332.

Baron, David P., and Ferejohn, John A. 1989. Bargaining in Legislatures. *The American Political Science Review*, 83(4), 1181–1206.

Barrett, Andrew W., and Eshbaugh-Soha, Matthew. 2007. Presidential Success on the Substance of Legislation. *Political Research Quarterly*, 60(1), 100–112.

Bartels, Larry M. 1985. Resource Allocation in a Presidential Campaign. *Journal of Politics*, 47(3), 928–936.

Bartels, Larry M. 1991. Constituency Opinion and Congressional Policy Making: The Reagan Defense Build Up. *American Journal of Political Science*, 85(2).

Bartels, Larry M. 2008. *Unequal Democracy: The Political Economy of the New Gilded Age*. Princeton, NJ: Princeton University Press.

Bartels, Larry M., and Zaller, John. 2001. Presidential Vote Models: A Recount. *PS: Political Science & Politics*, 34(1), 9–20.

Baum, Matthew A., and Kernell, Samuel. 1999. Has Cable Ended the Golden Age of Presidential Television? *American Political Science Review*, 93(1), 99–114.

Beaulier, Scott A., Hall, Joshua C., and Lynch, Allen K. 2011. The Impact of Political Factors on Military Base Closures. *Journal of Economic Policy Reform*, 14(4), 333–342.

Beckman, Matthew N. 2010. *Pushing the Agenda: Presidential Leadership in U.S. Lawmaking 1953–2004*. New York: Cambridge University Press.

Behr, Roy L., and Iyengar, Shanto. 1985. Television News, Real-World Cues, and Changes in the Public Agenda. *Public Opinion Quarterly*, 49(1), 38–57.

Berdahl, Clarence A. 1949. Presidential Selection and Democratic Government. *Journal of Politics*, 11(1), 14–41.

Berinsky, Adam J. 2007. Assuming the Costs of War: Events, Elites, and American Public Support for Military Conflict. *Journal of Politics*, 69(4), 975–997.

Berinsky, Adam J., Huber, Gregory A., and Lenz, Gabriel S. 2012. Evaluating Online Labor Markets for Experimental Research: Amazon.com's Mechanical Turk. *Political Analysis*, 20(3), 351–368.

Berry, Christopher R., Burden, Barry C., and Howell, William G. 2010. The President and the Distribution of Federal Spending. *American Political Science Review*, 104(4), 783–799.

Berry, Christopher R., and Gersen, Jacob E. 2010. Agency Design and Distributive Politics. *John Olin Law and Economics Working Paper No. 539.*

Bertelli, Anthony M., and Grose, Christian R. 2009. Secretaries of Pork? A New Theory of Distributive Public Policy. *Journal of Politics*, 71(3), 926–945.

Bickers, Kenneth N., and Stein, Robert M. 1996. The Electoral Dynamics of the Federal Pork Barrel. *American Journal of Political Science*, 40(4), 1300–1326.

Bickers, Kenneth N., and Stein, Robert M. 2000. The Congressional Pork Barrel in a Republican Era. *Journal of Politics*, 62(4), 1070–1086.

Bond, Jon R., and Fleisher, Richard. 1990. *The President in the Legislative Arena*. Chicago: University of Chicago Press.

Bond, Jon R., and Fleisher, Richard. 2000. *Polarized Politics*. Washington, DC: CQ Press.

Bond, Jon R., Fleisher, Richard, and Wood, B. Dan. 2003. The Marginal and Time-Varying Effect of Public Approval on Presidential Success in Congress. *Journal of Politics*, 65(1), 92–110.

Bond, Jon R., and Smith, Kevin B. 2008. *The Promise and Performance of American Democracy*. 8th edn. New York: Thomson-Wadsworth.

Bonica, Adam, Chen, Jowei, and Johnson, Tim. 2012. Estimating the Political Ideologies of Appointed Public Bureaucrats: An Application to the Senate Confirmation of Presidential Nominees. Presented at the Annual Meeting of the Society for Political Methodology, Chapel Hill, NC.

Books, John, and Prysby, Charles. 1999. Contextual Effects on Retrospective Economic Evaluations the Impact of the State and Local Economy. *Political Behavior*, 21(1), 1–16.

Brams, Steven J., and Davis, Morton D. 1974. The 3/2's Rule in Presidential Campaigning. *American Political Science Review*, 68(1), 113–134.

Bryce, James. 1924 [1888]. *The American Commonwealth*. Vol. 1. New York: The MacMillan Co.

Buhrmester, Michael, Kwang, Tracy, and Gosling, Samuel D. 2011. Amazon's Mechanical Turk: A New Source of Inexpensive, Yet High-Quality Data? *Perspectives on Psychological Science*, 6(1), 3–5.

Busch, Marc L., and Reinhardt, Eric. 2005. Industrial Location and Voter Participation in Europe. *British Journal of Political Science*, 35(4), 713–730.

Calabresi, Steven G. 1995. Some Normative Arguments for the Unitary Executive. *Arkansas Law Review*, 48(1), 23–104.

Cameron, Charles M. 2000. *Veto Bargaining: Presidents and the Politics of Negative Power*. Cambridge: Cambridge University Press.

Cameron, Charles. 2002. Studying the Polarized Presidency. *Presidential Studies Quarterly*, 32(4), 647–663.

Campbell, Andrea, Cox, Gary W., and McCubbins, Mathew D. 2002. Agenda Power in the U.S. Senate, 1877 to 1986, in *Party, Process, and Political Change in Congress: New Perspectives on the History of Congress*, eds. David Brady and Mathew D. McCubbins. Stanford, CA: Stanford University Press.

Canes-Wrone, Brandice. 2006. *Who Leads Whom? Presidents, Policy, and the Public*. Chicago: University of Chicago Press.

Canes-Wrone, Brandice, and De Marchi, Scott. 2002. Presidential Approval and Legislative Success. *Journal of Politics*, **64**(2), 491–509.

Caro, Robert A. 2012. *The Passage of Power: The Years of Lyndon Johnson*. New York: Alfred A. Knopf.

Carpenter, Daniel P. 2001. *The Forging of Bureaucratic Autonomy: Reputations, Networks, and Policy Innovation in Executive Agencies, 1862–1928*. Princeton, NJ: Princeton University Press.

Charnovitz, Steve, and Hoekman, Bernard. 2013. US-Tyres: Upholding a WTO Accession Contract – Imposing Pain for Little Gain. *World Trade Review*, **12**(2), 273–296.

Chen, Jowei. 2013. Voter Partisanship and the Effect of Distributive Spending on Political Participation. *American Journal of Political Science*, **57**(1), 200–217.

Clarke, Harold D., and Stewart, Marianne C. 1994. Prospections, Retrospections, and Rationality: The "Bankers" Model of Presidential Approval Reconsidered. *American Journal of Political Science*, **38**(4), 1104–1123.

Clinton, Bill. 2004. *My Life*. New York: Alfred A. Knopf.

Cohen, Jeffrey E. 2006. The Polls: The Coalitional President from a Public Opinion Perspective. *Presidential Studies Quarterly*, **36**(3), 541–550.

Cohen, Jeffrey E. 2010. *Going Local: Presidential Leadership in the Post-Broadcast Age*. New York: Cambridge University Press.

Cohen, Jeffrey E., and Nice, David. 2003. *The Presidency*. New York: McGraw Hill.

Cohen, Marty, Karol, David, Noel, Hans, and Zaller, John. 2008. *The Party Decides: Presidential Nominations before and after Reform*. Chicago: University of Chicago Press.

Conover, Pamela Johnston, Feldman, Stanley, and Knight, Kathleen. 1986. Judging Inflation and Unemployment: The Origins of Retrospective Evaluations. *Journal of Politics*, **48**(3), 565–588.

Conover, Pamela Johnston, Feldman, Stanley, and Knight, Kathleen. 1987. The Personal and Political Underpinnings of Economic Forecasts. *American Journal of Political Science*, **31**(3), 559–583.

Cox, Gary W. 2010. Swing Voters, Core Voters, and Distributive Politics, in *Political Representation*, eds. Ian Shapiro, Susan C. Stokes, Elisabeth Jean Wood, and Alexander S. Kirshner. New York: Cambridge University Press.

Cox, Gary W., and McCubbins, Mathew D. 1986. Electoral Politics as a Redistributive Game. *Journal of Politics*, **48**(2), 370–389.

Cox, Gary W., and McCubbins, Mathew D. 1993. *Legislative Leviathan: Party Government in the House*. Berkeley: University of California Press.

Cox, Gary W., and McCubbins, Mathew D. 2007. *Setting the Agenda: Responsible Party Government in the U.S. House of Representatives*. New York: Cambridge University Press.

Cronin, Thomas E., and Genovese, Michael A. 2004. *Paradoxes of the American Presidency*. 2nd edn. New York: Oxford University Press.

Dahl, Robert A. 2001. *How Democratic is the American Constitution?* New Haven, CT: Yale University Press.

Dallek, Robert. 2003. *An Unfinished Life: John F. Kennedy, 1917–1963*. Boston: Little, Brown and Company.

Daniels, R. Steven. 2013. The Rise of Politics and the Decline of Vulnerability as Criteria in Disaster Decisions of the United States, 1953–2009. *Disasters*, 37(4), 669–694.

Davidson, Roger, Oleszek, Walter, Lee, Frances, and Schickler, Eric. 2013. *Congress and Its Members*. 14th edn. Washington, DC: CQ Press.

Deering, Christopher J., and Smith, Steven S. 1997. *Committees in Congress*. Washington, DC: CQ Press.

Delli Carpini, Michael X., and Keeter, Scott. 1996. *What Americans Know about Politics and Why It Matters*. New Haven, CT: Yale University Press.

Den Hartog, Chris, and Monroe, Nathan W. 2011. *Agenda Setting in the U.S. Senate: Costly Consideration and Majority Party Advantage*. New York: Cambridge University Press.

Destler, I. M. 2005. *American Trade Politics*. 4th edn. Washington, DC: Institute for International Economics.

Dickinson, Matthew J. 1999. *Bitter Harvest: FDR, Presidential Power and the Growth of the Presidential Branch*. Cambridge: Cambridge University Press.

Dickinson, Matthew J. 2005. The Executive Office of the President: The Paradox of Politicization, in *The Executive Branch*, eds. Joel Aberbach and Mark Peterson. New York: Oxford University Press.

Dougherty, J. Hampden. 1906. *The Electoral System of the United States*. New York: G.P. Putnam's Sons.

Dynes, Adam M., and Gregory A. Huber. 2015. Partisanship and the Allocation of Federal Spending: Do Same-Party Legislators or Voters Benefit from Shared Party Affiliation with the President and House Majority? *American Political Science Review*, 109(1), 172–186.

Edwards, III, George C. 1989. *At the Margins: Presidential Leadership of Congress*. New Haven, CT: Yale University Press.

Edwards, III, George C. 2000. Building Coalitions. *Presidential Studies Quarterly*, 30(1), 47–78.

Edwards, III, George C. 2004. *Why the Electoral College Is Bad for America*. New Haven, CT: Yale University Press.

Edwards, III, George C., Barrett, Andrew, and Peake, Jeffrey. 1997. The Legislative Impact of Divided Government. *American Journal of Political Science*, 41(2), 545–563.

Edwards, III, George C., Wattenberg, Martin P., and Lineberry, Robert I. 2008. *Government in America: People, Politics, and Policy*. 13th edn. New York: Pearson Longman.

Epstein, David, and O'Halloran, Sharyn. 1999. *Delegating Power: A Transaction Cost Politics Approach to Policy Making Under Separate Powers*. Cambridge: Cambridge University Press.

Erikson, Robert S. 1989. Economic Conditions and the Presidential Vote. *American Political Science Review*, 83(2), 567–573.

Erikson, Robert S., Bafumi, Joseph, and Wilson, Bret. 2001. Was the 2000 Presidential Election Predictable? *PS: Political Science & Politics*, 34(4), 815–819.

Erikson, Robert S., MacKuen, Michael B., and Stimson, James A. 2000. Bankers or Peasants Revisited: Economic Expectations and Presidential Approval. *Electoral Studies*, 19(2–3), 295–312.

Evans, Diana. 2004. *Greasing the Wheels: Using Pork Barrel Projects to Build Majority Coalitions in Congress*. New York: Cambridge University Press.

Fenno, Jr., Richard F. 1978. *Home Style; House Members in Their Districts*. New York: Little, Brown and Company.

Ferejohn, John. 1974. *Pork Barrel Politics: Rivers and Harbors Legislation, 1947–1968*. Stanford, CA: Stanford University Press.

Finger, J. Michael, and Harrison, Ann. 1996. Import Protection for U.S. Textiles and Apparel: Viewed from the Domestic Perspective, in *Political Representation*, ed. Anne O. Krueger. Chicago: University of Chicago Press.

Fiorina, Morris P. 1981. *Retrospective Voting in American National Elections*. New Haven, CT: Yale University Press.

Fleisher, Richard, and Bond, John. 2004. The Shrinking Middle in the U.S. Congress. *British Journal of Political Science*, 34(3), 429–451.

Flora, Colin, and Parker, David. 2007. BRAC Attack: Delegation, Politics, and the Closing of Military Bases. Paper presented at the annual meeting of the Midwest Political Science Association, Palmer House Hotel, Chicago, IL, April 12.

Frisch, Scott A., and Kelly, Sean Q. 2011. *Jimmy Carter and the Water Wars: Presidential Influence and the Politics of Pork*. Amherst, New York: Cambria.

Gailmard, Sean, and Jenkins, Jeffery A. 2007. Negative Agenda Control in the Senate and House: Fingerprints of Majority Party Power. *Journal of Politics*, 69(3), 689–700.

Galvin, Daniel J. 2009. *Presidential Party Building: Dwight D. Eisenhower to George W. Bush*. Princeton, NJ: Princeton University Press.

Galvin, Daniel J. 2013. Presidential Partisanship Reconsidered: Eisenhower, Nixon, and Ford and the Rise of Polarized Politics. *Political Research Quarterly*, 66(1), 46–60.

Garrett, Thomas A., and Sobel, Russell S. 2003. The Political Economy of FEMA Disaster Payments. *Economic Inquiry*, 41(3), 496–509.

Gartner, Scott Sigmund, Segura, Gary M., and Barratt, Bethany A. 2004. War Casualties, Policy Positions, and the Fate of Legislators. *Political Research Quarterly*, 57(3), 467–477.

Gasper, John T., and Reeves, Andrew. 2011. Make It Rain? Retrospection and the Attentive Electorate in the Context of Natural Disasters. *American Journal of Political Science*, 55(2), 340–355.

Gelman, Andrew. 2008. *Red State Blue State Rich State Poor State*. Princeton, NJ: Princeton University Press.

Gelman, Andrew, and King, Gary. 1993. Why Are American Presidential Election Campaign Polls So Variable When Votes Are So Predictable? *British Journal of Political Science*, 23(1), 409–451.

Gilliam, Jr., Franklin D., and Iyengar, Shanto. 2000. Prime Suspects: The Influence of Local Television News on the Viewing Public. *American Journal of Political Science*, 44(3), 560–573.

Gimpel, James G., Lee, Frances E., and Thorpe, Rebecca U. 2012. Geographic Distribution of the Federal Stimulus of 2009. *Political Science Quarterly*, 127(4), 567–595.

Goidel, Robert K., and Langley, Ronald E. 1995. Media Coverage of the Economy and Aggregate Economic Evaluations: Uncovering Evidence of Indirect Media Effects. *Political Research Quarterly*, 48(2), 313–328.

Goldstein, Ken, and Freedman, Paul. 2002. Campaign Advertising and Voter Turnout: New Evidence for a Stimulation Effect. *Journal of Politics*, 64(3), 721–740.

Gordon, Sanford C. 2011. Politicizing Agency Spending Authority: Lessons from a Bush-Era Scandal. *American Political Science Review*, 105(4), 717–734.

Grimmer, Justin, Messing, Solomon, and Westwood, Sean J. 2012. How Words and Money Cultivate a Personal Vote: The Effect of Legislator Credit Claiming on Constituent Credit Allocation. *American Political Science Review*, 106(4), 703–719.

Grose, Christian R., and Oppenheimer, Bruce I. 2007. The Iraq War, Partisanship, and Candidate Attributes: Variation in Partisan Swing in the 2006 U.S. House Elections. *Legislative Studies Quarterly*, 32(4), 531–557.

Harrington, David E. 1989. Economic News on Television: The Determinants of Coverage. *Public Opinion Quarterly*, 53(1), 17–40.

Hauk, Jr., William R., and Wacziarg, Romain. 2007. Small States, Big Pork. *Quarterly Journal of Political Science*, 2(1), 95–106.

Hazards and Vulnerability Research Institute. 2009. The Spatial Hazard Events and Losses Database for the United States. Columbia: University of South Carolina. Available from http://www.sheldus.org.

Healy, Andrew, and Lenz, Gabriel S. 2014. Substituting the End for the Whole: Why Voters Respond Primarily to the Election-Year Economy. *American Journal of Political Science*, 58(1), 31–47.

Healy, Andrew, and Malhotra, Neil. 2009. Myopic Voters and Natural Disaster Policy. *American Political Science Review*, 103(3), 387–406.

Healy, Andrew J., Malhotra, Neil, and Mo, Cecilia Hyunjung. 2010. Irrelevant Events Affect Voters' Evaluations of Government Performance. *Proceedings of the National Academy of Sciences*, 107(29), 12804–12809.

Heclo, Hugh. 1975. OMB and the Presidency – The Problem of 'Nuetral Competence'. *The Public Interest*, 38, 80–98.

Hibbs, Jr., Douglas A. 1987. *The American Political Economy: Macroeconmics and Electoral Politics*. Cambridge, MA: Harvard University Press.

Ho, Kevin. 2003. Trading Rights and Wrongs: The 2002 Bush Steel Tariffs. *Berkeley Journal of International Law*, 21(3), 825–846.

Hogan, Michael J., Long, Michael A., and Stretesky, Paul B. 2010. Campaign contributions, lobbying and post-Katrina contracts. *Disasters*, 34(3), 593–607.

House, Chatham. 1995. *The Presidential Branch: From Washington to Clinton*. Chatham, NJ: M.E. Sharpe.

Howell, William G. 2003. *Power without Persuasion: The Politics of Direct Presidential Action*. Princeton, NJ: Princeton University Press.

Howell, William, and Brent, David. 2013. *Thinking about the Presidency: The Primacy of Power*. Princeton, NJ: Princeton University Press.

Howell, William G., Jackman, Saul P., and Rogowski, Jon C. 2013. *The Wartime President*. Chicago: The University of Chicago Press.

Howell, William, and Lewis, David. 2002. Agencies by Presidential Design. *Journal of Politics*, **64**(4), 1095–1114.

Howell, William G., and Moe, Terry M. 2013. Inefficacy, Anxiety, and Leadership. Social Science Research Council.

Howell, William G., and Moe, Terry M. forthcoming. Enhanced Presidential Proposal Power: Con, in *Debating Reform: Conflicting Perspectives on How to Fix the American Political System*, eds. R. Ellis and M. Nelson. 3rd edn. Washington, DC: Congressional Quarterly Press.

Howell, William G., and Pevehouse, Jon C. 2007. *While Dangers Gather*. Princeton, NJ: Princeton University Press.

Huang, Taofang, and Shaw, Daron. 2009. Beyond the Battlegrounds? Electoral College Strategies in the 2008 Presidential Election. *Journal of Political Marketing*, **8**(4), 272–291.

Huber, Gregory A., Hill, Seth J., and Lenz, Gabriel S. 2012. Sources of Bias in Retrospective Decision Making: Experimental Evidence on Voters' Limitations in Controlling Incumbents. *American Political Science Review*, **106**(4), 720–741.

Hudak, John. 2012 (May). The Politics of Federal Grants: Presidential Influence over the Distribution of Federal Funds. Ph.D. thesis, Vanderbilt University, Nashville.

Hudak, John. 2014. *Presidential Pork: White House Influence over the Distribution of Federal Grants*. Washington, DC: Brookings Institution Press.

Hudak, John, and Stack, Kevin M. 2013. The President and the Politics of Agency Enforcement: The Case of Superfund. Typescript.

Hufbauer, Gary, and Lowry, Sean. 2012. Policy Brief: US Tire Tariffs: Saving Few Jobs at High Cost. *Peterson Institute for International Economics*, April 1–14.

Hufbauer, Gary Clyde, Berliner, Diane T., and Elliott, Kimberly Ann. 1986. *Trade Protection in the United States: 31 Case Studies*. Washington, DC: Institute for International Economics.

Jacobson, Gary C. 2004. *The Politics of Congressional Elections*. Vol. 6. New York: Pearson Longman.

Jacobson, Gary C., Kernell, Samuel, and Lazarus, Jeffrey. 2004. Assessing the President's Role as Party Agent in Congressional Elections: The Case of Bill Clinton in 2000. *Legislative Studies Quarterly*, **29**(2), 159–184.

James, Scott C. 2000. *Presidents, Parties, and the State: A Party System Perspective on Democratic Regulatory Choice, 1884–1836*. Cambridge: Cambridge University Press.

James, Scott C., and Lawson, Brian L. 1999. The Political Economy of Voting Rights Enforcement in America's Gilded Age: Electoral College Competition, Partisan Commitment, and the Federal Election Law. *American Political Science Review*, **93**(1), 115–131.

Jones, Bryan D., and Baumgartner, Frank R. 2005. *The Politics of Attention: How Government Prioritizes Problems*. Chicago: University of Chicago Press.

Kagan, Elena. 2001. Presidential Administration. *Harvard Law Review*, **114**, 2245–2385.

Karol, David, and Miguel, Edward. 2007. The Electoral Cost of War: Iraq Casualties and the 2004 US Presidential Election. *Journal of Politics*, **69**(3), 633–648.

Kernell, Samuel. 1997. *Going Public: New Strategies of Presidential Leadership.* Washington, DC: Congressional Quarterly Press.

Key, Jr., V. O. 1966. *The Responsible Electorate: Rationality in Presidential Voting, 1936–1960.* Cambridge, MA: Belknap Press of Harvard University Press.

Kiewiet, D. Roderick. 1983. *Macroeconomics and Micropolitics: The Electoral Effects of Economic Issues.* Chicago: University of Chicago Press.

Kiewiet, D. Roderick, and McCubbins, Matthew. 1988. Presidential Influence on Congressional Appropriations Decisions. *American Journal of Political Science*, **32**(3), 713–736.

Kinder, Donald R., Adams, Gordon S., and Gronke, Paul W. 1989. Economics and Politics in the 1984 American Presidential Election. *American Journal of Political Science*, **33**(2), 491–515.

Kinder, Donald R., and Kiewiet, D. Roderick. 1981. Sociotropic Politics: The American Case. *British Journal of Political Science*, **11**(2), 129–161.

Kittur, Aniket. 2008. Crowdsourcing User Studies with Mechanical Turk, in *CHI 2008*, eds. H. Chi and Bongwon Suh. New York: ACM Press.

Koza, John R., Fadem, Barry F., Grueskin, Mark, Mandell, Michael S., Richie, Robert, and Zimmerman, Joseph F. 2013. *Every Vote Equal: A State-Based Plan for Electing the President by National Popular Vote.* 4th edn. National Popular Vote Press.

Kramer, Gerald H. 1971. Short-Term Fluctuations in U.S. Voting Behavior, 1896–1964. *American Political Science Review*, **65**(1), 131–143.

Kramer, Gerald H. 1983. The Ecological Fallacy Revisited: Aggregate- versus Individual-Level Findings on Economics and Elections, and Sociotropic Voting. *American Political Science Review*, **77**(1), 92–111.

Kriner, Douglas L. 2010. *After the Rubicon: Congress, Presidents, and the Politics of Waging War.* Chicago: University of Chicago Press.

Kriner, Douglas L., and Reeves, Andrew. 2012. The Influence of Federal Spending on Presidential Elections. *American Political Science Review*, **106**(2), 348–366.

Kriner, Douglas L., and Reeves, Andrew. 2015. Presidential Particularism and Divide-the-Dollar Politics. *American Political Science Review*, **109**(1), 155–171.

Kriner, Douglas L., and Shen, Francis X. 2007. Iraq Casualties and the 2006 Senate Elections. *Legislative Studies Quarterly*, **32**(4), 507–530.

Kriner, Douglas L., and Shen, Francis X. 2010. *The Casualty Gap.* New York: Oxford University Press.

Kriner, Douglas, and Shen, Francis. 2014. Responding to War on Capitol Hill: Battlefield Casualties, Congressional Response, and Public Support for the War in Iraq. *American Journal of Political Science*, **58**(1), 157–174.

Landis, Michele L. 1998. "Let Me Next Time Be 'Tried By Fire'": Disaster Relief and the Origins of the American Welfare State 1798–1874. *Northwestern University Law Review*, **92**(3).

Lanoue, David J. 1994. Retrospective and Prospective Voting in Presidential-Year Elections. *Political Research Quarterly*, **47**(1), 193–205.

Larcinese, Valentino, Rizzo, Leonzio, and Testa, Cecilia. 2006. Allocating the U.S. Federal Budget to the States: The Impact of the President. *Journal of Politics*, **68**(2), 447–456.

Lauderdale, Benjamin E. 2008. Pass the Pork: Measuring Shares in Bicameral Legislatures. *Political Analysis*, **16**(3), 235–249.

Lazarus, Jeffrey, and Reilly, Shauna. 2010. The Electoral Benefits of Distributive Spending. *Political Research Quarterly*, **63**(2), 343–355.

Lee, Frances E. 2000. Senate Representation and Coalition Building in Distributive Politics. *The American Political Science Review*, **94**(1), 59–72.

Lee, Frances E. 2003. Geographic Politics in the U.S. House of Representatives: Coalition Building and Distribution of Benefits. *American Journal of Political Science*, **47**(4), 714–728.

Lee, Frances E. 2004. Bicameral Institutions and Geographic Politics: Allocating Federal Funds for Transportation in the House and Senate. *Legislative Studies Quarterly*, **29**(2), 185–214.

Lee, Frances E. 2009. *Beyond Ideology: Politics, Principles, and Partisanship in the U.S. Senate*. Chicago: University of Chicago Press.

Lee, Frances E., and Oppenheimer, Bruce I. 1999. *Sizing Up the Senate – The Unequal Consequences of Equal Representation*. Chicago: University of Chicago Press.

Levitt, Steven D., and Poterba, James M. 1999. Congressional Distributive Politics and State Economic Performance. *Public Choice*, **99**, 185–216.

Levitt, Steven D., and Snyder, Jr., James M. 1995. Political Parties and the Distribution of Federal Outlays. *American Journal of Political Science*, **39**(4), 958–980.

Levitt, Steven D., and Sndyer, Jr., James M. 1997. The Impact of Federal Spending on House Election Outcomes. *The Journal of Political Economy*, **105**(1), 30–53.

Lewis, David. 2003. *Presidents and the Politics of Agency Design: Political Insulation in the United States Government Bureaucracy, 1946–1997*. Stanford, CA: Stanford University Press.

Lewis, David E. 2008. *The Politics of Presidential Appointments: Political Control and Bureaucratic Performance*. Princeton, NJ: Princeton University Press.

Lewis-Beck, Michael S., and Stegmaier, Mary. 2000. Economic Determinants of Electoral Outcomes. *Annual Review of Political Science*, **3**, 183–219.

Lewis-Beck, Michael S., and Tien, Charles. 2008. The Job of President and the Jobs Model Forecast: Obama for '08? *PS: Political Science & Politics*, **41**(4), 687–690.

Light, Paul C. 1998 [1982]. *The President's Agenda: Domestic Policy Choice from Kennedy to Clinton*. 3rd edn. Baltimore, MD: Johns Hopkins University Press.

Lindbeck, Assar, and Weibull, Jörgen W. 1987. Balanced-Budget Redistribution as the Outcome of Political Competition. *Public Choice*, **52**(3), 273–297.

Linz, Juan J. 1990. The Perils of Presidentialism. *Journal of Democracy*, **1**(1), 51–69.

Lohmann, Susanne, and O'Halloran, Sharyn. 1994. Divided Government and U.S. Trade Policy: Theory and Evidence. *International Organization*, 48(4), 595–632.

Lowi, Theodore J. 1985. *The Personal President: Power Invested Promise Unfulfilled*. Ithaca, NY: Cornell University Press.

Machiavelli, Niccolo. 1998 [1532]. *The Prince*. 2nd edn. Chicago: University of Chicago Press.

MacKuen, Michael B., Erikson, Robert S., and Stimson, James A. 1992. Peasants or Bankers? The American Electorate and the U.S. Economy. *American Political Science Review*, 86(3), 597–611.

Malhotra, Neil, and Kuo, Alexander G. 2008. Attributing Blame: The Public's Response to Hurricane Katrina. *Journal of Politics*, 70(1), 120–135.

Mann, Thomas E., and Ornstein, Normal J. 2013. *It's Even Worse Than It Looks: How the American Constitutional System Collided with the New Politics of Extremism*. New York: Basic Books.

Markus, Gregory B. 1992. The Impact of Personal and National Economic Conditions on Presidential Voting, 1956-1988. *American Journal of Political Science*, 36(3), 829–834.

Marshall, Bryan W., and Prins, Brandon C. 2007. Strategic Position Taking and Presidential Influence in Congress. *Legislative Studies Quarterly*, 32(2), 257–284.

Marshaw, Jerry. 1985. Prodelegation: Why Adminsitrators Should Make Political Decisions. *Journal of Law, Economics, and Organization*, 1(1), 81–100.

Martin, Paul S. 2003. Voting's Rewards: Voter Turnout, Attentive Publics, and Congressional Allocation of Federal Money. *American Journal of Political Science*, 47(1), 110–127.

Mason, Winter, and Suri, Siddharth. 2012. Conducting Behavioral Research on Amazon's Mechnical Turk. *Behavior Research Methods*, 44(1), 1–23.

Mayer, Andrew C. 1982. Base Closures Law and Politics. *Armed Forces & Society*, 8(3), 463–469.

Mayer, Kenneth R. 1995. Closing Military Bases (Finally): Solving Collective Dilemmas Through Delegation. *Legislative Studies Quarterly*, 20(3), 393–413.

Mayhew, David R. 1974a. *Congress: The Electoral Connection*. New Haven, CT: Yale University Press.

Mayhew, David R. 1974b. Congressional Elections: The Case of the Vanishing Marginals. *Polity*, 6(3), 295–317.

Mayhew, David R. 2005. *Divided We Govern: Party Control, Lawmaking, and Investigations*. 2nd edn. New Haven, CT: Yale University Press.

McCarty, Nolan M. 2000. Presidential Pork: Executive Veto Power and Distributive Politics. *American Political Science Review*, 94(1), 117–129.

McCarty, Nolan M., Poole, Keith T., and Rosenthal, Howard. 2006. *Polarized America: The Dance of Ideology and Unequal Riches*. Cambridge, MA: MIT Press.

McCubbins, Mathew D., and Schwartz, Thomas. 1984. Congressional Oversight Overlooked: Police Patrols versus Fire Alarms. *American Journal of Political Science*, 28(1), 165–179.

Milkis, Sidney. 2013. The Modern Presidency, Social Movements, and the New Party System. Paper Presented for the Annual Meeting of the American Political Science Association, August 29–September 1, Chicago, IL.

Milkis, Sidney M., and Rhodes, Jesse H. 2007. George W. Bush, the Republican Party, and the "New" American Party System. *Perspectives on Politics*, 5(3), 461–488.

Milkis, Sidney M., Rhodes, Jesse H., and Charnock, Emily J. 2012. What Happened to Post-Partisanship? Barack Obama and the New American Party System. *Perspectives on Politics*, 10(1), 57–76.

Moe, Terry. 1985a. "The Politicized Presidency" in *The New Direction in American Politics*, eds. John E. Chubb and Paul E. Peterson. Washington, DC: Brookings Institution Press.

Moe, Terry M. 1985b. Control and Feedback in Economic Regulation: The Case of the NLRB. *American Political Science Review*, 79(4), 1094–1116.

Moe, Terry M., and Howell, William G. 1999. The Presidential Power of Unilateral Action. *Journal of Law, Economics, and Organization*, 15(1), 132–179.

Moe, Terry M., and Wilson, Scott A. 1994. Presidents and the Politics of Structure. *Law and Contemporary Problems*, 57(2), 1–44.

Molotch, Harvey, and Lester, Marilyn. 1974. News as Purposive Behavior: On the Strategic Use of Routine Events, Accidents, and Scandals. *American Sociological Review*, 39(1), 101–112.

Mutz, Diana C. 1992. Mass Media and the Depoliticization of Personal Experience. *American Journal of Political Science*, 36(2), 483–508.

Muûls, Mirabelle, and Petropoulou, Dimitra. 2013. A Swing State Theory of Trade Protection in the Electoral College. *Canadian Journal of Economics*, 46(2), 705–724.

Nagler, Jonathan, and Leighley, Jan. 1992. Presidential Campaign Expenditures: Evidence on Allocations and Effects. *Public Choice*, 73(3), 319–333.

Nasr, Vali. 2013. *The Dispensable Nation: American Foreign Policy in Retreat*. New York: Doubleday.

Neustadt, Richard E. 1990 [1960]. *Presidential Power and the Modern Presidents: Politics of Leadership from Roosevelt to Reagan*. First Free Press paperback edn. New York: Free Press.

Newman, Brian, and Siegle, Emerson. 2010. The Polarized Presidency: Depth and Breadth of Public Partisanship. *Presidential Studies Quarterly*, 40(2), 342–363.

Norpoth, Helmut. 1985. Politics, Economics, and the Cycle of Presidential Popularity, in *Economic Conditions and Electoral Outcomes*, eds. Heinz Eulau and Michael Lewis-Beck. New York: Agathon.

Paolacci, Gabriele, Chandler, Jesse, and Ipeirotis, Panagiotis. 2010. Running Experiments on Amazon Mechanical Turk. *Judgment and Decision Making*, 5(5), 411–419.

Patterson, Thomas E. 1990. *The American Democracy*. New York: McGraw Hill.

Pearson, James. 1975. Oversight: A Vital yet neglected congressional function. *Kansas Law Review*, 23(2), 277–288.

Pika, Joseph A., Maltese, John Anthony, and Thomas, Norman C. 2006. *The Politics of the Presidency*. Revised 6th edn. Washington, DC: Congressional Quarterly Press.

Pildes, Richard H., and Sunstein, Cass R. 1995. Reinventing the Regulatory State. *The University of Chicago Law Review*, **62**(1), 1–129.

Popkin, Samuel. 1994. *The Reasoning Voter: Communication and Persuasion in Presidential Campaigns*. Chicago: University of Chicago Press.

Read, Robert. 2005. The Political Economy of Trade Protection: The Determinants and Welfare Impact of the 2002 US Emergency Steel Safeguard Measures. *The World Economy*, **28**(8), 1119–1137.

Reeves, Andrew. 2011. Political Disaster: Unilateral Powers, Electoral Incentives, and Presidential Disaster Declarations. *Journal of Politics*, **73**(4), 1142–1151.

Reeves, Andrew, and Gimpel, James G. 2012. Ecologies of Unease: Geographic Context and National Economic Evaluations. *Political Behavior*, **34**(3), 507–534.

Riker, William H. 1962. *Theory of Political Coalitions*. New Haven, CT: Yale University Press.

Rivers, Douglas, and Rose, Nancy L. 1985. Passing the President's Program: Public Opinion and Presidential Influence in Congress. *American Journal of Political Science*, **29**(2), 183–196.

Rosenstone, Steven J., Behr, Roy L., and Lazarus, Edward H. 1996. *Third Parties in America: Citizen Response to Major Party Failure*. Princeton, NJ: Princeton University Press.

Ross, Joel, Zaldivar, Andrew, Irani, Lilly, Tomlinson, Bill, and Silberman, M. Six. 2010. Who Are the Crowdworkers? Shifting Demographics in Mechanical Turk. CHI2010: Imagine all the People, Atlanta.

Rossiter, Clinton. 1960. *The American Presidency*. 2nd edn. New York: Mentor Books.

Rowley, Charles, Thorbecke, Willem, and Wagner, Richard. 1995. *Trade Protection in the United States*. Brookfield, VT: E. Elgar.

Rudalevige, Andrew. 2002. *Managing the President's Program: Presidential Leadership and Legislative Policy Formulation*. Princeton, NJ: Princeton University Press.

Rudalevige, Andrew. 2006. *The New Imperial Presidency: Renewing Presidential Power After Watergate*. Ann Arbor: University of Michigan Press.

Salkowe, R. S., and Chakraborty, J. 2009. Federal Disaster Relief in the US: The Role of Political Partisanship and Preference in Presidential Disaster Declarations and Turndowns. *Journal of Homeland Security and Emergency Management*, **6**(1), 28.

Savage, Charlie. 2007. *Takeover: The Return of the Imperial Presidency and the Subversion of American Democracy*. Boston: Little, Brown and Company.

Schick, Allen. 2000. *The Federal Budget: Politics, Policy, Process*. Washington, DC: The Brookings Institution Press.

Seligman, Lester, and Covington, Cary. 1989. *The Coalitional Presidency*. Chicago: Dorsey Press.

Sellers, Patrick J. 1997. Fiscal Consistency and Federal District Spending in Congressional Elections. *American Journal of Political Science*, **41**(3), 1024–1041.

Shaw, Daron R. 1999a. The Effect of TV Ads and Candidate Appearances on Statewide Presidential Votes, 1988–96. *American Political Science Review*, 93(2), 345–361.

Shaw, Daron R. 1999b. The Methods behind the Madness: Presidential Electoral College Strategies. *Journal of Politics*, 61(4), 893–913.

Shaw, Daron R. 2006. *The Race to 270: The Electoral College and the Campaign Strategies of 2000 and 2004*. Chicago: University of Chicago Press.

Shepsle, Kenneth A., and Weingast, Barry R. 1981. Political Preferences for the Pork Barrel: A Generalization. *American Journal of Political Science*, 25(1), 96–111.

Shepsle, Kenneth A., and Weingast, Barry R. 1987. The Institutional Foundations of Committee Power. *The American Political Science Review*, 81(1), 85–104.

Shoemaker, Pamela J., and Reese, Stephen D. 1996. *Mediating the Message: Theories of Influence on Mass Media Content*. White Plains, NY: Longman Publishers.

Shor, Boris. 2006 (Apr). *The Political Geography of Distributive Politics in the United States*. Ph.D. thesis, Columbia University, New York.

Skinner, Richard M. 2008. George W. Bush and the Partisan Presidency. *Political Science Quarterly*, 123(4), 605–622.

Snowberg, Erik, Meredith, Marc, and Ansolabehere, Stephen. 2014. Mecro-Economic Voting: Local Information and Micro-Perceptions of the Macro-Economy. *Economics & Politics*, 26(3), 380–410.

Sood, Rahul, Stockdale, Geoffrey, and Rogers, Everett. 1987. How the Media Operate in Natural Disasters. *Journal of Communication*, 37(3), 27–41.

Stein, Robert M., and Bickers, Kenneth N. 1994. Congressional Elections and the Pork Barrel. *The Journal of Politics*, 56(2), 377–399.

Stein, Robert M., and Bickers, Kenneth N. 1995. *Perpetuating the Pork Barrel: Policy Subsystems and American Democracy*. New York: Cambridge University Press.

Suzuki, Motoshi, and Chappell, Jr., Henry W. 1996. The Rationality of Economic Voting Revisited. *Journal of Politics*, 58(1), 224–236.

Sylves, Richard, and Búzás, Zoltán I. 2007. Presidential Disaster Declaration Decisions, 1953–2003: What Influences Odds of Approval? *State & Local Government Review*, 39(1), 3–15.

Tama, Jordan. 2011. *Terrorism and National Security Reform: How Commissions Can Drive Change During Crises*. New York: Cambridge University Press.

Tomkin, Shelley Lynne. 1998. *Inside OMB: Politics and Process in the President's Budget Office*. Armonk, NY: M.E. Sharpe.

Tufte, Edward R. 1978. *Political Control of the Economy*. Princeton, NJ: Princeton University Press.

Twight, Charlotte. 1989. Institutional Underpinnings of Parochialism: The Case of Military Base Closures. *Cato Journal*, 9(1), 73–106.

Velez, Yamil, and Martin, David. 2013. Sandy the Rainmaker: The Electoral Impact of a Super Storm. *PS: Political Science & Politics*, 46(2), 313–323.

Vock, Daniel C., and Malewitz, Jim. 2013. Disaster Declaration Denials Exasperate Governors. *Stateline: The Daily News Service of The Pew Charitable Trusts*, August 23.

Waterman, Richard W. 1989. *Presidential Influence and the Administrative State*. Knoxville: University of Tennessee Press.

Weingast, Barry R. 1979. A Rational Choice Perspective on Congressional Norms. *American Journal of Political Science*, 23(2), 245–262.

Weiss, Daniel J., and Weidman, Jackie. 2013 (Apr). *Disasterous Spending: Federal Disaster-Relief Expenditures Rise amid More Extreme Weather*. Tech. rept. Center for American Progress, Washington, DC.

Wilkins, Lee, and Patterson, Philip. 1987. Risk Analysis and the Construction of News. *Journal of Communication*, 37(3), 80–92.

Wilson, Graham K. 1977. *Special Interests & Policymaking: Agricultural Policies and Politics in Britain and the United States of America, 1956–1970*. New York: Wiley.

Wilson, Woodrow. 1908. *Constitutional Government in the United States*. New York: The Columbia University Press.

Wood, B. Dan. 2009. *The Myth of Presidential Representation*. Cambridge: Cambridge University Press.

Wright, Gavin. 1974. The Political Economy of New Deal Spending: An Econometric Analysis. *The Review of Economics and Statistics*, 56(1), 30–38.

Yildirim, Huseyin. 2007. Proposal Power and Majority Rule in Multilateral Bargaining with Costly Recognition. *Journal of Economic Theory*, 136(1), 167–196.

Index

Page numbers in *italics* refer to figures and tables.

military policies (*cont.*)
  defense spending, 66, 71, 114, 179,
    183n30
  in wartime, 20–22, 35–37, 60, 84–85,
    160
Milkis, Sidney, 24n61, 42, 178
Mills, Wilbur, 65n47
mine reclamation grants, 122
Minnesota, 7
Mississippi, 56, 138, *139*
Missouri, 148
Mo, Cecilia, 37
Moakley, Joe, 79n83
Moe, Terry, 13, 19
Mondale, Walter F., 57, 155
Multi-Fiber Arrangement, 56
Mutz, Diana, 32n8
myopia in voters, 134–135
Myth of Presidential Representation, The
  (Wood), 42

NASA research grants, 116
National Climatic Data Center, 86
National Economic Council, 60
National Popular Vote bill, 176–177
national *vs.* local interests, 33–39, 41n41
natural disaster relief. *See* disaster relief
Nebraska, 15n30, 39
Nelson, Ben, 15n30, 118
Neustadt, Richard, 37
Nevada, 7, 94, 122
New Hampshire, 23, 94, 100, 106–107
New Jersey, 88–90
New Mexico, 7, 94
New York, 105, 130–132
New York Times, 126, 164
Nixon, Richard, 46, 55–56, 69, 117, 175
Norman Y. Mineta San Jose International
  Airport, 108
North Carolina particularism
  in 1960, 54
  in 1980, 56
  in 2004, 141
  in 2008, 113–114, 138, *139*
  in 2012, 21n51
Nzelibe, Jide, 13, 13n23

Obama, Barack
  administration
    budgetary strategy of, 21, 35, 114n8,
      164

  earmarks by, 4–6
  electoral particularism of, 7–9, 10, 21
  immigration policy of, 172–173
  description of, 24n61, 177
  election of, 38, 40, 135
  on line item veto, 111
  on partisanship, 3
  public opinion survey on, 149–152,
    205–206
  on universalism, 12
O'Brien, Ed, 60
O'Donnell, Kenneth, 54n9
Office of Management and Budget (OMB),
  118, 119, 121
Ohio particularism
  in 1984, 57
  in 2004, 60, 64, 65, 141, 142, 166
  in 2008, 11, 94, 137–138
  in 2012, 7–9, 21, 35, 38, 111–112, 164
Oklahoma, 91, 100
Omnibus Deficit Reconciliation Act of
  1993, 122
O'Neill, Tip, 33, 71
Ornstein, Norman, 19
Orwell, George, 2n3
oversight, congressional, 72–74, 78, 180

parliamentary system, 17
parochialism, congressional, 10–15, 19–20,
  45, 113–114, 126
particularism
  conditions for, 16–18, 23–24, 29–30
  congressional parochialism *vs.*, 2, 4,
    10–11, 67, 180
  in federal grant program
    disaster funding, 26, 44, 84–87,
      91–93, 95–101, 108–109, 171
    research grants, 116–117
    transportation grants, 101–109
    within-state targeting, 131, 141–145,
      155–159
  origin of, 2–4
  risks of, 25–28, 181–182
  universalism *vs.*, 10–15, 19–20
  wartime, 20–22, 60, 173
  See also coalitional particularism;
    electoral particularism
partisan particularism
  in budgetary strategy, 117
  in disaster declarations, 26, 89–90,
    98–101